D0270249

Writing on the Road

CAMPERVAN LOVE
AND THE JOY OF SOLITUDE

SUE REID SEXTON

WAVERLEY BOOKS

This edition published 2020 by Waverley Books, an imprint of
The Gresham Publishing Company Ltd.,
31, Six Harmony Row,
Glasgow, G51 3BA, Scotland, UK.

www.waverley-books.co.uk
info@waverley-books.co.uk

Text copyright © 2016 Sue Reid Sexton.

First published 2016. Reprinted 2016, 2017, 2018, 2019, 2020.

The author hereby asserts her moral right to be identified
as the author of this work.

All rights reserved. No part of this publication may be reproduced,
stored in a retrieval system or transmitted in any form or by any
means, electronic, mechanical, photocopying, recording or otherwise,
without the prior permission of the copyright holders.

Conditions of Sale:
This book is sold with the condition that it will not, by way of trade
or otherwise, be resold, hired out, lent, or otherwise distributed or
circulated in any form or style of binding or cover other than that
in which it is published and without the same conditions being
imposed on the subsequent purchaser.

ISBN: 978 1 84934 383 1

Also available as an eBook
ePub format ISBN: 978 1 84934 387 9
Mobi format ISBN: 978 1 84934 388 6

A catalogue record for this book is available from the British Library.

Printed and bound in the EU.

For Kirsty and Jessica

and for Liz

Contents

'Can I love someone … and still think/fly?'

Susan Sontag

Thanks

Thanks are due to Liz Small of Waverley who had the idea for the book in the first place. This allowed me to indulge my passion for campervanning and gave me the excuse to take yet more trips. I got to share it with the world too.

Thanks also to the rest of Waverley especially designer, Mark Mechan, who created the beautiful cover. By coincidence it bears a resemblance in style to the railway posters of Austin Cooper who happens to be one of my ancestors.

I'm indebted to the various garage mechanics who fixed the parts of my vans which baffled me, especially Bill of Stag Garage in Lochgilphead who spent hours getting one of my vans onto his breakdown truck without causing further damage. Others would have had less patience. Also thanks go to 'Willie' in Govan for rescuing a trip that would never have happened without his help.

Arthur Blue deserves an honourable mention for risking his life to get me back into one van when I'd locked myself out. Also David Reid for unfailing practical back-up and friendship, Sue McCann for good sense and wisdom and Louise Rohan for letting me charge my laptop many times so I could avoid formal campsites and keep wild camping. Trips to Kintyre were always happier when she and Eric were around to share walks.

Kintyre was never as good without at least one trip to Killiegruer Caravan Site near Glenbarr where Anne Littleson always provided a warm welcome and never objected when I parked parallel to the sea and at right angles to everyone else.

John Burnett was tireless in his encouragement for the project and our discussions over tea and baked potatoes were a joy.

Jan Nimmo and Paul Barham deserve special thanks for introducing me to Kintyre in the first place, but mostly for being my staunch supporters through thick and thin. Thanks for believing in me.

Colin Salter's help on the manuscript was invaluable and I'm indebted to his wife, Rosie Doyle, for being my first reader and offering so much help.

Thank you to the many people I encountered in laybys who always had something new to tell me.

Finally, a huge thank you to my daughters, Kirsty and Jessica, for their forbearance when left to their own devices while I trundled off into the wilds. It was also a delight to have them along when they came too.

Rough Guide

This book is about many things. It's the result of a ten-year love affair with campervans and countless trips in them around Scotland and occasionally further south. Most of these have been solo excursions. If you've always wondered what it's like to go solo then read on.

In the first half of the book, which I have called 'Outer', I explain why I do it and what I do when I'm away. You'll find information on the practical aspects of campervanning like where to park overnight, how *not* to buy a van, and what to cook. I've made lots of mistakes. You might be able to avoid your own by reading about the pitfalls I've encountered. I've also included some of the deeply invigorating and rejuvenating experiences I've had because those are the reasons I do it.

I've written in most detail about trips I took during the writing of this book. This is mainly because it was easier to write about being in a campervan when I was actually in one. I've also called upon much earlier trips, some even taken as far back as childhood.

The second half of the book, 'Inner', has more to do with the human side and the experience of being alone in wild places and writing. There are sections about the creative process, with tips on meditation and staying present, and how to survive and thrive.

Campervans are my lifeline. I can't imagine a life without one.

Part One

Outer

Arrival

Hammering up the western side of Loch Lomond, I reach across the passenger seat of the campervan, flick the door open and shove a broken washing machine out the door. I picture it landing and bursting into a million pieces, and a series of resounding crashes filling the air as it careers backwards along the road, sparks flying. Finally, in the wing mirror, I watch it burst into flames and the faulty inner drum rolling across the road. Narrowly missing the oncoming Glasgow bus, the drum bounces off a rock, leaps over some campers whose bonfire is just getting going, and sploshes into the loch with a hiss.

Ah, how I love this journey! Onwards to salvation before nightfall!

Voices on the radio begin to splutter and fade, the signal lost as the mountains rise around me. I turn it off so I can concentrate more fully on proactively losing all those stress-factors.

Next up are multiple soggy towels from the bathroom floor including the virulent pink bath mat which lands on the tarmac with a pop like a belly flop. Then the dishes. A chipped plate flies Frisbee-style into the bushes, a mug explodes in smithereens on the road, and those bent forks and corroded spoons tinkle and dance around it.

This is fun. I wonder why I've never thought of it before.

The most troubling member of my household I put in a soap bubble which I blow, gently, skywards over the trees, across the loch and into the distant woods on the other side.

Deadlines and unkind words I scribble on the back of all those bills and set fire to them on the dashboard, one by one.

Being a Scottish summer, the day is still bright, but my journey is long, so I press down hard on the pedal to outstrip the travels of the sun and get me to my destination before it goes down behind the islands.

I pop another strawberry in my mouth and consider the secrecy of the season, how in winter the grass is brown and the hillsides bare along these shores, and through the dark and sleeping branches of trees Ben Lomond rises from the water's edge. But in summer the trees ooze with green life and shroud the West Highland Way and its walkers. Almost a hundred miles of path, this famous hiking trail goes north from Milngavie, outside Glasgow, along the loch's eastern shore, across the mountains and on to Fort William in the Highlands. This evening the loch itself is part hidden behind leafy branches that sway in the slipstream of passing lorries. The sun still glints off the water which is visible intermittently between the trees. From behind the swell of shrubs, the roofs of other campervans flash past, gathered in laybys at the loch's edge, the faint whistle of a kettle caught on the breeze. The hills are warmly lit, the road veers closer to the loch, the trees thin out and the true twinkling expanse of the water reveals itself. Two motorboats buzz across it, weaving circles round each other.

I let the sun warm my elbow in the open window like a proper trucker, breathe the warm air deep into my lungs and sigh it all back out again. I drive the next few miles in a state of smugness as I follow my journey forwards in my mind's eye through Tarbet with its castle-like hotel, past Arrochar's chip shop, the car park for the Cobbler (not a pub but a mountain with a peak like an anvil), and up Rest-And-Be-Thankful. In older campervans than this one I've rested at the top and been thankful we made it, like the original foot or horse travellers of this precipitous glen. On past a mist-covered loch in a hanging valley, through the vast super-straight valley which follows to Cairndow, where Loch Fyne appears for the first time, then through the trees at the loch's edge to Inveraray with its humpy-backed bridge and a fairy-tale castle with a bloodthirsty history.

Inveraray Co-op is still open and sells chocolate, vital fuel for any van trip. I have a quick stretch of my legs, then plug in the MP3 player and flick through the tracks, plumping at last for Dvorak's Cello Concerto. With the volume as high as is healthy for my ears, I sing along to as many parts as I can manage at the top of my voice, a flute here, a clarinet there, and the jubilant, wistful, wilful strains of the cello.

In the comparatively sizeable town of Lochgilphead with its giant school premises set on the approach road, I pause Mr Dvorak and contain myself, trying to look especially sensible as I pass the police station on the seafront. I take the two roundabouts with special care and continue south past Ardrishaig where I wave a cheery hello to the house of a friend. The lights are always on but he's rarely home, and besides, I'm in a hurry. Beyond the last building, I unpause the music and a scene of great valour, desperation and horseback triumph begins to play out in my head provoked by the concerto's final movement. I sing my merry and heroic way to Tarbert, Loch Fyne, which marks the beginning of the final stage of the journey.

This is different from the earlier Tarbet and has an extra 'r': Tarbert. Many more towns in Scotland bear these names, which are derived from the Gaelic 'An Tairbeart' meaning isthmus. Tarberts don't usually name their lochs after themselves but this Tarbert spans the land between East Loch Tarbert, a natural harbour off the far grander Loch Fyne, and West Loch Tarbert a narrow sheltered loch which opens onto the Sounds of Jura and Gigha. Lochs, for the uninitiated, are lakes and a sound is a strait of water, neither loch nor open sea, though water is never straight and strait has two letters missing, surely.

I digress.

The road entrance to this Tarbert is suitably grand, a slow descent towards a harbourful of yachts, launches and fishing boats. Like many places around this coast, it used to be swirling with seagulls, less so now, which is a concern. Global warming or perhaps overfishing have come home to roost. The evening is peaceful, the harbour greying in the fading light. I park briefly on the quayside and toss the entire contents of my teenage daughter's bedroom into the harbour and watch piles of dirty washing, biscuit wrappers, festering mugs and unused A4 notepads sink to the bottom. Then I say hello to the swans lingering by the quayside with their young, and am ignored. Perhaps they sense my dangerous mood. A chill is setting in and the somewhere I have to be is either twelve or fifteen miles further on, depending on the availability of my chosen layby and whether I feel like stopping when I get to it, or continue for the ride and a gamble on a better place.

I cross from the east of Kintyre to the west. I am on the final stretch of the journey so I conduct it in reverent silence and as slowly as I can travel without arriving in darkness. The engine therefore hums instead of roars, as if I was tiptoeing past all those sleeping houses and not being propelled by a series of small explosions. Not a car passes me, so I have the view to the west and the beginning sunset, the falling night and the vast expanse of the rolling hillsides to myself. After a series of villages and villagettes, the road rises one last time before cresting the hill and offering the big blue sea in all its magnitude. At the bottom of the hill there's a strange house with funny little turrets, the gatehouse to Ronachan House, both previously part of a rehab centre. Beyond it, where the road meets the sea, there's a small car park and beside that, on the seaward side, a 'dun' or fort which is now just a stump of a hill, barely noticeable and completely covered in grass, which is not surprising seeing as it's been there since forever.

If I travel in the day, I always stop here for a tea on the rocks, as in sitting on the rocks with my feet in the water and a mug of tea in my hand, cold at one end, hot at the other. I say a first hello to the sea and wave to a departed friend who had a fondness for both whisky and the island of Jura on the other side of the water where some of the best whisky is made. Ronachan means 'place of seals' and I have indeed seen grey seals here, sunbathing on rocks or playing in the water beside them like human kids on holiday and making sounds surprisingly similar. Today there are none. The island of Islay stretches south and the Paps of Jura rise like cartoon hills beyond the darker strip of the island of Gigha where a couple of wind turbines are just visible against the sky. The sun is setting in the north west.

This is my arrival point in Kintyre, even though Kintyre actually officially begins quite a distance back. From here the road runs more or less down the west coast beside the sea. With the light fading, this spot is my first choice for an overnight stay, an ideal late-arrival-early-departure stop, but there is a giant lorry in it and an occupied steamed-up car. I toss my house keys past the oystercatchers on the beach and into the water. The sea accepts them with a glug, and I leave almost as soon as I arrive and continue along the shoreline, marvelling at the pale smoothness of the light and the glassy water so unnaturally silent. It's the colour of glacier water which it obviously isn't, and an odd mixture of tones with the peachy glow of the dying sun. It defies any understanding of distance from the shore across it to the islands. Luckily, from this point on, because the road runs by the sea it has many long open parts where other cars can easily overtake me.

A few miles further on, I pull into a layby on a bend just above the beach and park where I've parked many times before, facing north and parallel to the sea, a few shrubs between me and it. I shake myself down, then hurry along the sandy path to the beach, across the stripes of pebbles and seaweed to where wavelets lap the sand.

And I stand. I stand and listen to the great silence of the sea, save for its occasional whisper on the shore, and the warning calls of seabirds further along the beach where little terns are nesting. The sliver of sun slips down the long northwards slope of the North Jura peninsula until it is gone. The light fades a little as it passes behind the Kilberry peninsula and I wait for darkness. But it doesn't come. There is no full stop to the day. My senses are confused, which both tickles and worries. I trudge quietly back to the van.

I eat a light meal of six oatcakes, an apple and some cheese, then crouch on the edge of the bench inside my van summoning up the energy to pull out the sleeping bag and hot-water bottle. My body is suddenly heavy with exhaustion. A deer steps into the layby as cool as you like, her eyes just visible in the dusk. She seems unworried, perhaps not aware of my presence. I wish my camera was close and primed, but the slightest movement from me and she'll run. She nibbles a few leaves from the bushes then strolls back onto the road, pauses as if listening for traffic and to consider her direction, then turns south towards Campbeltown and vanishes from view. I sink lower with delight on the bench. What a treat, to be granted witness to this simple intimate moment.

Almost immediately, the silhouette of a bird of prey rises into the darkening sky above the scrubby trees and hovers on long, almost parallel wings, a tight shaft of a tail just visible behind. A buzzard? A golden eagle? I wish fervently it's the latter. It's hard not to feel blessed by the sighting of a giant golden eagle, and it would make a better story for the pub, or the next hidebound Twitchers' Tea Party. I've seen golden eagles in Kintyre twice before, but only in daylight. The word 'majestic' was invented for them. But tonight there isn't light to see well enough to tell the difference. It's most likely a buzzard which, though probably ten a penny round here, are still fun for city-dwellers like myself. I watch it search the length of the forest opposite the layby, dropping and rising, falling and climbing, until finally it dives into the black woods. I stare at the deep blue of the sky as it darkens and wait for the bird to mount the sky again, but it doesn't show itself.

I pull my purple sleeping bag and red fluffy hot-water bottle from the bunker, fill both and plunge into the night.

Earthling

Wild camping, or stopping overnight but not in a campsite, is old hat to me now. In Kintyre it's like an old familiar and much-loved hat that I knitted for myself from super-soft chunky merino. For those who don't knit, this means comfort and ease and a perfect match between hat and head. Wild camping in Kintyre is my favourite habit in my best location, my baseline for a total let go and my campervan's most natural habitat.

But it isn't always easy to do, and in areas that are new to me I still feel the bareheaded exposure of the hatless. Roadside overnights can be challenging but for me this can make them invigorating too.

One summer a few years back, I left Glasgow early in the morning and drove to Kintyre at a leisurely pace. I pulled over every so often to drink tea, read, write and take in the view. The journey is a little over three hours without stops, but it was the middle of August and the day was warm and breezy. I could do what I liked, so I did, and took my time at it.

I was making for Machrihanish Caravan Park, which is on the site of the old Argyll Colliery on the west coast of Kintyre near the road's end. In the old days when the mine was still active, underground tunnels were hacked a thousand feet or so deep under the ground and a full mile (staggering) from the minehead out under the sea. The mine was closed in 1967 and the campsite established not long after. I came here as a little girl with my mother and brothers to stay in a rented brand new caravan. At that time, the coal had unfortunately not been completely cleaned up on the surface and my poor mother spent the whole holiday wiping little black footprints from the carpet. It's not like that now. Today there is lovely green grass on a bed of solid clean pebbles, and panoramic views. There are toilets and hot showers, and hook-ups for your electricity supply, if you want it. This was to be my third stay there in a camper, the first in a long while.

I arrived in Machrihanish around three but on a whim passed by the caravan park and went on to the centre of the village. I parked in a car park right on the beach and set my feet in the sand. The tension ran through my body towards my feet and into the ground like an electric current being earthed. The wind tugged my hair from my face. I watched a crowd of black-and-white oystercatchers flee at my arrival and quickly settle further to the south, while a brave little wagtail hopped a few steps towards me to examine me more closely. Further along the beach a young woman sat on a picnic rug as her children grabbed sandwiches, then ran to the water to paddle. The sea was clear as crystals and the sand soft and golden and lined with seaweed that was crisp in the sunshine when I poked it with my foot. A huge outcrop of rock divided this beach from the next and lent a sense of privacy, despite the open view across the water to Islay in the distance.

I took off my socks and shoes and ground my feet into the sand, then chose a piece of shoreline to paddle in away from kids and oystercatchers, so as not to disturb them. The shock of the water was sudden. I could feel the blood withdraw from my skin and the nerves tense around the tiny bones in my feet. Waves of goose pimples climbed my legs. I imagined they were like the barnacles on the rocks nearby, tight together and jagged to the touch. I held my breath against the shock, then pulled my cut-off jeans higher over my knees and pushed further into the water until it was gripping my calves. That's how it felt anyway, like hands around my legs, and when I poked the skin most sensation had been lost. Goose pimples travelled my torso. Near the picnic, some seagulls were squabbling over a lost sandwich that flew into pieces in midair. I covered my eyes against the sun and accidentally dropped one trouser leg in the sea.

'Damn,' I muttered.

I watched the light play on my feet through the tiny waves and the little bubbles circle them on the surface, and dropped the other trouser leg into the water too. No point in being lopsided. Then I turned inshore where the water closer to the edge actually felt warm compared to that only a little further out. Wonderful nature. I picked a couple of tiny shells from the beach and stuck them in my pocket, turning them over and over as I made my way back to the van. Then I leant against the bumper and waited for the sand on my feet to dry and fall. It was time to go back to the campsite.

The best spot in Machrihanish Caravan Park, indeed arguably the only one worth having if you're on your own and need a view in place of human company, is on a rise looking out to sea. You can turn your back on civilisation and float your imagination to anywhere in the world. At the foot of it there's a burn called the Machrihanish Water. This is its final meandering before it finds the sea a few hundred yards further on. A 'burn', in typical Scottish back-to-front poetic style, is a small river or brook.

As I drew up I saw a row of campervans and motorhomes lined up along the rise like an army surveying a battlefield. I didn't want to join anyone or their army, not even a band of nice relaxed holiday-makers, and there seemed no space anyway. Being behind the front line and gazing chiefly at other vehicles wasn't an attractive option. I simply hadn't considered this possibility, so I panicked and drove on, slowing on a long straight stretch to think. The nearest campsite I knew of was a twenty-five mile drive north again and advertised itself as 'family friendly' which usually means great for letting kids run wild, but not the imagination.

I turned the van again and drove back to the campsite, but I just couldn't turn the steering wheel and get myself over the threshold and through the gate. All that blinding white plastic, those perfectly friendly neighbourly conversations. I panicked for the second time and carried on.

And on past the first house in the village, then the golf course and the pub, the beach and the toilets and finally the last house before fields open up. The road narrowed to single track and I thought about a road with no tarmac a little further on which wove its bumpy way to another wilder beach. I had walked it a few times before and knew that at the back of this other beach there's a flat, solid piece of grass, perfect for parking. But it would be too dark at night and I'd be scared. I stopped and backed into a two-car parking spot by the road to gather my thoughts and still my heaving chest.

The wind had turned easterly and cooled so I got out the folding chair, made tea, found my notebook and sat down outside the back of the van. I decided to ignore the campsite problem for a while. Worrying about it made it harder to focus on a solution. Anyway, I had a story I was mulling over and was keen to get back to it. That was what I was there to do. That was what I should be doing. Getting down to it. I was determined not to waste time.

This was fine for a while, but the wind kept grabbing the page so I moved round to the westerly, leeward, side of the van and put on a jumper. From there my view to the south was blocked by a knobby hillock of grass, but I could see islands in the distance across the water.

I wasn't long back in the writing seat when I heard a loud harrumphing sound from the water. A seal was blinking his dark eyes at me amongst the waves. His head was perfectly spherical and dark, like an old leather football lost at sea. I whistled to him, though I'm no good at whistling, and he bobbed and blinked back. He swam a little towards the village, diving below the surface. I could see the water shifting against his form. Then he rounded and went further out to sea and his ball of a head popped up again. He gazed at me and snorted, then dived deep where I couldn't trace him. The last time he re-emerged, closer to shore again, I leant against the van and sang to him, a little self-consciously I admit because you never know where the wind will take your voice. Perhaps he didn't like my singing, maybe he'd seen what he wanted to see, but he left and didn't come back. As I waited and searched fruitlessly for him in the waves, I kept mistaking some distant lobster pot floats for his head. Then I noticed where I was standing.

I mean, I knew where I was. I was in the south west of Kintyre by the sea. I'd often been past that particular layby, but I hadn't actually stopped and spent any time. Now I stood facing northwards, but usually I gazed west from this coast. The land swooped round to the west a couple of miles back and had changed my perspective, but I hadn't fully realised. Everything had changed. The light was different. I was confused by the direction of the light and read the time wrongly. It felt like noon when really it was late afternoon. The sun was in the wrong place.

The surface of the sea was agitated by the growing wind. Dark patches of squalls moved from east to west. I imagined the little family on the beach packing up their picnic rug, drying their feet on soggy towels, pulling socks over sandy skin and wandering home tired and happy. The coast ran away from me, the long scoop of shoreline dwindling under a headland in the distance. The sun shone brightly on one part while dark clouds hovered over another, then the wind changed the whole scene again.

The big sky soared above. Puffs of cumulonimbus ballooned on high and floated across its perfect blue. The surface of the water below was busy with movement and the flat heaviness of it seemed vast and somehow magnetic, forcing me to strain my eyes to the inaccessible faraway. I was suddenly aware of being on the tips of my toes. I retreated to the lee of the van again and lost myself in my story.

A solid focussed hour passed during which I made decisions about the plot, and a character took shape after being somewhat evasive. Like friends and family, some characters just refuse to behave, but in the end these guys are often the most fun to write about or be with. I therefore woke from this concentrated effort with a feeling of contentment, though the story itself was dark. My tea had gone cold and a biscuit wrapper and bookmark had travelled a few yards up the grassy hillock, so I strode out after them to clean up and quickly found myself on top of it. From there I saw the sudden drop that fell six feet behind the van. At the bottom of it more rocks jagged up and a couple of sandpipers flew off as I towered over them. The drop wasn't deep, but enough to wreck a van. A tiny bout of vertigo gripped me and my sense of wellbeing dissolved. I grasped my arms in front of me and swayed. The tide was sucking out and in around the seaweed-laden rocks below and I felt myself lean out and back again in sympathy. The wind had dropped a little and a small fishing boat was making its way north across the expanse of water. Everything was big, except the boat and me, everything in its place, except perhaps me. The overnight problem niggled.

I ran back to check the camper's handbrake and left the gears in first, then made dinner and ate it in the lee of the van, hoping this would steady my churning stomach.

The sun was moving northwards and the wind had dropped in anticipation of twilight. I washed my dishes and tidied them away, then counted the house windows from which I could be seen. There was a small one on the side of a cottage by the shore a few hundred yards back and a conservatory up the hill behind me which was yellow with electric light. Other houses were too far distant and the fish research facilities further south were probably closed for the night. As the light began to fade I pulled the curtain over on the village side for privacy and having done so felt extremely safe. Calm began to return. Birds called to one another like mothers calling their children home, and I watched the colours of the sky change and glow, the pinks and oranges reaching far over my roof as well as burning a reflected path across the water to my door.

There were no superlatives great enough for the hugeness of it all. Splendiferous, fantasmagoric, or mind-bogglingly magnificent. I laughed at my attempt to find anything that caught the moment and tossed my notebook aside. The universe appeared to be offering me a pathway to heaven and had somehow already lured me to the most beautiful spot on the planet in which to spend a night. I sighed and sat. God was sending out his special rays from the dying sun. Or maybe I had just failed to find my way to a campsite and chanced upon something far better. Either way I decided to stay the night.

I stored the folding chair and the various bits and pieces that always seem to spread themselves around every available surface inside the van, and dug out my jammies. These night-time preparations took me some time because the view up the west coast of Kintyre, was so beguiling that I kept leaning on the door and gazing, just gazing, completely bewitched and feeling somehow loved by the place, which I'm perfectly aware is completely illogical.

The thought of doing something slightly dangerous like being alone and female in a van with a dodgy lock without the proximity of other humans for protection or an electric hook-up for light, filled me with happiness. The wonderful aloneness. I whooped silently in excitement, as if I'd been given an unexpected present. Then my beloved seal, because he was already beloved, stuck his head up through the salmon pink path of the fading sun.

'Hey, big guy!' I called out.

He blew bubbles at me, then the waves folded over him. I got out the binoculars and tried to follow his movements but only managed to find the plastic lobster pot buoys instead. A lone shag stood on a rock a little way off with its wings outstretched facing into the sunset. I stood facing it too as the islands became dark shapes and the pale sea lapped at the rocks beneath me.

I got comfy on the bed with a book and a bag of nuts but the silhouettes of gulls against the many-coloured sky proved more interesting than the words on the page. The firmament was all shades, even green in some places. I had left the back door open because I just couldn't let go of the splendour beyond it. The air was delicious, the hum of waves such a pleasure to my ears. The wind was rising again and whistling through the gaps in the van.

Then two fat headlights shone through the curtain and illuminated my little sanctuary. Frenzied shadows crossed the wall. Through a gap in the material I saw the outline of a large windowless van hurtling towards me from the village. It pulled up with a roar, turned into the layby alongside me and ground to a halt. With one last growl the engine died. A complete silence fell.

It seemed even the wind dropped for a period. I held my breath. A door handle clicked. I leapt off the bed and closed my own door, being careful to turn the handle upwards into the lock position. I straightened the curtains and shut the ones on the other side too. Men's voices reached me, somebody laughed. A heavy side door rumbled open. I heard the fizz of a can being pulled. More voices, all men. I didn't dare look. Feet scraped the gravelly ground.

'Did you bring a knife?' said someone who was extremely close to my window. There was a muffled reply and the sound of something heavy, like a suitcase full of body parts, landing on the ground.

'Ooft! Watch out with that, man.'

That was all the sense I could make of their talk. I pulled the pillow round my ears and closed my eyes, then changed my mind: I might need to defend myself.

Five more minutes of boots shuffling on grit, the suddenness of people sharing a joke, a second can opening, a third, then the sliding door sliding shut. Boom.

I waited another thirty seconds then peeked. It was a giant white van, the kind everyone hates being stuck behind on a narrow road. Its sides were a mishmash of coloured stickers with words like 'Thrilla Gorilla', 'Shaggs', 'Billabong' and 'Vans' all over it.

I should get a 'Vans' one, I mused for a second.

'Ripcurl', 'Surf Shack', 'Fat Willy's' and 'Dude'. There was a poem in there, for sure. Perhaps not one by me.

I didn't know any surfers. I didn't know if they were likely to be dangerous. I thought probably not, but couldn't be sure. I waited for more sacks of body parts to land but heard nothing for five minutes, so I guessed they were asleep. No wonder, if they'd been surfing all day, though even I could tell the surf hadn't been up around my bit of sea. I opened the skylight, listened to the waves on the rocks and tucked myself more firmly into the sleeping bag.

This had happened once before, the first time I took my two daughters camping. They were only three and five. We had the whole hillside campsite to ourselves until at eight in the evening six large bikers arrived on six giant motorbikes. For five minutes I was on high alert, ready to protect us. But the bikers threw up their tent (only one, so it must have been quite smelly in there) climbed inside and were gone, silent for the rest of the night. They waved to us in the early morning when they left.

The surfers were the same. Their sliding door woke me at dawn. The wind was up and also, no doubt, the surf. They were in for a good day. I imagined them hurrying along to Westport Beach, about three miles long and popular with surfers, walkers and their dogs, where nothing stood between them and America.

The van rocked gently and fresh air slipped through a space at a window and tickled my forehead. I was sorry I hadn't said hello. I made a silent apology. It is sensible to be circumspect, but layby encounters are generally good. Yet I was equally pleased they had gone and I had the whole grand view up the west coast to myself in the quiet magnificence of dawn.

Campervan Love

This is a love story, of sorts, but with vans. I'll tell you the end of this tale first, so you know where it's going: I will never be able to live without a campervan. Owning a van has become a vital element of my private and working lives. In fact, as a writer, those two compartments are actually one, but the van fulfils a variety of needs, escape being the most obvious. Returning to myself is another.

Another vital aspect is knowing with some certainty that, as long as I have the van, I will be able to write. I am therefore happy as soon as I set foot in it.

I use my small campervan as a mobile office, a writing retreat and a base camp for interesting days out, amongst other things. I usually, though not always, travel solo, sleep in it solo and spend hours alone in it, often in the middle of nowhere. In addition to a roof, four wheels and all the other features that make a van a camper, in other words a bed, cooker and sink at the absolute minimum to earn the title, my campervan must have a table and some means of sitting at it. I need windows so I can stare out at the view, and a good view, Kintyre for instance, but anywhere I can get on with it and ignore everyone, and be ignored, will do.

The beginnings of this tale and the itinerant and solitary habits which resulted can be traced as far back as the end of my parents' failed love story, after their separation and bitter divorce, once my dad realised he wasn't 'never going to see [us] again'. Around that time, he bought a Bedford Dormobile, pale blue and cream on the outside with blood-red interior upholstery, and he drove us to beautiful Ardnamurchan. Similar to Kintyre in that it's a long peninsula with a lighthouse at the end, Ardnamurchan Point is the most westerly part of mainland Scotland and has two very distinct ring dykes, which are a delight to many an amateur geologist because they are so easily seen. If you climb the rocks beside the road just before you arrive at Sanna and look back the way you came, you'll see a perfect circle of crags. This includes the rock you'll be perched on which is part of the edge of a massive volcano, fortunately extinct.

I don't think my dad knew about these, or perhaps I was deemed too young to bother telling, but he parked our van and us at the side of the little road and set up camp for a week. This was myself aged about five and my two older brothers aged six and seven. My youngest brother was too small to come with us and my two half-siblings weren't born or even imagined.

We spent most of our time on the beach, a place where hours slipped by unnoticed while we pottered, paddled and built sandcastles. How he filled the water tank or dealt with other practicalities like disposing of washing-up water or waste, storing fresh food and so on I have no idea. I wish he was here to tell me. It seems quite a feat for a middle-aged man on his own. I'm pretty sure we were filthy little ragamuffins by the end, but also very happy.

I have a photo he took of the van with the three of us standing beside it, me looking a tad cocky with my big brother's elbow precariously close to my ear. We were at Sanna Bay, just beyond the geological rings and quite close to several beautiful beaches full of white sand. At that time, the houses were still inhabited all year round. When I came back on a cycling trip twenty years later, only one house was occupied, by an elderly couple, and the rest had been bought up as holiday houses. In the sixties, when I went with my dad, you could still stop and camp anywhere you fancied and for as long as you liked. In the photo there's a saucepan on the bonnet which was put there, I think, having had its contents returned to the sea, an ink-squirting cuttlefish which we kept captive under the back wheel for a couple of days. I think it squirted when scared so whenever we approached in our clumsy children's way, it vanished into a cloud of purple, so I've no recollection of what it looked like. I don't remember caring much about its fate either, being much more scared of it than it would have been of me.

Cornflakes and carnation milk were the order of the day, carnation milk being condensed but not (massively) sweetened, like UHT only more so. Probably also present were burnt sausages, slightly wrinkly tomatoes and hard-boiled eggs, all specialities of my dad's. The roof of the Dormobile was one that rose sideways with a canvas collapsible part of red-and-white stripes, like the red-and-white stripy folding chair I carry in my own van. The chair was my gran's and probably ages with the Dormobile. Stripes must have been in that year.

Inside this lovely Bedford there were two upper bunks, one on either side, red fabric scoops like old-fashioned army camp beds. Fun but not actually comfortable and probably hellish if you need a pee in the middle of the night, though I've no memory of that. I can't remember an on-board toilet either and, there being no trees at Sanna, I've no idea what we did. I do remember being sent for fresh milk to the nearest farm, which was always a treat, but scary in case I got it wrong. I often got things wrong.

After this trip, I think when I was about six, my dad and new step-mum took us in this van all the way across Europe (as I understood it) to Venice. This was nerve-wracking, but my dad was that sort of guy; it wasn't the van that made me jumpy. I remember being fascinated by ants in the Alps which were swarming around a little hole in the concrete about the size of my tiny six-year-old finger. I also remember trying to explain to some grown-ups that I had two mums and them laughing. Remarrying was new in those days, especially in Catholic France, and I didn't fully understand. No doubt I was trying to make sense of what my dad remarrying might mean, and at six knew nothing of the birds and the bees.

I don't think they had the Dormobile all that long, but a couple of years later my maternal grandparents bought their first camper which I assumed would make up for my loss. As grandparents they were lovely but quite strict and, being a child, I was a natural anarchist or perhaps an anarchic naturalist. Either way, I also assumed they had rediscovered a connection with all things natural themselves and were going to be chilling and slumming it a bit and generally being more human and accessible instead of the tidy and proper people they were. How wrong I was. Going in their van meant just that – going, as in being driven, in a van. My grandpa was the plastic surgeon who set up the Canniesburn Unit in Glasgow, so extremes of cleanliness were his norm. It was a seen-and-not-heard situation for us kids where you had to be careful what you touched and whether your fingers were clean when you touched it. This time it was usually me and my little brother, the older two having been dispatched to boarding school by my dad under the draconian agreements of my parents' divorce. These campervan trips were adult fun, in other words boring and serious, and you had to keep your dress clean and be polite. I don't think I ever spent a night in them either. The vans were largely plastic and not good old metal, wood and canvas like my dad's Bedford, and therefore unnatural and consequently, to my young mind, substandard. There were also territory issues, again seemingly based on age. I remember sitting in the back, alone, staring miserably out as fence posts whizzed past, wishing I could hypnotise myself out of my current reality. I've been told my grandparents had two campervans, though not at the same time obviously, but I have only hazy memories of either of them. Perhaps my self-hypnosis worked. But I believe they were both Bedfords, the pioneers of campervanning at the time along with the iconic VWs.

So already, by the age of ten, I'd had two formative campervanning experiences. The most significant was an early attachment to 'natural' vans in natural places, the other inspired a need for imaginative escape from my surroundings and company, especially while inhabiting a campervan. A now-familiar template, or perhaps a Pavlovian-style response, was established.

Several years passed. As a young, youngish and then less young adult, camping was a poor alternative. When my two kids were small I took pride in being able to pack them, a tent and all the accoutrements of camping into my tiny car within an hour, after which I would head for the safety of a campsite. Having arrived I'd set up the tent and pump the mattress full of air, while they ran free and happy. 'There's a lot of air on this hill,' said my asthmatic daughter on our first trip, which took us to the hills above Skelmorlie on the Clyde coast, where the campsite wasn't quite flat and there was a considerable wind. I'd make a simple dinner on the same primus stove my mother used when she did the same for me and my brothers. Her trips were more fully planned. There were, after all, four of us, but she still cooked on a single burner and had better washing habits than my dad. Though separated, my parents shared a tenacity in their determination to make our lives interesting and outdoors. Like them, I too was separated from my children's father from early on and wanted my kids to love being in the open. I wonder too whether my parents would fall into bed near us exhausted with all the effort. For me there was the sudden decision to go, then the driving, putting up the tent, pumping up mattresses and wiping mud off hands and faces before sausages and beans could be served up, faces wiped again and teeth brushed. I was always grateful they were young enough for an early bedtime.

More years passed. Circumstances changed. I remarried. Along with my new husband, I filled my house with four step-children. Including my own two, this meant eight people in one house. What was I thinking? It all seemed quite valiant and vital for a while. So many people trying to find their way and needing, as we saw it, the stability he and I could provide. But in fact the chaos which ensued soon began to wear us down too. Regular escape became vital and we took every opportunity to get away and nearly broke the bank with train fares and flights to various locations, and good hotels when we got there. But this was no solution and posh hotels don't bring the kind of relaxation that works for me. Escape from real life isn't my thing either. I wanted to escape, but to a more real sense of life. Escape from endless household chores and unsatisfied and incomprehensible teenagers yes, but also escape towards something good and healthy and sane. Escape was vital in both senses of the word.

We almost bought a flat in the south of France, but having no love for one particular place, I suggested a campervan which we could keep over there and move about. We hummed and hawed, and hawed and hummed again. There was a lot of talk and very little action. We considered moving abroad entirely, but as I worked with the English language I would probably have wound up unemployed. With a campervan and frequent holidays, we could test the water first. I searched online and thought about it long and hard until I figured out what we needed and what could be risked financially. My husband was my partner in this, but I was the leading party and, because I was the mover and shaker of this plan, I chose a van which moved and shook and didn't resemble a posh hotel in any way.

It was never meant to be suitable for France, only as a starter in Scotland. The day I set off to view it, he had to stay and work. We also had a disagreement in the morning, not about campervans, more likely about towels or people being rude, I can't honestly remember, but instead of staying home to sort the problem, I kept my appointment. I had spent considerable time on this, a friend had arrived to drive me over to Fife, a distance of about eighty miles, and the vendor was waiting. Thus, from the very beginning, campervanning became the new pressure valve.

But heading off to buy it on my own was an unfortunate mistake. It made our first vehicle mine, and not ours. Buying together would have bonded us in a proper *folie à deux*. Going it alone meant he took some persuasion and four days of glorious sunshine at a music festival to love this van. His resistance was also to do with its age and the fact that it had necessarily had many previous owners who most probably weren't all that clean. Being slightly dirty is at best unavoidable in a campervan and often *de rigueur*. This is not how my husband liked things to be.

I have to admit that, in the pain of that morning's argument, the vendor of the van seemed comfortable company. At least fifteen years my senior, his wife had died three years earlier and I suspect his van and his adventures in it around Scotland that he told me about had been some kind of salve. In contrast to certain other people, he totally got what I saw in this beautiful, though elderly, campervan. I found him in a compound of vehicles and bikes of all kinds, neatly arranged in readiment for fixing, use or sale and surrounded by a high wire fence. I'd have happily spent an afternoon wandering about in it and learning about all the various vehicles and their history. These places always interest me, especially in their lack of waste, the way ordinary things are salvaged from extinction and solutions are found to apparently intractable practical problems. He was totally engaged with his ongoing life and it felt good to start my new campervanning adventure under his blessing.

His van was ideal. It too was a Bedford but it had a Suzuki engine, a combination said by my scrapyard friend to be indestructible. I believe this to be true but I have no proof, because two years later this van came a cropper when my daughter's boyfriend mistook it for a four by four and broke the irreplaceable exhaust manifold on a rock in the middle of a field. I could even tell you what an exhaust manifold is, but I won't waste time here. The lack of it means no forward motion.

This gem of a van was a 'high top' or 'hi-top' as it is often spelt. This means you can stand up if you're my height, which is a joy if you're cooped up in there for too long on wet days. Of course, this never happens in Scotland. It had a 'rock and roll' bed so you could take it to music festivals and dance. No, so you could easily roll the bench forward into a bed for sleeping, and rock it back up again when there's writing to be done. The bed was surprisingly comfortable and had the added advantage of backing against the rear door which you could open from the inside by reaching behind your pillow if you woke to find a scorching hot day and you were being boiled alive behind all that glass. There was a lot of window. When you think that the tea-making facilities were only a few feet away from the foot end of the bed you can see the type of luxury I'm talking about here.

The van's height was to accommodate a second bed. Half of this upper sleeping area was removable. It could be stored on top of the permanent part or you could leave it at home, as I generally did. I never slept in it because it didn't provide enough height for sitting up. Very cramped. It was once used by my poor eldest who passed a warm midgey night up there, tossing, turning and complaining 'til dawn while her sister and I slept fitfully below. Not fully realising her plight, and being similarly invaded ourselves, there was nothing to be done but await the dawn. It was the midgiest night ever because of the heat which midges, Scotland's tiny but deadly national insects, love. This was compounded by our location, a sheltered and damp spot close to water. Heaven for midges and hell for us. They were swarming at the windows. We had no toilet but outside, you see, to make matters worse. Hellish. We emerged into the day covered in a mass of tiny pink spots: the dreaded, maddening, distracting and annoying, though usually harmless, midgie bite. We moved to a breezy spot and dozed all afternoon. I thought at the time my daughter would be put off campervanning for the rest of her life, but on the same fatal trip across the rocky field which ended its life, two couples slept in that van in the rain. There was probably no room for midges, and I prefer not to imagine the smell.

The upper torture chamber, otherwise known as the extra bed space, provided a great throw-everything-in space, storage being extremely important in campers. Many vans are entirely inadequate in this respect. I'm a throw-everything-in sort of a gal, planning for every eventuality and forever fearing some vital implement, probably a book, could be forgotten. The days of the one-hour pack-up into a tiny car were long gone, so the van and I were ideally suited. This van could have had a chemical Porta Potti, had I had the sense to buy one. A main advantage of any van in any location is the existence of an on-board toilet, so you can wave goodbye to watching your fluid intake and scanning the horizon for toilets, or at least bushes big enough to hide your big behind behind, so to speak.

There was a cooker and a sink and a large water tank which was filled from an entrance on the outside just along from the petrol tank. It had a cap very similar to the petrol cap too, and yes, you've guessed it, one of us, not mentioning any names, filled the water tank with petrol. Oh dear. Well, alright then, it was my husband as was. He'd been playing that game of making out I treated him like he was stupid, which I wasn't because he's not, usually. I thought it best to let him read the sticker above the water tank by himself. 'WATERTANK' it said. There was no need to say anything thereafter.

But I guess we all make mistakes and there are many opportunities to do so in campervans. Unfortunately there was no repairing that particular damage, but luckily there was ample space on the worktop for a small portable water tank. Where there's a will there's a way.

This beautiful Bedford van was open-plan which means the cab was not separate from the living accommodation. Additionally, the engine was between the front seats, a perfect location from a mechanic's point of view because the engine was so accessible, but a disaster if you wanted to travel listening to the quiet movements of concertos, or indeed the noisy ones. And it's amazing how tiring it is to be next to the equivalent of a road hammer-digger for any length of time. But it certainly warmed the van on a cold day.

The two years we had this lovely Bedford proved the feasibility and importance of a campervan to us, and the vacant six-month period after its demise proved this again without a doubt.

One of the Bedford's loveliest features was its almost total all round visibility. The windows were real glass so there was no distortion to your horizon, and there were further windows in the high top so you could stand and gaze as well as doing it sitting down. Unfortunately this was not true of the next van which had mostly plastic windows, all small and all below head height if you were seated on the bench at the table. This disability added up to no proper viewing in bad weather or while working at the table. However, like the Bedford, it did have a side door which was very comfy for sitting in the sun, and an awning which magically helped cool down the whole van when it was hot.

I found this new van online after another extensive search. This time I wanted more comfort, a toilet for me and good washing facilities for him. It was the van that would take us to France as planned. We went to view the van together and both took the chance to test drive it along a little back road in Stirlingshire. We explored its insides in the privacy of the owner's driveway, while they discreetly left us to it, and discussed the pros and cons of its various features. We imagined our future, and finally went together to the cashpoint and took out the deposit. It was ours, though the balance came from my late father's bequest, and while it seemed huge compared to the Bedford, I knew it made better sense for the two of us travelling together.

Our new van was a long-base Fiat Ducato with 'captain's' seats for driver and passenger which means they could be turned towards the bench and table behind for greater sociability. It cost about eight times more than the previous van but, in a bid to please my squeamish husband, it had all mod cons: an oven we never used, a three ring cooker, a safe (never used), a better shower than the one at home except for requiring its water tank filled, toilet, two sinks, loads of storage space, hot water, central heating (sometimes), a twelve CD player for exceptionally long predictable journeys down motorways, a satellite dish and a TV connection had we chosen to reinstall the TV.

It also had a remarkably uncomfortable bed. My back suffered in this one as the bottom end of the bed consisted of the front driving seats, complete with lipped edges, and a specially designed square cushion to jam in between them. The van was an otherwise cleverly and professionally converted ordinary big white van, high-topped as is best. Apart from the bed, it felt extremely posh, and even the bed was luxurious and bohemian when left made up for four boozy days and nights at a festival.

We added three large batteries so that we could travel and not use campsites and I could write on my laptop for lengthy periods without needing to worry. Lined up along the inside of the door were stickers naming all the exotic places the previous occupants had been to on their honeymoon: Liechtenstein, Venice, Monaco and the like. The kerb-side door sported a professionally painted picture of palm trees and ships, all very romantic and kitsch. This was probably the clincher for me in the decision to buy it, even though it wasn't to my taste. It seemed fantastically eccentric and distinctive. But the people who sold us it had gone to the bother of pricing a cover-up job and had already done away with whatever had been on the bonnet. Bare naked ladies? Hash leaves? We never found out but reckoned the remaining artwork was good insurance against theft. We certainly attracted attention.

This van was a compromise on my part, being much bigger and fancier than anything I would ever have chosen. I never really needed such luxuries as a shower or even so much space, but it was extremely comfortable for two people to live in and we never felt cramped, even on long trips. He liked it, especially the comfortable driving seat and the way it turned towards the table. We felt self-contained, secure and for the most part happy in it, especially once he'd accustomed himself to the limitations of its interior and stopped bumping his head. It took practice but soon we had a natural way of moving about in it, a daily routine when we were away, and allotted tasks like filling the water tank (him) and making up the bed (me). It was great for solo writing trips too because I could sleep on the bunk which was against the back door and leave the table up at night with all my writing paraphernalia ready for the morning.

It was in this van that he says he had the happiest time he can remember, ever. That's quite something. We were parked in a fairly basic campsite by a river in the little town of

Limoux in Aude in southern France for a whole three weeks in late September. I wrote all morning while he cycled in the surrounding hills, then we visited my sister and family who lived nearby. Life seemed, for a while, to be in perfect balance. Then the campsite closed for winter and we had to return home. My kids were young adults and calling me. I wanted to be there for them. He wanted to stay.

Those three weeks felt almost like a holiday romance, of a kind, a companionable bubble safe from the realities of our six teenage and young adult children, from work and maintaining our home, and from decisions about what to do with our lives because it seemed like we were actually doing it.

On the way through France, we stopped in a service station, or *aire* as they call them in France, which simply translates as 'area'. He went to stretch his legs and when he came back announced he wanted to take a job he'd been offered in Turkey, for three months. I sat in stunned silence. As we drove through France then England, the weather changed from warm autumn sun, to breezy, to wet and breezy, to wild, and so on until the wind was horizontal and the rain lashing the windscreen. Fearing our high top van would be overturned, we stopped at the lovely service station at Tebay, about forty miles short of the Scottish border, and parked in the sloping car park. It was dark and the campsite was shut, so we slept in the shelter of a massive lorry. We ate breakfast beside the little pond there and watched the ducks chase each other, but the sky had already darkened.

In A Romahome

I'm on the Road to the Isles in a tiny car park about two thirds of the way along the northern side of Loch Cluanie heading west, where I'm writing about our old Fiat Ducato, now sold. Fort William, at the top of Loch Linnhe, is directly to the south, at six o'clock, while Fort Augustus is equally directly east, at three o'clock, at the foot of Loch Ness. Both towns and both lochs, Linnhe and Ness, are part of the Great Glen and run roughly southwest to northeast. Loch Cluanie is one of several other lochs which run roughly east to west and close to the Great Glen, intersecting at angles of roughly forty-five degrees, obviously. What is less obvious to the naked eye is that the landmass north of the Great Glen is moving imperceptibly northeast, while the bit south of it is heading southwest. They are rubbing along each other in opposite directions. This is considered a fault, but it always strikes me as amazingly beautiful.

There are other geological faults in the surrounding glens and minor earthquakes are not uncommon. Loch Cluanie is on the northern side of what is known as the Great Glen Fault and is heading northeast. It is almost entirely deserted and moody, a place where great storms can be seen approaching for miles, as can better weather. It is also a giant reservoir which was built after the Second World War as part of the hydroelectric scheme. The Isles this road leads to are the Inner Hebrides, Skye in particular.

Mountains rise on the opposite side of the loch directly

from the water and there appears to be no road over there, but a house sits on an exposed promontory from the southern shore a little to the west of me, offering a perfect photo opportunity to the several people who have stopped so far this morning. The day is warm enough for the back door of my van to be open, allowing me to eavesdrop on any other vehicles that dare to park.

By some weird chance, a similar Fiat Ducato campervan to the one we used to own has entered the car park. The visitor has French number plates. The layout is therefore reversed, but I can see the vans are closely matched. The side door is open and the captain's seat swivelled. It is newer than ours, silver with a red-and-blue motif along the side and an electric side step. Dead posh 'n' that, even posher than ours was. I should congratulate them on making it so far from home. We travelled all the way to Limoux several times in our Ducato, so I know it's a slog. From across the car park (not far) they don't sound French. They are as quiet as a long-married couple which is what they appear to be. Like them, we also attached a bike rack to the rear. Our falling apart as a couple was reflected in our lack of maintenance of this van. When it came to selling it there was a deal of fixing to be done, including a dodgy side door that had fallen off its runners.

I've just caught a glimpse of a dimply French thigh and pants. Someone is getting changed. French knickers ain't what they're cracked up to be. And these people are speaking French but with a light accent. Very clear. Odd the sounds that travel – I can hear plastic bags crackling, I think I hear munching, but now a car is roaring past and has obliterated everything.

My husband and I were even less able to maintain our private lives than our van and separated shortly after the publication of my first novel. This was very sad indeed, as I'm sure you can imagine. There will be more on going solo later, but let's stick with the vans just now.

When we parted, I sold the Ducato. Despite separating, we met to fix the broken seat, the sliding door that would no longer slide, the central heating that only worked on days with no 'y' and other little bits and pieces. This was weird, desperately sad and painful, but necessary, and quite quickly the van was in much better condition than when we'd bought it two-and-a-half years before. We'd made very good use of it and been on more trips than I can remember, both together and apart, but it was expensive to run, tricky to drive on little winding Scottish roads and not necessary for a single person. I got the same price we'd paid for it and began a life of simplicity and thrift with no van or car. After a blur of struggling to adjust and being horribly unhappy, I bought another van for a tenth of the price.

Three months had passed and he was not back. I couldn't rectify his loss, but I could sort the absence of a van. This helped take the edge off the hurt.

I found my very own first Romahome online too. It was an internet romance. The smallest campervan you could buy at the time, I'd passed one near my home for years and always wondered what it was like inside. My scrappie friend came with me to view it, so that I could check whether its natural home was in fact a scrapyard. To my great delight, he pronounced this little Bedford solid, for it was indeed another Bedford with another apparently indestructible Suzuki engine. There was no rust underneath it because it had been sprayed at an early age with some kind of protectant. The owner was an elderly man who lived in an even more elderly cottage which over the years had gradually been surrounded by an industrial estate and retail outlet in the eastern extremes of the Glasgow conurbation. Fixing vehicles had been his life and the yard he'd worked in was next door to his house but in use by someone else. He'd bought the van so he could go on fishing trips with his son, but the insurance had proved too expensive. He sold the van to me for next to nothing.

This little campervan was dinky and cute and a little drippy on the inside. It had less than 1000cc, 970 to be exact, and very limited suspension. But don't be fooled by the tininess of Romahomes. Within a load volume of just under a hundred and six cubic feet it had a king-size bed or two narrow singles. There was a cooker, a fridge and a toilet, a fresh-water container with a foot-operated pump, a hook-up for the mains, two sockets and two electric lights. The kitchen cupboards were adequate but there were also four large bunkers beneath the benches and a huge area in the Luton which is the bit above the cab. There were two large windows made of glass for easy viewing, and a table on which to write a novel. The seat covers were extremely posh, like tapestry in tasteful but cheery colours. You exited the cab in the normal way via the driver's door and entered the campervan part from a little door at the back. There was a narrow gap between the chair backs in the cab and no glass partition between front and back, which was handy when I accidentally locked the back door of the living quarters with the keys inside and me outside. By breathing in and some undignified up-ending I managed to squeeze through from the front cab, slide across the table in the back, and roll onto the bench where I'd left the keys.

The over-the-table skylight in this Romahome was covered with a metal sheet so I installed a brand new Perspex one, and although it continued to leak at one edge, I was at least mobile again and mostly dry. This was a very good thing and confirmed for me the absolute necessity to my sanity of having a campervan no matter what. It also proved to me that previous vans had not existed for the sole purpose of abandoning my husband and family, which they had occasionally suspected, and in fact so had I. Having a van served several purposes all of its own, as we shall see.

The front seat covers of my new van were threatening to divulge their innards so, on a trip to Oban, I bought two cheap t-shirts, one with Spiderman on the front (kids' jammies), the other a cute kitten crop-top. These I put over the seats to retain their stuffing. When I came later to sell the van, I noticed the new owner retained these ridiculous monstrosities. I know this because I found the buyer online but by some weird coincidence she was the girlfriend-of-the-son-of-the-woman-who-lives-two-doors-down-from-me, and therefore for a while the van was still often parked outside my house. At some point during this time my neighbour on the other side took a fancy to Romahomes too and bought a Citroen Romahome, which has the same back living quarters but sits on a Citroen C15, making our side of the street look like some strange club.

But I am ahead of myself. We need to identify these vans by name for future reference, even though I don't actually think naming vehicles is the act of a rational human being. For the purposes of this book, however, I think it will make things easier and save confusion.

To recap on my pre-loved, previously-owned-by-me vans: the first Bedford high top, an Autosleeper of midge-collection fame with an (in)destructible engine, had RAL in its registration number. This reminds me of 'rallentando', a musical term which is Italian for a gradual decrease of speed. Very appropriate. Of course RAL is also the beginning of rally, a long distance race and therefore the opposite of rallentando, so I think we'll encapsulate both notions and go for 'Rally', now to be known as Rally Bedford.

The big Ducato's registration plate included FUG. My marriage was most definitely in one for part of that time at least, but perhaps Fugue would be kinder: we were in fact singing the same tune, but contrapuntally, so to speak. Therefore Rally for the Bedford and Fugue for the Ducato.

Then along came Vera. On being driven home for the first time, my new Bedford Romahome had the terrifying habit of leaping to left and right at the slightest provocation, like a highly sensitive racehorse. There appeared to be a complete absence of suspension. It also veered heavily to the left. Vera.

Vera's number plate included UFC. Some might say this van was therefore affiliated to one of many possible 'United' football clubs, but having lived in a sectarian squabble during my marriage, I chose to think of it as Unattached Football Club, or Unlimited Fun Club.

Vera did staggeringly well on the steep hills of Cowal, a peninsula in the west which calls itself 'the gateway to the Scottish Highlands'. I use the word 'staggeringly' advisedly. We often went up Cowal's hills in first gear with both of us, Vera and I, puffing and panting. I'd be shouting encouragement from the wheel as I watched the temperature gauge rise and Vera would be belching out black smoke as she fell through the gears. Because of Vera's old engine (over two decades) I thought it wise not to cause her (and me) the stress of the traffic on the busy long way round from Glasgow to Kintyre via Loch Lomond, Arrochar, Inveraray and all the other tourists stops on that popular scenic trail. Cowal, by contrast, is accessible via a choice of two ferries. Board at Gourock on the southern shores of the Clyde estuary and cross the Lower Clyde Basin to Dunoon or Kirn. The drive overland across Cowal is sparsely populated and has limited phone coverage. These are usually advantages to the writer in search of inspiration, but always a worry if you think you might need help. The route is also considerably shorter and passes through forests, moors and mountains, along rivers, tributaries, lochs and reservoirs and affords magnificent, if a little dizzying, views from several great heights down the Kyles of Bute. It always amazes me that such wilderness is so close to Glasgow, as if the Highlands have travelled south which, being located south of the Great Glen, they have.

Kyle, incidentally, is another word for strait, as in the water variety and there is one on either side of Bute. Of course, to get these amazing views from Cowal, you have to climb a couple of death-defying hills. It was the thought of these hills which decided me against buying a similarly ancient Romahome I'd found near a disused mine in darkest Lanarkshire shortly before I found Vera. It refused to go above fifty miles per hour on a flat road with no bends, and belched out so much smoke you could be forgiven for assuming it was powered by coal. These hills would have been the death of it, and possibly me.

After crossing Cowal there is the pleasure of a second ferry trip from Portavadie to Tarbert at the top of Kintyre. Two ferries makes the journey pricey but you may spot dolphins or basking sharks in Loch Fyne on the way. These are a fairly frequent sight if you are determined enough and look carefully, but sightings are still sporadic enough to make you feel lucky. The journey is also short enough to sit on deck whatever the weather and gaze south at Goat Fell, the highest peak on Arran, and north up huge Loch Fyne towards Inveraray.

Vera Romahome was never popular with my husband who did in fact return for a while. It's understandable he wasn't keen. Vera was such a massive step down from Fugue, being double Fugue's age and a bit bashed and broken, like its owner for a while, and the accommodation didn't offer much in the way of luxury, though the bed was comfy.

Two years later, when he'd left again, even I tired of Vera's noise and tardiness. Like Rally Bedford, the engine was under the seats, mostly the passenger seat, so passengers tended to overheat or my shopping bags (and cheese) would melt. It was exhaustingly noisy and vibrated a lot. Vera was rather elderly, about twenty-four years old by the end, a wee old lady of a van. Her new owner is an environmentalist, which is probably just as well. I hope she managed to fix her up.

I then bought Vanessa Hotplate, which is the camper I have now. Vanessa Hotplate's name is emblazoned on her two-gas-rings-one-grill cooking arrangement. Vanessa is also a Romahome, indeed the Romahome part was only slightly younger than Vera's, but the cab and base was only ten. A young thing. This is the joy of Romahomes, theoretically. They are 'demountable', in other words the back part can be raised slightly on legs, similar to the jack you'd use to fix a flat tyre, and made to stand independently. You can then drive the base out from under it, freeing the owner to travel without the weight and encumbrance of the back. This is not particularly useful to me when on holiday or a writing retreat, or indeed in the city, because the entire van, including cab and living quarters, is so small anyway. As an added bonus, the wheelbase is narrow, much slimmer than normal vehicles. The result is that Vera and Vanessa can both race through the spaces in those broken 'sleeping policemen' that are so popular around the south side of Glasgow where I live, without feeling a thing. She can also do U-turns in narrow roads with grace and ease.

Vera, my first Romahome, was a Bedford whose living quarters were specifically designed for her and therefore the top and bottom fitted snugly together with no air gaps. Vanessa Hotplate, however, is a hybrid. Her home part (think snail) is Romahome, but her base is a Daihatsu Hijet pickup. This is an almost but not quite total match. The result is she sits a little high on her base making her potentially extremely unstable, as you'd expect with a name like Vanessa Hotplate.

The depth of her instability was brought home to me on a trip down the M74, the main motorway through the south of Scotland. I was going to a friend's music gig near the border. There was a strong wind when I left the house, but nothing Vanessa couldn't handle. Or so I thought.

Twenty miles down the road the wind was wild and unpredictable. I was buffeted violently by side winds all the way to Abington. At one point, after the shelter of a thick wall of evergreens, I came out into the open and traversed a high bridge over the Douglas Water. I thought for a not very brief second that it would be my last bridge and that Vanessa and I were going over the edge into the abyss. I slowed to thirty miles per hour (from thirty-five) and saved the day, but I had no idea when the next exit would present itself or whether my little van would be upright long enough to get me there. I was shaken to the core. I had checked temperature and rain forecasts, but not wind factor. Curses. This was a stupid ill-thought-out expedition into unknown territory with unknown equipment in unknown conditions.

I was travelling directly south. The wind hit me from the west at a ninety degree angle. Most of the time I was being blown off the road rather than into the paths of other vehicles. But the gusts were fierce, sudden and erratic and let up as swiftly as they arrived. I had to react quickly to each blast and then re-react, straightening up the wheel, with equal speed when it left. Otherwise I was in danger of throwing myself into the fast lane and the paths of juggernauts. Who'd have thought driving a small campervan could ever be an extreme sport?

Since then I've taken various measures to harness her. She was like Vera Bedford only worse. I'd fitted both vehicles with new suspension stabilisers, but Vanessa took more than that to respond and needed special tyres with reinforced sides which were then pumped up to an extra high pressure. She is still a tad flighty, especially in those side winds which I try to avoid by always checking the weather properly, but I am used to her little ways and so far we have come to no great harm.

Vanessa has a glass-backed cab. The last owner had fitted a board across this on the inside of the living space. This was because of the disparity between back and front and the resulting large gaps. It was the only way to make it airtight. And it was a very thorough job. Absolutely no draughts were getting through. Not fully understanding why the board had been fitted, but completely unable to park because of zero rear visibility, I removed the board, a fibreglass space filler that was underneath and the rubber that surrounded the space filler. I scraped all the paint off the glass panel at the back of the cab too. Then I could see. At last. But there were consequences. On my first trip in Vanessa, the living part of the van filled up with beasties and bugs of every imaginable kind which had been sucked in between the cab and the back, through the gaps round the window and into my living space. They were spread the length and breadth of it, quite often in pieces. It was a scene of casual mass murder. They were mostly dead, obviously, after such a shock, but some had survived. Unfortunately it was also late in the day when I found their writhing bodies, and I'd hoped to slip straight into bed. Instead, with head-torch strapped to my forehead, I swept up as many as I could find, squashed those not already departed to a better world, picked them out from between the cushions with a pen and squirmed inwardly if any of them fell across my hand. I could hear some of them still buzzing after lights out. The following day I headed to the nearest hardware shop for gaffer tape with which I covered the gap. I used several layers of it and spanned well beyond what was needed, which sorted the problem for a while. However, it wasn't long before the force of the wind when driving regularly unstuck these repairs so I never travelled without gaffer. I simply couldn't figure out a better solution than continually adding tape, but in fact the tape proved indispensable thereafter for anything that broke.

Then a small community design organisation wanted to borrow Vanessa for a project. They were even prepared to pay me for the pleasure. I had already agreed before I fully grasped the fact that most people require better draught-proofing than unstickable sticky tape. These people were *designers* too. Oh dear. I purchased a large tube of expanding foam, took a deep breath (DIY isn't my strong suit) and squeezed yellow gunk into the gap. It looked like the inside of a Crunchie bar and solidified to almost as hard. When the van moved it sounded like a gang of hysterical chimps were on the roof. Luckily, through time and also motion, the foam has been compacted enough to merely gasp occasionally at bumps in the road while still retaining most of its ability to stem draughts or invasions by kamikaze insects.

There is also a crack to the inside pane of one of the plastic doubled-glazed windows. Unbelievable numbers of live beasties have made their way into the chamber within, only to die a slow and probably hot death unable to find their way back out. It's a veritable graveyard in there. I have no way of rescuing them in life or after it, short of renewing the whole window. There is even a small but perfectly formed peach-coloured grasshopper entombed upside down. I noticed, after the first winter, that there were fewer of them, so I'm assuming a particularly intelligent spider got inside, ate his dinner and managed to find his way back out.

Vanessa has no obvious water leaks like Vera's apart from a little one at the front end of the graveyard window. The ceiling was lined with white wallpaper covered in pastel-coloured butterflies when I got her, oh my, and stains, damp stains with unexplained sources which have not, thank goodness, got worse since my stewardship. And a small patch of mildew above the cooker. But it's mostly fine. Vanessa's previous owner also installed bright leafy curtains and made new bench cushions which she covered in waterproof red-and-white polka-dotty material. The cushions were not firm enough and I didn't fancy sleeping on plastic. I therefore swapped them with Vera's tapestry ones when I sold Vera. The result was, I think, a cheerful pastiche. However, the same designer crowd who borrowed Vanessa, also stripped away the butterflies, installed new tartan curtains, uncomfortable wooden benches, a new board across the window between front and back despite all my efforts to fix it (or perhaps because) and painted certain other interior parts black or red. When I reinstalled the tapestry cushions there was a gothic effect which was too weird for my liking. I again removed the wooden cover on the window and painted everything white. Now light enters and stays, or so it seems, and I feel outside when I'm inside, but in a good way.

Vanessa Hotplate's registration number includes the letters HMH which I've been reliably informed by a friend who is an MBE no less, stands for Her Majesty's House. This is also rather appropriate, although it may be illegal to call it that and could even risk the half-inching of Vanessa Hotplate by Her Majesty Herself for those quiet moments in the wilderness I'm sure even she would benefit from.

This is the van in which I now sit to write and gaze down Loch Cluanie, and on which the nice man in the French van came to congratulate me.

'Perfect for one person,' beamed the French-Canadian. That explained the accent and the pants. He also informed me his van was French, as labelled, and that they kept it in France and flew over from Canada every year for lengthy holidays, Scotland being this year's destination. I thought it was generous of him to admire my lunch box on wheels, with such a disparity between mine and his, but he was not in fact the first posh-vehicled *homme* to congratulate me, even with what appeared to be genuine admiration.

On a single-track road on another trip in sunny Cowal, I pulled into a passing place to let a golden Porsche through. The golden Porsche stopped in the golden sunshine and indicated I should wind down my window, which luckily was still working at that time.

'That is one fantastic vehicle,' said the driver, smiling in admiration. 'Who's it made by?' We chatted for a bit about size, cuteness, escape and manoeuvrability until another car wanted through and we had to part company. I drove on three inches taller in my driver's seat and singing along loudly to anthems on the radio.

You do get much fancier Romahomes nowadays, including some that sleep more than two people, but even the smallest ones will cost you in the region of thirty grand. They have heating and air conditioning, working fridges, built-in gadgets, parking bleeps, waste water tanks, fly screens and blinds. But I'd lose all those endearing air-leaks and damp patches, so where would be the fun?

Other Love

Out here among the song birds,
the ducks and the geese,
I hide beneath a hedgerow,
crouched under a pink and yellow sky
to gaze at trees all shades of green
and brown brackened hills.

Nothing is too far away or close,
all is as it always was
and time does not exist,
so you could not have finished us.

This book is mainly about solo campervanning. But it's also about writing, loss, love and the pleasures of solitude. It was begun at a time of extreme turmoil in my life when suddenly I was single again. I was just coming to terms with what this meant when, with rather less abruptness, he and I were back together, only to fall off the cliff again soon after.

Like all couples, we used to have no doubts at all. Then that was all there was. Eventually, I grew tired of cliffhangers. Don't we all in the end?

When I first started campervanning, he and I were still living under the same roof, and my two daughters and any combination of his four children were there too. Our house had five bedrooms but whatever size or shape the house, eight people in one place is not easy, whether the other seven are your blood relatives or not. The requirements of this set-up eventually became intolerable. Change of some kind was imperative and inevitable.

In case you are in doubt about the horrors of so-called 'blended' families, imagine the worst teenage behaviour and consider the high mathematical probability of those habits and incidents appearing in a house of six young people aged between twelve and twenty and from two sets of parents. Many parents experience mass towel disappearance, extreme chocolate theft, tantrums (occasionally violent) and sudden inexplicable absence accompanied by sudden inexplicable loss of phone coverage. Many parents feel helpless. Many young people rage or wander or forget. Add the impossibility of parental control in a situation where other households are involved, each with different rules which confuse everyone and conflict with your own, and you'll get a glimmer of how this can become untenable.

'I never found a companion that was so companionable as solitude,' said David Henry Thoreau. I agree, but suddenly it became imperative that I enjoy solitude more often than previously. It's so much easier to enjoy being alone with the 'safety net' of belonging with another person. It is less fun when solitude is your constant buddy who refuses to go away.

There was always a suspicion that I used campervan excursions to escape, as a way of avoiding difficulties that would be better confronted at home, and indeed there is always that danger. It's a powerful manoeuvre in any relationship with a partner, family member or friend to remove yourself physically from it. But after selling Fugue Ducato, which was an experience that was definitely 'ours', I bought Vera. This doesn't prove there was no element of running away. It's possible I was running away from him, or indeed from my everyday self, but we all need a safety net from time to time and mine is a van. I needed it whether he was with me or not.

Other people play golf or ride horses. Thoreau went to the woods. I go off alone in a campervan.

Part of the deal for me is the freedom to roam afforded by campervanning itself. I get happy just getting into the cab, and I gather I'm not alone in this. The other element is, of course, writing and the certainty that, if I go off in the van even for an afternoon, I will almost certainly write. Writing stabilises me. Communing with myself and/or nature stabilises me. Being free to wander stabilises me. It's a win/win/only-occasionally-lose situation.

My husband actively encouraged me to write. He even metaphorically shoved me into a room to do it, closed the door behind me and only opened it to pass through tea. Then as soon as my first novel was published, he withdrew all his support. Perhaps he felt threatened by my success; I'll never know. He moved out two months later and I thought I might never write again.

Of course in the short term this was true. It's extremely difficult to function in nearly every way when something as devastating as marital break-up happens. It was all I could do to fulfil obligations regarding events and workshops and to keep body and soul together.

This is where notebooks are invaluable. First of all, you can write out your distress, just sick the whole thing up onto the page, tear it up and throw it away; secondly, you can chart your progress into the abyss and back out again; and thirdly, you can keep taking notes.

Always keep taking notes, however brief. They will remind you of the wider thinking that surrounded that tiny memorandum when you return to it later. Taking notes gave me the comfort that something in my life was not getting lost forever. It was a symbolic and an actual investment in my future. Notebooks are a store for ideas, thoughts and observations. I was using notebooks long before I ever started writing seriously, my whole adult life in fact.

So for the nine months following his first departure, I wrote sporadic notes and generally researched and mulled over the next book. I tried to get down to the actual writing of it many times but met with a demoralising blockade of inertia which nothing would shift. Normally this would worry me but I was too busy either being miserable or trying not to be.

The week he moved back in, I miraculously started writing again. You would think, if you didn't know any better, that I needed him in order to write; that I was unable to write without him. This is what I resigned myself to believing for a while. I was delighted to be writing again, but it also felt like proof of my inadequacy at being mistress of my own fate, and therefore a defeat. This was in fact not true. Historically, when there was a disagreement, I would instantly down tools and try and fix the problem, or I'd just give up, and seethe with resentment of course. This time I managed to keep going, but writing was a far more lonely experience because he was no longer interested in cheering me on. His support was lost.

And then, so was my marriage. Almost a year to the day, he moved out again.

This time I decided to fight on two fronts. First, I was going to stay happy and in control of my life, and not go to pieces. Second, I was going to go on writing, no matter what. I absolutely refused to give that up ever again. At last I valued what I was doing. These two things were, of course, closely intertwined.

In the following year I finished several drafts of the new novel, and ghost-wrote two other books, a memoir and an autobiography. I was relentlessly productive. I met every deadline that presented itself. I even made money and new friends. I'd already spent several months mourning the loss of my marriage. I couldn't afford to do it again. In short, I learnt that my top priority was writing, and that I could write even in his absence, even in an emotional hurricane. I was not dependent on him to be able to write, but most importantly I could in fact write, and write well, in the midst of the tempest.

None of this was easy. My first attempt at being alone in isolation ended soon after it started with a sudden tearful departure for home. But this was followed by a steely determination to regroup and carry on writing, and to continue to overcome my grief.

I tell you this to clarify, but also because I don't believe for a second that there's anything unusual in my story. A great many marriages break up, roughly half in the UK at the moment. The statistics are worse for second marriages, and this was a second marriage for both of us. This is the background to something rarely spoken about: being alone, and how it can be done, and done well.

I was a counsellor for ten years and it was with no small sense of irony that I now applied a maxim common in the therapeutic world at that time – 'It's all grist to the mill' – meaning whatever happens in the counselling room can be used to further the client's understanding of themselves. I took this to imply that this excruciating pain I was experiencing was all useful stuff for fiction writing. Great. Nothing wasted then.

Annoyingly, after the break-up it became much harder to be alone in the van, or even in the house, or indeed anywhere, once I was alone in life. 'Solitude is fine but you need someone to tell that solitude is fine,' said Honoré de Balzac. Thanks Balzac, but there was no-one to tell except my very patient daughters, and absolutely no choice. I had to persevere. I could either drown or swim. I chose to swim.

That choice was partly due to my inability to drown my sorrows in drink. I almost always get disproportionately ill when I drink even relatively small quantities of alcohol, so taking to booze wasn't an option. My best way forward was to swim directly through the storm with my eyes wide open, which was preferable by far to throwing myself into ill-health in a pub, or hiding in a dark room.

It was a very conscious choice. It meant giving myself deliberate distractions like travelling, keeping the company of good people, giving myself permission to leave any situation if sadness arrived, and withdrawing quietly from those people who were unhelpful in this respect. This is a diary entry from this period: 'I seem to be moving all the time. Can't sit still. Can't be still. Can't stay in the house for too long – the initial high of solitude doesn't sustain itself and old doubts creep in.'

I had this strange sense that it wasn't only my metaphorical eyes which were open but my actual physical ones too. I do feel like that year was lived in inglorious technicolour. I therefore took loads of photos including a series of selfies taken in the various rooms I stayed in on my travels. Like my journals, I wanted to chart my way back to safety.

I felt much more at home in the natural world than in my city life. Its quiet predictability felt safe: night always came and so did the day which followed; the rivers continued to run and the leaves grew back on the trees in spring. Seagulls behaved like seagulls. But I was afraid that I would inadvertently merge with it. The difference between life and death felt meaningless when picnicking alone by the sea where time often ceases to hold significance. In the ecstasy of great natural beauty it would have been easy to forget the dangers of exposure or the cruelties of animal life, or the importance of staying alive. The wilderness was seductive in its certainty, like a convincing speaker whose unkind message is so masked in eloquence to make good people cheer.

But while I feared drowning, I made sure I grabbed all the best bits of my marriage and dragged them along with me, things like a clearer sense of belonging in the world, feeling like I was worthy of love and a good companion, and sanctuary from the fears I conquered in his company.

Here are four little lines I scribbled in my notebook when he first left.

> So lucky. Liberation.
> Conflagration.
> Parachutes of rescue.
> Solid ground.

They reflect the initial sense of relief from the constant tension and battles, and the gratitude I felt to friends and family who supported me. There was peace and rescue, and a cleansing fire which made it possible to find new strength. Even in the sudden void, which felt like falling from a great height through a storm, it wasn't all bad, and eventually the wind began to subside.

Wilderness

I had come to Assynt, one of the wildest, most remote parts of Scotland, away up in the very north west. I was just under fifty-three miles south-southwest of Cape Wrath as the crow flies, or perhaps the gull, except gulls don't fly in straight lines. This area will not be kind in winter and is peopled mainly by animals that know how to survive in long dark nights and wet summers with no night at all, such as gannets, red deer, wildcats, otters, whales, dolphins, golden plover, and even golden eagles. The landscape is heathery moorland but there are also extensive grasslands and areas of sudden startling green which reflect earlier cultivation, habitation and geology.

It is rugged and varied, formed from a mixture of rock types such as Torridonian sandstone, Lewisian gneiss and Cambrian basal quartzite. Not being a geologist, these words for the spectacular variety in the landscape seem to match their beauty but I can't claim to understand them. What I do get, however, is the fact that some of these rocks date back three thousand million years and more, which is astounding.

If that weren't enough, Assynt is said to be the most travelled landmass on the planet and many of its geological features are strikingly dramatic, for instance Stac Pollaidh (pronounced Stack Polly) and Suilven (say Soolven), two of the many peaks which rise suddenly from their more undulating surroundings. During the ice age, the sides of these mountains were worn away, while their tops, sticking up through the surface of the ice, remained untouched. Stac Pollaidh is a shortish climb as the road runs fairly close to the summit, but the path is very steep near the top and the view quite terrifying when you peer over the craggy summit and find yourself buffeted violently back again by the extreme prevailing wind. Not one for the vertiginous either as the drop is more or less vertical. However, if you turn your back to the blast, the views in all the other directions will take your breath away. I think it was the distances from the top of Stac Pollaidh which most struck me. Moors, lochs, mountains and valleys seemed to stretch off into time as well as vast geographical space. Distance was impossible to grasp. Cul Mor, Canisp and Suilven rose steeply, like Stac Pollaidh, out of the swelling brown moorlands. Loch Sionasgaig (Shona's gaig) glinted deep blue amongst the heather in the foreground. Cloud shadows moved like spectres across the undulations of the land and loch. More prosaically, gazing at Cul Mor (Cool More) and Canisp was like being in the top bunk in the hostel and sharing secrets with the occupants of three other top bunks. The peaks seemed closer than the plains and troughs between them. I felt lucky to be alive.

I had problems with the van's electrics. Vanessa's previous owner had put the battery in the place where the toilet should have been. When I got a garage to move it, the connection to the engine was somehow lost. This meant it no longer recharged as I drove, which is what's meant to happen. I only discovered this shortly before leaving so I chose to stay in a campsite. Clachtoll Beach had been recommended by a friend, and with good reason. Outside the van, five hens ran from camper to camper in search of titbits, and with some success going by the size of them. A flock of starlings worked across the grass too, enjoying the beasties thereunder. The tent nearest to my van was at least thirty yards away, as was the shower block. There was a washing machine and two kitchen sinks, and a water tap by my electric hook-up, amongst other luxuries. As well as all these conveniences there were spectacular views to a wide open sea fringed nearby with impressively jaggy cliffs. To the west, at some distance, lay the strip of land which is Harris and Lewis in the Western Isles, a good thirty miles away. To the south west lies the Coigach peninsula and the great mountain of Ben Mor Coigach which stands majestic above it. Ben Mor Coigach means 'big mountain of Coigach' and Coigach is Gaelic for 'five fields'. The five are also villages associated with these fields which all begin with 'A'. The best known is probably Achiltibuie, which means 'field of the yellow house'. Beyond Coigach is the Gairloch peninsula and on a clear day you can see the northern end of Skye, a whole fifty miles away.

It's easy to get lost in the distance here. Back at Clachtoll, there is also a sandy cove down an easy path, tiny cottages nestling amongst rocky outcrops, cushions of purple heather across the surrounding hills, and a two-thousand-year-old broch. What more could a campervanner want?

Brochs are round windowless buildings shaped like cooling towers, sometimes rising to as much as fifty feet high, as the Clachtoll broch once was. The doorway is tiny with a huge almost right-angled triangular stone over it. Apparently there are as many as five hundred brochs in the north west of Scotland in various states of dilapidation, as you'd imagine, what with them being so ancient and the weather being so treacherous. Near the Clachtoll broch is what appears to be a chambered cairn. However, I was informed that it isn't a cairn at all but the entrance to a tunnel that runs all the way to the broch but which went on fire and collapsed, thereby sealing in various ancient jewels. A more reliable person told me it was built a few years ago by a local man, complete with concrete to shore it up (it is near the shore after all), for the purposes of hiding his fishing gear, though why he'd have to hide his fishing gear was never explained.

The owners of the campsite were extremely friendly. I had

even been googled before I arrived, which was weird but nice. A great deal had also been done locally to make the traveller's stay a good one. For instance, there were a series of interesting little gates, one of which was run by a pulley system with a buoy as a weight, that guided walkers through some gardens, past a small football pitch and badminton field, and out onto the common ground above the bay. Several of these gates sported signs declaring 'WALKERS WELCOME'. It was wonderful to be directed by these and a series of discreet but blood-red arrows.

There was a small information centre with natural and human history on display and a selection of plastic buckets and spades to borrow for the beach, and a 'salmon hut' and ice room with information about local fishing traditions, all of which were permanently unlocked and had polite requests to close the door when you go. They did, however, have life-size models in there which, if you're not expecting them, will scare the living daylights out of you. Apart from that there was an overall sense of generosity and pride in what people were doing there.

However, I had been seduced. This was all just so pleasant and easy that I forgot about the torment of writing. I forgot I wasn't just there to get any old words down about tourist attractions but actually do what I had been doing until I arrived: diving into the depths of my soul and blabbing on about campervanning. Darn.

What I was having was the very pleasant experience of being safe there with lots of mod cons. And I was mostly invisible to the rest of the campsite, despite being on my own in an area everyone else seemed to have chosen to avoid, which naturally made me pretty obvious. The sun was beating down. I had everything I needed. This was lovely. It's what everyone wants when they go on holiday.

But, eh, I wasn't on holiday. I was on a writing retreat, I

suppose, if I had to define it. If it hadn't been for the electrical problem, I wouldn't have been there at all. I'd have been in some layby gazing at the sky and not laughing at the toddler chasing the hens, or trying to figure out whether the couple in the piebald tent were Spanish or German.

Years ago, I cycled out to Ardnamurchan from the northern coast of Loch Linnhe. It was my first solo trip and I was younger and fitter and didn't need an engine to turn my wheels. One brilliantly sunny day I came across a bearded man walking on the road, another solo traveller. We were alone on the road and I was puffing up the long steep hill of Glen Tarbert (yes, another Tarbert) while he was sauntering down it, so I stopped for a chat. He was walking the considerable distance back from the nearest shop at Strontian to his kayak which was parked in a small uninhabited bay over a nearby hill with no road access. He was circumnavigating the coast of Scotland all by himself. It was 1986 and a few weeks after the Chernobyl disaster. He had taken so many provisions with him he had managed to be out of human contact for two whole weeks during which time the dreadful disaster happened. Until he strode out for a shop, he had no idea about Chernobyl or that the government had announced that Scottish mountain water was likely to be contaminated and to avoid it. He was alarmed but had decided to carry on drinking the water anyway. What else could he do? He'd already been drinking it since the awful event. I was completely in awe at his excursion and his acceptance of his fate. I wanted to marry him and take him home, but I knew that was counterintuitive: we were both on solo paths.

All these years later I'm wondering who he was and why he had undertaken such an arduous trip alone. A quote comes to mind: 'Only those who will risk going too far can possibly find out how far one can go.' This was TS Eliot of all people. He sums up the crux of the problem, I think: really actually going too far would mean you didn't survive to tell the tale. This is a dangerously fine line, but the closer we are to it, the more alive we feel.

Shortly after my husband last moved out I did an accidental road trip by car. It began with a visit to my daughter who was studying in Preston in the north of England but, unable to face going home, I continued south and eventually arrived at the furthest ends of Cornwall. After four strenuous days of reworking a novel in a rented cabin in someone's garden and speaking to almost no-one but myself, I turned north again, picking up a copy of *Into the Wild* by Jon Krakauer in the wonderful Carlisle Book Shop. Its subject is Chris McCandless, a young man who liked to wander about in wildernesses and for the most part was careful to learn how to avoid dying there. Unfortunately he made a fatal mistake in the Alaskan wilderness and died there aged only twenty-four. I was deeply moved by his life, as many others have been. A last photo of him sitting outside the abandoned bus in which he was later to die, shows him to be strong and healthy in body and mind, a picture of the extreme beauty of which human beings are capable. Was I looking at mankind in its natural state? It seems to me the purest way to live, the difficulties of social living completely avoided and the challenges of survival the only focus, apart from the beauty and splendour of the environment. This is not what I do in my campervan. I'm alone, but clearly I'm safe, eating food from shops and someone always knows where I am.

I have a similar photo of a boyfriend on my first proper excursion into wilderness. He too was stunningly beautiful in this context. Our trip was by hitchhiking and finally on foot to a tiny abandoned cottage on the peninsula of Slyne Head on the west coast of Ireland. He and I lived there for a month or so and survived on bread, butter, boiled vegetables and tea. Ours was a lesser version of Chris McCandless's various survival adventures, and we were two, not one, but it was a giant experience for an eighteen-year-old city girl like me. It was a happy time and became a building block as I negotiated what was fundamentally meaningful in my life. Wilderness, simplicity and basic survival became reference points which both ground and feed me.

By contrast, in Assynt (pronounced with the emphasis on the A) I was loving the sunny weather and the easy lifestyle of being on that very chilled campsite, but I knew this was not what I'd set out to do. I also knew this happiness would vanish if I went home with nothing important either experienced or written. Not feeling close enough to death wasn't the problem. It was just that all that comfort had made me emotionally sleepy and that has very little to do with the crystal realities of life which I like to pursue. I was miles from my adventure at Slyne Head and light years from McCandless's joy in survival.

I was, however, only vaguely aware that I wasn't doing what I had set out to do. Then one day I set off from the campsite for a late afternoon walk, bringing with me a camera, a pair of binoculars, my varifocal glasses, a sheet of paper and a pen. To match all my viewing apparatus there was a clear pale-blue sky and a fresh but not cold breeze. The sunlight was softening a little and on my way back it turned everything it touched into gold. Without fully realising it, I was trying to 'see' with greater clarity.

Physically I could see for miles. The Minch, that great stretch of sea between the northwest Highlands and Lewis and Harris in the Outer Hebrides, was again a deep dark-blue and its expanse was a real joy after the elegant but tall grey streets of Glasgow, or even Glasgow's lush green parks with their towering chestnuts and sycamores. Space was magnificent. I crossed the garden of the many welcoming gates and climbed a wild area full of shorn sheep who were fat, curious and unafraid. Half a mile on I reached a cliff, or an almost cliff. It was a massive flat rock lying at an angle, fifty feet deep perhaps and a hundred feet long. Two long sharp claws of rock reached out parallel to it into the sea, like a giant sea eagle.

The wind was strong enough to whisk my glasses off my head when I perched them there. I raised my binoculars and examined the land to the north. Here was evidence of 'lazy beds' a traditional farming method which leaves stripes on the land when it has gone. This was evidence again that this area was once far more densely populated. I checked also for ancient roads and the remains of houses and believe I found both. Then I turned to the south where a shorter peninsula lay just beyond Clachtoll Beach. It was covered in these same agricultural stripes all the way to the insanely geometric chunk of rock at the end. I wondered how it must have felt to go out there in rain or sun and grow food for your family in such grand surroundings. The backdrop to these fields is the Coigach peninsula and all those mountain peaks. As well as Ben Mor Coigach itself, there stood Stac Pollaidh, Suilven, Cul Mhor and Cul Beag, all fading into the purple haze of the descending evening. On the shoreline beneath Ben Mor Coigach, my binoculars picked out a house. Life so far away brought so close. I can't recommend a pair of really powerful binoculars highly enough. They will take you to places you might never otherwise be able to reach, like into the nest of the golden eagle which I found quite by accident while searching for ravens in Kintyre. It was a complete fluke and an exciting one. Ravens are frequent visitors and easily identifiable by their size and their aerial acrobatics, but golden eagles are rare and finding their nest was a surprise.

The Clachtoll information centre urged visitors to take their binoculars and gaze out to sea for basking sharks, dolphins, whales and the like, so I spent a good fifteen minutes travelling into and out from the shore with them while perched on the slope above that cliff, but no cigar. Instead I got truly lost in the patterns of the waves and how they differed depending on their proximity to the shore, the direction of the light, squalls and so on. Lost in the patterns of the natural world out there, lost in those left by earlier people on the land, lost in the shaping of the sand, lost, quietly, gently I was lost.

What a great feeling!

And not remotely close to death.

What I suffer from, or am blessed by, is a lesser version of this: 'We like companionship, see, but we can't stand to be around people for very long. So we go get ourselves lost, come back for a while, then get the hell out again.' This was Ken Sleight, a river guide and desert rat, explaining his own and Chris McCandless's experiences in wild living. It resonates with me, although admittedly in a greatly diminished form. Wild places often feel like home when I'm there, even though I normally live in the large all-mod-cons city of Glasgow. I was utterly at peace on the cliff top because I couldn't see or be seen by people, only sheep, who don't require anything of me. Don't get me wrong: I love people. I'm very sociable when I'm around them, but every so often I get weary and need to touch base with the wilderness.

So, revived, I returned to the camper, got in the back and after a delicious dinner of pasta, pesto and cherry tomatoes, set to work again. Somehow my inner muse or child or wayward spirit, whatever you want to call it, had taken me to what I needed.

Campervanning is like life and like relationships: you have to enjoy what you have and maximise what you can do with whatever is available. My van had decided not to charge the leisure battery any more as I drove. This meant I couldn't use my laptop battery then recharge it from the leisure battery, then recharge the leisure battery by driving to town for supplies, which is my habitual way. It was therefore reasonable to be here in this lovely campsite attached to the national grid via their hook-up. I was making the most of that situation.

But the truth is: my experience was being watered down in subtle ways. Waste is a central one. I couldn't toss my peapods into bushes (or my pee) because there weren't any and even if there were I'd have been thrown off the site for being unsightly, 'scuse the pun, or unhygienic. This meant the peapods were in the bin mixed in with other recyclables because, although there was a recycling bin there, I had nowhere to store these waste products separately in my tiny van before removal. This simple cycle of renewal was broken. There was also the constant, low-level buzz of voices and vehicles arriving and leaving, all inoffensive but distracting. There was no silence in which to hear the birds, the shoosh of the wind, and so on. Grass in campsites has to be kept low and the ground hard, so the myriad of little flowers, grasses and beasties that normally inhabit the earth, even the earth beside a layby, are all absent. The carefully limited use of utensils was less urgent with a sink full of hot water only a few yards away. The clear night sky had vanished beyond the yellow light at the toilet-block door. As a collection of influences, they added up to a distance between me and my simple basic and often neglected humanity.

Life in a layby campervan has no words, only those I write or choose to read; no artificial intelligence, no constant babble of piped music, TV, radio; no constant stream of adverts or the relentless capitalism which pervades our every waking hour. Most of this is absent in the type of informal campsites I favour, for instance Clachtoll in Assynt and Killiegruer in Kintyre, but the minimal socialisation required even in these lovely places is not of the wilderness. These interactions are often tinged with the assumption that we are all the same and that this is good. Most people enjoy this feeling. We are not all the same. It is important that we are not all the same. Any pressure which tells us we should be is by its very nature stifling of individuality and therefore lateral thinking or anything creative or innovative. At the very least it's bad for our mental health.

All this yearning for wilderness: it was time to move on from lovely Clachtoll.

I mentioned this to the lovely proprietor, that his campsite was wonderful but I'd be leaving the following day, that I needed to wild camp for a bit.

He looked at me sideways. 'But that's dangerous,' he pointed out.

Lots of people say this. I completely disagree. 'I've done it loads of times before,' I tell him cheerfully.

'Not round here,' he said. 'There's a man near here who will let down your tyres if he catches you at it.'

'Where exactly?' I asked.

He told me. 'Thanks for the warning,' I said, and determined not to go there.

There is no point in getting riled about some people being unreasonable, especially landlords, or indeed local councils who don't want campervans all over the place. How people in these parts manage during the six-week Scottish school holidays is a miracle. Their single-track roads must be chocca with giant campervans, often driven by people who have never driven a vehicle that large before, so I understand local people must get fed up. Letting tyres down is hardly a solution. I suspect in this instance it was a tall tale.

There are some parts of the country which do not welcome wild campers of any kind, tent or van. A distinction must be made here between the comforts of even a slightly drippy van in a storm and the vulnerability of a tent, and also the bravery or recklessness of tent-dwellers on a mountainside as opposed to softie campervanners in laybys. I use the term 'wild' in this context to mean not in a campsite. There is one such estate near Loch Fyne which I was warned about. The landowner is said to insist vans and tents move on whatever time of day he finds them, so why risk that? Other places are happy for campers to be there. The stretch of road between Claonaig and Skipness on the east coast of Kintyre is one. I learnt of this on the recommendation of a hitcher I picked up who was on his way there. After fixing a minor problem with my radiator, this helpful though unwashed young man told me a pair of retired teachers had been camping at Claonaig in a small tent all summer, over two months by then, and there were plenty of natural places for campervans to stop at the edge of the stony beach. I went straight there and stopped for five days in distractingly fine sunshine without wind, and wrote screeds.

Incidentally, there were loads of dolphins in Assynt. I saw them later from the back of the van one afternoon as they swam up and down just off the shore for the best part of an hour. Meanwhile far off across the water I saw the huge unmistakable spout of a whale. Blessed.

Can You Fix It?

The problem with buying a campervan is the romance. Similar to finding a life partner, it is easy to be deluded and unrealistic, to imagine a perfect future of endlessly unfolding delight and adventure, only to be brought down to earth with a great thud when you discover the object of your desire has feet of clay, or at least axles of rust.

The power of campervan dopamine should not be underestimated. The burgeoning market in campervan 'stuff' is testament to this: fridge magnets are only the beginning. Just as everyone has a book in them, so we all, apparently, have a fantasy van which is going to make modern life ok. This is simply not the case. Neither of these truisms have even a toe in the sea of reality. To paraphrase an old saying, 'buy in haste, repent at leisure', which was never more true.

The news about dopamine, according to studies on gamblers in America as reported in the *Guardian*, is that it is implicated in near success as well as actual success. This means it encourages you to go on trying when all good sense would otherwise tell you to stop. This means, perhaps, that once you discover your van's slow puncture, gas leak or dripping petrol tank, you will also have the overwhelming desire to fix it. Naturally, eventually, when you have all three of these ailments plus a leaky roof and doors that fly open as you round bends, the dopamine affect is severely tested and may even reach its natural limit.

Or not. Research done by the University of Texas tells us

that dopamine is a chemical messenger similar to adrenaline. It affects the brain processes that control movement, emotional response, and the ability to experience pleasure and pain. Regulation of dopamine is crucial to our mental and physical health. Theirs and other studies have also focussed on addiction, in which dopamine is also a culprit. For instance, many people hooked on drugs say they get no pleasure from their drug but still feel compelled to take it. This may be where dopamine comes in. Similarly, war veterans suffering from Post Traumatic Stress Disorder also have surges of dopamine when reminded of the sounds of battle, something which is obviously deeply distressing for them.

What I'm getting at here is that dopamine can make us pretty illogical about what's good or bad for us. Without it there are many things we wouldn't do, like buying a beaten-up old campervan for cash in the deserted back court of a disused shopping centre. (Wasn't me, by the way, but I think they'd prefer to remain nameless.)

Beware.

Additionally, campervans are complicated machines, being vehicles and houses all in one very enclosed space, which means things often go wrong. Therefore, don't even think about it if DIY makes you panic. You don't need to be a specialist in campervan electrics or even simple car mechanics. Though these things would help, they're not essential. A willingness to fix things as they break and perhaps a taste for the Heath Robinson, will be useful. Theoretically, if you have money this is mostly not necessary but then, if this is the case, you've probably bought a large van WITH BUILT-IN COMPLICATIONS by the sheer size of it.

Again, campervans are like life, or like love life anyway. Some relationships are straightforward, others make your eyes cross with the level of 'maintenance' required. Only you can know if it's worth it. I like to keep my campervanning life as simple as possible, probably because I had a Winnebago of a relationship. (Winnebago are famous for their giant coach-built mobile homes which are popular with American celebrities and are really houses on wheels.)

You may, however, love these kinds of campervan complications. There are plenty of people who dedicate their lives to huge houses (or difficult partners) and then to their huge (and difficult) motorhomes. Motorhomes are not the same as campervans. They are clearly something different altogether. The clue is in the name. MotorHOME and CAMPERvan. Homes are for living in and motorhomes are things in which it is possible to live for extended periods of time and which have wheels and motors. They are therefore bigger and better equipped and not fun to drive, especially on those narrow roads in Assynt. Campervans are for camping out and involve certain compromises on daily conveniences, especially space, but also gadgets. So what are we doing here? Playing houses or roughing it?

Personally I'm roughing it so I can't really advise you about playing houses, though Fugue Ducato afforded real living-in possibilities and two of us did just that for the best part of a month twice. Roughing it in style is what I prefer, but there's a balance to be found between cost, comfort, hassle, flexibility, freedom and peace of mind. Just little things. But it's up to you which of these things you personally need, and what you can do without.

A while ago, some friends of mine considered buying an ordinary van and building their own campervan or motorhome within it. This was patently silly as neither of them was much good at fixing things, only aspirations to be so. They had fun trawling the net for ideas and guidance, types of vans, layouts and tips on how to build them. Eventually this convinced them of our own madness and the project was abandoned. One website they showed me sticks in my mind. It was called

'Deep Red, a self-build motorhome'. This reads almost like a novel title and tag-line, and looking at it convinced me that building a motorhome is as difficult as writing a novel. The two projects are probably comparable in scale, though writing a novel is perhaps the cheaper option. 'Deep Red' is actually the name of an exceptionally thorough online guide to the transformation of a big red van into a comfortable living space on wheels. It shows every stage of one retired couple's work from design to completion and even includes details and pictures of every part used and every single tool. No spanner unturned, so to speak. It was their thoroughness which scared off my friends. And rightly so. This work does take a particular kind of mindset, one which neither of them had. Like me, they preferred chilling in a ready-made van. Personally I prefer to maximise my writing time by doing the minimum of fixing, rather than getting embroiled in the meticulous business of working out precise details for the optimum living space. As a result, no dopamine was triggered for any of us in this instance.

Winston Churchill seems to have been well-acquainted with the vagaries of dopamine. He once said, 'Success is the ability to go from one failure to another with no loss of enthusiasm.' But I think you have to choose your task wisely in the first place, one which matches ability to eagerness. I'm always keen on ready-made, except when it comes to jumpers, which I like to knit, the more intricate the pattern the better.

Believe it or not, even sensible people can go gaga over a new old van. It's the obvious things like always take it for a test drive no matter how often the vendor tells you it's a great wee runner but not insured for you. It may look so stunningly perfect in every way and surely it's rude to go inside cupboards, even that one at the front that houses the engine … but STOP! Open it. Drive it. Turn on the taps. Open all the windows, doors, drawers and cupboards; try the cooker, the fridge and the heating. Test everything. Fixing bits of campervans is tedious, unless you're that kind of enthusiast. Minimise the work, maximise the writing time. Small things can ruin trips.

As an illustration of Churchill's principle of dopamine, I give you the example of my brother Colin and his wife Rosie, who bought a second-hand van around October. They went immediately to the petrol station to fill it, only to have a helpful stranger rush across the forecourt to tell them their petrol was running straight out the bottom. Various other problems came to light as a result of which the van spent more time in the garage than out for the following six months. They had the occasional day trip, though the van remained mysteriously heavy on petrol, but their first overnight trip finally came about the following July. Yes, October to July. Five nights were spent in Northumbria, photos of which were beamed out to the world on Facebook to great congratulations from all and sundry. Two nights in, I received this dopamine-fuelled message from Rosie: 'Totally hooked. Never want to be without a campervan again.'

When they returned, Rosie spoke with great animation. Bliss was a word that cropped up often, frequently alongside 'out' as in 'blissed out'. She also declared, in total amazement, 'The sense of freedom is just extraordinary!' Like me, she gets happy just as soon as she finds herself behind that wheel.

One word of caution: on Rosie's first overnight trip alone for a work event, she again experienced that bliss of freedom and was halfway home when she considered the possibility of turning round and taking this sense of freedom to its natural conclusion. It was a *Thelma and Louise* moment. Fortunately for us all, she didn't.

I'm absolutely delighted with their campervan success, blissed out you could say, not least because I think even I would have given up long ago on their van, so many and varied were their van's problems, some of which I've cited above. Deep respect is due. I look forward to many happy meetings with them in campsites and laybys.

There are some basics regarding safety that all vans must possess. All doors must open/shut with ease and when required. External doors should not be openable using the centrifugal forces of sharp bends or when traversing sudden bumps. Water should stay in water tanks or outside entirely. Petrol should stay in petrol tanks. Engine fumes are banned completely. Gas should burn quietly or remain in its container. Toilets should not leak, not even slightly. Bad smells (toilets, camping gas or petrol) spell danger. If you find one, something is not where it should be and you need to act quickly.

The point is: the older your van the more likely the various parts will be worn out and could even be irreplaceable. This is obvious, but just as pertinent a point is: the fancier your van, the larger the number of special conveniences it may contain which translates into more things that can go wrong. It's not quite as dangerous as buying a boat where if even the simple things go amiss you risk entering Davy Jones' Locker, but the truth is, even in campervans, one minor problem can wreck your plans. One problem generally leads to another, quite often of a whole new variety.

For instance, I have my own toilet failure story in my current campervan, Vanessa Hotplate. I love that van but a leaking toilet is intolerable.

Problem number one: while camping in a remote spot, my elderly Porta Potti was suddenly leaking. The simple solution was to take it to a public toilet, empty it and check for the cause.

This led to problem number two: the chemicals in the Porta Potti need a special chemical draining point found only in campsites, though normally I dump it down the toilet at home.

Hence I encountered problem number three: by dawn

the smell was so pungent that it woke me up. No way of stopping smell or knowing how far the leak has spread. Toilet in bunker lined with home-made insulation. Immediate problem with no solution. Short sentences due to holding breath at memory. Ick!

I got out quick and set off immediately to fix this. However, none of the public toilets were open yet.

Problem number four: in any case, all public toilets on that journey had signs banning the emptying of chemical toilets. Metaphorical and actual doors were slamming shut or refusing to open right, left and centre. I was in the Highlands. Toilets up there are usually attached to septic tanks which can't cope with chemicals.

Obviously there was a solution to all of this: go to a campsite and empty the offending canister into their special chemical toilet facility or perhaps even buy a new toilet. But it was still too early to arrive at a campsite. I should probably have gone home at this point but I was still determined to make my trip work. I headed to the nearest campsite and waited for it to open.

I had really needed to stay in bed that morning and this took me to problem number five: I was tired and needed a rest.

Back to problem number one. I'll stop numbering them now because they do just keep developing once they start.

As well as being tired that day I was feeling quite frazzled and unsociable for other reasons and not the joyous fun-loving devil-may-care person I needed to be to persuade campsite officialdom (which is often weirdly strict) to allow me to use their chemical facilities but not have me staying overnight. There are certain expectations and protocols in most sites, often around hygiene, whose rules I would automatically have broken by dint of the fact that my toilet had leaked and the van needed some thorough cleaning. Also, anyone not conforming to the motorhome norm seems to be generally viewed with suspicion in big campsites. I was too tired to confront all this adequately.

I did however locate five super-dooper toilets of indeterminate size for sale at outlandish prices in a campsite near Fort William, and one other for £50 less near Oban, but none of these was suitable. Most of that day's writing time was lost, which was frustrating when my time away is so limited. The muse was seething with resentment in the back of the van. The toilet problem had swamped the whole trip and almost no work had been done. I returned to base camp, that's to say home, much sooner than I'd hoped.

The hinge of the cupboard door had also broken, leaving the possibility of plastic plates, china mugs and cutlery rolling about on the floor …

And so on …

Those little things.

Increase the four cupboard doors and one back entrance in Vanessa Hotplate to the higher standards of Fugue Ducato, the big van, for instance, and you have thirteen cupboard doors, two extra external doors and four drawers. Escalate the toilet problem into two sinks, a shower, a hot water supply and a central heating system, and see how luxury becomes misery.

Check the size of your purse then take a chunk off what you think you can afford and that's the amount to spend on your van. I'd say all campervans require attention when first bought because vans are personal things for individual and often quite specific purposes. For instance, on my travels recently I met a professional photographer who had converted the shower unit in his van into a dark room. All things are possible.

When we first had Fugue Ducato it had some serious battery problems which only came to light while facing up a steep slope in a small campsite among some trees in France. I think we were feeding France's national grid instead of drawing from it. We had to jump start it *in reverse* without hitting any of the small trees which marked the edge of our small parking spot. The obvious result was expensive but before we got to repairs we had to get Fugue Ducato out of a very tight spot. I messed up my part in the joint effort to get it going by missing the all-important moment to let out the clutch. We managed in the end and the engine charged the battery up as we continued south. There was a second incident in Palabras on the French Mediterranean coast for the same reason. I remember the location because I named the incident a 'Palaver in Palabras'. We therefore never used the electricity in the new battery for the rest of the trip. This was actually very pleasant and romantic because we had to live by candlelight and I was writing by hand anyway, not laptop. Subsequently and at huge expense, we fitted a new electrical charging unit and three GIANT batteries. This of course was ideal for our contrapuntal lifestyle in which I left often to write. On several such trips I have wild-parked for five days straight and worked the entire time on a laptop without losing power, and could probably have stayed longer.

If you want to be really technical about it you can match gadgets to battery using mathematically calculated kilowatt hours. Personally I'd rather die or at least hand over such things to experts who will do you a full professional diagram if you really want one. Campervans are hybrids between house and vehicle and generally have two available sources of charge: motion via the engine or the national grid. It's completed and often hidden in tight spaces, so having a diagram isn't entirely daft. Nowadays campervans and motorhomes will almost always come with TV aerials and indeed every other electrical convenience. An alarming number of people watch TV in campervans. I'm always amazed by this and actually laughed when I found Fugue Ducato's TV cables. For me watching TV is the absolute antithesis of campervanning, but then I don't watch it at home either.

I was even more horrified recently when fantasising about upgrading to a vehicle worth seven times the cost of Vanessa. This would be a princely sum I can only dream of, so I might as well. I watched the *Which* online video guide to professional campervan conversions. These are workman's vans fitted to the highest specifications as campervans, or possibly motorhomes. In one memorable case, not only were there three TVs but one of them had been installed on the back of the cooker unit at the side door and could be watched from the comfort of outside. Outside? Really? Why?

Consequently, because of my snobbery in such matters, I could not possibly advise you on television installation. Radio I might consider. I listen to the radio, when there's reception, but only when I'm driving. I bring equipment for listening to music while stationary but rarely do, because then I'd miss the sounds which surround me, like gulls laughing overhead, the wind gusting in the trees or the rain tinkering on the roof, and this would break the connection between me and my surroundings. I can listen to the radio any time.

A word here on garages: if you find one prepared to fix your old campervan, be nice, be appreciative and send all your friends to them so they stay in business. Most garages prefer modern cars with expensive things to fix which take them less time. Nevertheless, there are some garages who appreciate my efforts to keep an old van on the road and will accommodate me. Some things are unfixable, like the exhaust manifold on my old Bedford, while others just need a little initiative. Even with big Fugue Ducato, it takes a specialist to fix the inside of vans and install batteries and converters and things. Boat chandlers are often handy, if expensive, for such things as kitting out or repairing small spaces and for gas supplies. I think my favourite van-fixer has to be 'Willie' in Govan who on a warm Saturday morning fixed the exhaust no-one else would touch by welding a length of pipe into the offending gap. It took him less than an hour and cost me next to nothing. Re-use, recycle and all that. Keep old vans going. All the other garages were either closed or their mechanics shook their heads as if they were pronouncing the van dead and told me the broken exhaust had been modified and couldn't be bought, and so was unrepairable.

Standard garages can do your MOT but most will avoid the inside like the plague. Some garages do specialise but they tend to aim at the more expensive end of the market, giant vans with fancy but fragile gadgets, and there is a growing number of companies who will fix out your van from scratch or sort the one you've got, but for big money. General motor electricians especially are already in short supply and campervan specialists even more rare. For instance, I took Vanessa Hotplate to such a specialist and paid a reasonable sum of money to have the electrics checked. After two hours they couldn't find the problem and said they'd need to charge me extra for getting an electrician in … I wasn't impressed. As in all things, trust is important and they'd blown mine. After some searching, I found a vehicle electrician who instantly understood my problem, that I had lost faith in Vanessa's electrics themselves. He fixed what was broken and demonstrated for me that every single electrical part of the van was working by showing me the reading on his electricity meter. This meant I could travel and turn on lights in confidence again. A more wonderful technician it would be hard to find.

Sometimes when you fix delicate old things, other parts get broken as a result. This is why most mechanics run and hide when they see elderly vans park outside their doors.

Despite Vanessa Hotplate's toilet problems and the unfortunate electrical dysfunction, Romahomes come top of the league for me as the perfect van for a solo campervanning writer. I especially favour the snub-nosiness of Bedfords or Daihatsus rather than the Citroens on which other

Romahomes often sit. They're also popular with children because of their similarity to Dinky cars. I was lounging in a friend's front window the other day and admiring Vanessa Hotplate where she sat immediately outside. I could see right through the van to the other side of the street through both windows. A small enrapt face, mouth open in wonder, suddenly appeared beyond the furthest away window. Shortly after, a boy and his mum crossed the road and stood outside my friend's window with a camera taking snaps and giggling together, completely oblivious to our presence. This, in addition to being photographed by a tourist halfway up the Mam Ratagan Pass, makes Vanessa Hotplate something of a star. It pleases me my campervan makes other people happy in this way. Recently I passed a convoy of two Bedford Romahomes on the Kintyre road. We waved to each other in frantic delight. I gather VW drivers do the same.

I totally love these vans, but one incident made me wonder.

On a beautiful summer evening in Kintyre, I was standing outside the van admiring the view out to sea from a layby halfway down the coast. I'd been indoors most of the day having a productive, enjoyable and prolonged writing session. It was about nine o'clock and my brain was running out of juice. Did you know your brain uses about twenty percent of your energy? In that moment I felt it. Then the wind grabbed the back door and slammed it shut. Bang! Which gave me no fright at all, I was so delightfully sleepy. It was time to find somewhere more discreet to park, but then the back door wouldn't open. The outer edge of the door had jammed itself behind the inner edge of the jamb. There was absolutely nothing I could do to shift it. I was looking at a night in the cab.

So I phoned my good friend Arthur Blue, who lived twenty-five miles away. When I was writing my second novel which was set around the Clyde River during the Second World

War, Arthur was my chief advisor on all things seaworthy and regarding Greenock. He is also a marine engineer and an all-round genius when it comes to anything practical or mechanical. He'd be an ideal companion in any campervan. Not entirely understanding my problem as I prattled over the phone, he offered to immediately set out with the appropriate tools, so instead I insisted on coming to him. Luckily I'd had the van keys in my hand when the door shut.

Arthur, who is eighty, got a stepladder and a special tool and climbed up onto the roof of my van, removed the skylight, which is about sixteen inches square, and lowered himself down into the van through the gap. Obviously he needs to eat more. Once inside, he checked the problem, then climbed back out the same way and went to get the correct tool. Up the ladder he went again and back through the skylight, then he let himself out the proper way, by the back door. Arthur Blue is a total hero. I do not want to be responsible for any mishap to Arthur, who will always put himself in the line of danger at the slightest provocation. It might therefore be more socially responsible of me to get a better van.

One further warning: I know two women who bought campervans and whose partners immediately disappeared into the sunset in these vans without a backwards glance. The first was an old converted minibus, the second a Mazda Bongo. Not even Romahomes. Beware of other people's inexplicable dopamine.

Tea And Toilet

I have been the butt of many a tea joke so it will come as no surprise that of the five presents given to me on the publication of my second book, two were tea. The others were two bottles of champagne and a box of such fancy chocolates it seemed (briefly) like hubris to eat them. Until this glorious day in the world of tea, there were but five varieties of the stuff in my van. There are at least twenty now that I have installed the multipack selection of delicate infusions. But tea is not really the issue here. Liquid is the issue.

I begin most of my days, at home or in the van, with half a lemon squeezed into a large glass of lukewarm water. I've been doing this for several years now following a short period of detox, and I think it works. I'd fallen into the trap of believing my brain would slow up as I aged. This is what people tell you, mostly young people when they disagree with what you're saying. Then one fine day on a campervan excursion in the south of France, I met someone who was doing a massive detox, nay, fast, and I thought, 'That can't be good for you.'

But a month later this person had lost weight and was very spritely and happy and extremely pleased with himself. Also sharp as a tack. So I thought I'd look into it.

I must stress here that I'm a great believer in the notion that dieting makes you fat. It also makes you obsessive, not to mention a tiny bit boring. Neither am I interested in fancy food fads or complicated cooking, though I enjoy the results. Food, especially within the restrictions of a small van, is functional. Obviously it's a stretch to say that the variety of my tea is purely functional, but I've never claimed to be consistent.

What I discovered was how the body functions in relation to food and that what my French friend had done was deliberately upset his body's balance and set it into emergency mode where it effectively eats its own fat. For part of his fast, his 'diet' required him to drink large quantities of lemon juice. This worried me considerably. It still worries me because lemon juice is powerful stuff. However, taken in moderation and especially in conjunction with cutting out (or down on) processed sugars and fats, diluted lemon juice can cleanse the inner conduits of the body.

Cleansing the body includes cleansing the brain and all the other communication systems within the body which of course makes them more efficient. So, my morning lemon juice ritual is effectively a way of keeping my brain as fully functioning as possible. If I neglect it, even for a couple of days, I find my thinking quickly becomes sluggish. The lemon juice habit is particularly important in the van because I need my brain to work to capacity.

Next up, usually half an hour after the lemon juice, is oolong tea. I discovered this by accident on holiday in Thailand – not a van trip, obviously. I wish! I stupidly assumed the hotel's tea would be normal 'breakfast tea' seeing as they were serving it at breakfast, but this was Thai breakfast, not Scottish. Instead of porridge or toast, there was chicken rice and noodles, and oolong tea. So, still in stupid mode, I added lashings of milk to my tea and the result was horrible. After three days of idiocy I decided to leave out the milk, and discovered delicious oolong tea.

It's a semi-green tea, some greener than others, which is fermented, though the fermentation process is stopped midway and the leaves dried as soon as they change colour.

Despite containing caffeine, it is thought to be one of the most beneficial teas on the planet. High in antioxidants, it's said to be good for weight loss, atherosclerosis, neurodegeneration, diabetes, stroke and rheumatoid arthritis and it's also anti-cancer. It's said to be good for skin problems such as eczema and allergenic skin conditions such as atopic dermatitis, both of which have bothered me in the past. It's also good for stress, though perhaps that's because it's tasty and refreshing, and there are rumours it may be good for mental alertness, but perhaps that's the caffeine. Whatever, a tea that's best without milk (which needs refrigeration) suits a writer in a small campervan extremely well. The only problem is my favourite brand comes loose and therefore the used leaves tend to clog up the very tiny plughole and waste pipe in the sink if I'm not careful how I dispose of them.

Next, perhaps an hour later, I'll be ready for real tea, ie that breakfast stuff some of us drink all day. I might even have two before lunch time and certainly at least one more during the afternoon. Thereafter, and probably interspersed between these various teas, I'll drink non-caffeinated teas, mostly herbal, occasionally fruity, but nothing too stimulating after six o'clock in the evening or I won't sleep at night. Fennel is good to settle my stomach if I've had too much builders' tea, camomile is refreshing and calming if I've been slogging in the sun, elderflower will calm you even in an emotional hurricane, and all tea requires boiling water which is good if you're not sure whether your water source is safe. All these teas are dry and won't go off as long as you keep them so.

All this palaver is designed to keep me hydrated and mentally alert from dawn 'til bedtime. It also serves to give me something to do while I'm trying to ignore the writing. Ignoring your writing is a very important component in any writing project. By ignoring I mean wandering off briefly to do something which is relatively mechanical but distracting enough to force you to put the writing to the back of your mind.

Throughout most of my writing projects I have employed something I learnt as a child in a piano lesson. I was trying to master a difficult but short piece but every time I came to one particular section I made the same mistake. Over and over I made this mistake, no matter how slowly and deliberately I played. It happened every time. My teacher was extremely patient. She had a technique of making me play things in crazy rhythms to break up habits like this. This was always fun and took the micky out of pieces of music that took themselves too seriously, and it usually worked. Not this time.

'Mars bars,' she said.

'What?' I said. 'What about them?' She wasn't in the habit of bribing me with sweets, so I knew no Mars bars were endangered by my presence at her piano.

We had a brief conversation about Mars bars and then about something that was stuck to the ceiling which I'd never noticed before. After a few minutes we took our attention back to the piano and I played the whole piece perfectly. It felt like a rewiring, or as though not just the fingers in my hand had been able to relax but also the synapses in my brain. Some other part of my being had taken over. This brief period of distraction gave the piano part of me time to rest, unjam the mental block and reorganise itself enough to go on – a kind of mini power nap for brains.

Therefore, the act of making tea, doing the washing-up, tidying the campervan or washing the windows (there aren't many) can be enough to reset my thinking on whatever knotty writing problem I'm confronting. When I return to it, the problem has lessened or even dissolved and the way forward becomes obvious without much effort. Writing is really just a series of decisions and this is one way I've discovered that facilitates difficult decisions. It can also give you that all tea-ed up, sicky feeling if you rely too heavily on black tea, so be careful to vary your distractions.

You may also develop great skill in computer mahjong and spider, find lots of new friends on Facebook, keep your family warm in home-knitted jumpers, send your phone bill through the roof and reduce your daily word count, if you use the wrong distraction techniques (or lose control of them as I have done with knitting). Everything in moderation.

Then there's food. I'm not interested in fancy cooking unless I have a full kitchen and the prospect of an appreciative band of eaters. Van food has to provide a balanced healthy diet while being easy to prepare and easy to clean up afterwards. No meat or frying because of the fat. Light snacks all day and one hot meal in the evening, however small. On some trips I manage to avoid sugar, apart from fruit, and to lessen my overall carbohydrate intake. I know sugar and carbohydrates are considered the greatest twin evils of the modern diet, but sugar has brought me great pleasure in the past and it's no mistake that my first husband owned an old style sweetie shop whose walls were lined with those lovely colourful jars full of treats of every colour, texture and shape. All nothing but sugar. Astoundingly, I still have most of my teeth.

I once survived a period of thinking I had to nibble small things all day in order to keep my concentration up for writing, but I put on so much weight I had to stop. Funnily enough, when I lost the grazing habit the writing kept going and perhaps even improved because my arteries were no longer blocked with debris.

Another oft-forgotten problem with food in campervans is space. On a trip to Kintyre with two friends who camped beside my van in a howling gale, I brought the usual simple and minimal quantities of grub. My friends arrived with every possible ingredient for what turned out to be a quite spectacular dinner, but this involved countless bags of ingredients (just in case) which quickly took over the van leaving nowhere to sit, lie down or even put your feet. Another word of caution: my friends and I were celebrating some successes, most probably our escape, at last, from civilisation, so I had brought along some bubbly. I got to our chosen camping spot two hours before them and stashed the bottle in the shade of the van to keep it cool. It had been shaken for four hours on the journey there, but two hours of being still should surely have been enough to still its fizz. Unfortunately not. As soon as I removed the muselet, which is the little cage bit over the cork, the cork itself exploded out of the top followed by a deluge of champagne. It soaked my hair, face, jumper and jeans, the cushion I was sitting on, one of my friends and most of the ceiling. What a catastrophe. We actually came to our senses pretty quickly and managed to capture quite a lot. It was a very festive occasion.

I'll come back to food and the dangers of cooking in campervans, but first the unavoidable flip side to all this consumption which is, erm, waste. You need to make your own decision about how you deal with this. The absence of a proper flushing water closet which simultaneously removes and cleans as if nothing toxic had ever arrived there, forces many people to come close to their most basic humanity in ways they may never have done previously.

Rally, the old Bedford, had no toilet and it never occurred to me to get one. This caused all sorts of trouble because it meant needing to be near facilities or at least bushes, which in the treeless windswept wilds of Scotland is not always possible. Fugue, the big Ducato, had a proper built-in flushing chemical toilet with a special toilet-roll holder and a nifty pull-down sink. No-one ever used this toilet except me and my small nephew and niece. All other visitors said they'd 'hang on', even my elderly mother in the middle of a cold night on a campsite whose shower block was a couple of hundred yards away.

Vera had a small chemical toilet which fitted neatly into a specially designed space. When I bought Vanessa Hotplate, there was a big fat battery in the space meant for the toilet, so the toilet had to go elsewhere. Unfortunately, the destination bunker was about one millimetre too shallow. If you have a weak stomach, turn the page now.

This tiny missing millimetre was enough to make the Porta Potti stand just proud of the bunker. The weight of the cushion and me on it, put too much pressure on the Porta Potti and it cracked, causing an awful leak. It happened in a spot with no emergency alternatives, in other words no public toilets or bushes, and in a place of great beauty and grandeur. I was surrounded by vast mountains, but simultaneously hemmed in by the proximity of a shifting blanket of mist and a cliff which rose immediately behind me. I was visible to various houses in the distance and I'm always aware how popular binoculars and telescopes are in these areas. My one-time neighbour in North Uist, when I lived there years ago, had a telescope openly and permanently trained on me. That's what wheels are for, to move elsewhere and find privacy and sanctuary.

In search of a new Porta Potti I then made a circular trip over the Skye Bridge to Skye's defunct gas pumps and camping supplies shops, but without success. Then I turned south for Armadale, where the sun shone brilliantly, and took a boat back across the Sound of Sleat to the fishing town of Mallaig. I called a friend south of there in the tiny village of Glenuig and arranged to call in. I was beginning to feel slightly crazy with all the frustrations and discomforts. The stench in the back meant nowhere to sit for tea. I needed sane company and felt better knowing she was in, enough to have a wander round Mallaig.

I love Mallaig. It's so fantastically bustling and busy and has a wide-open view over vast expanses of ever-changing sea to Skye, Rum and Eigg. On a previous trip, when I rented a house in Morar and holed up for a week one March to write, I sat in Mallaig's seafront car park for hours transfixed by the light. Years ago, when my Glenuig friend and I were younger, a handsome fisherman allowed us to win a bucket of fresh prawns from him in a pool game bet. I like the boats too, all shapes and sizes, some half-built or in for repair. Real things happen here. Such a vibrant harbour seemed the obvious place to find a portable toilet.

But unfortunately not. Distractingly, the pier-side chandlers had every other piece of equipment for small-space living, so I settled for an antiseptic spray, some washcloths and a small round green washing-up bowl, though I wasn't exactly sure what I was going to do with these things. I just liked the shop and the lifestyle it served too much to leave empty-handed.

Onwards to Glenuig where I cleared out the offending toilet bunker and dumped the bunker's insulation in a bin bag. I cleaned and sprayed and cleaned and sprayed again. My friend lives on a croft and keeps two little fat pigs which churn up the earth and fertilise it, a great example to us all. They live at the bottom of a steep slope which surrounds the house on three sides and is covered in flowering plants of all kinds. She and her late-husband built glass extensions on two sides of their house to make the most of the hill-side location and its views across the valley and the bay. As with any working garden, there is 'stuff' everywhere and all things are used several times. Large white plastic feed or seed tubs and their Frisbee-like lids were dotted everywhere, some as plant pots, some abandoned once used. I spent an hour trying to match tops with bottoms until I found one with the same capacity as my toilet. Then the emptying began.

Smelly.

Poisonous in every way.

Ugh!

My host offered a serious reprimand on using chemicals in the first place, but was kind enough to take the poisonous tub off my hands with a promise to dispose of it more sensibly than I seemed able. She also wanted to know what was wrong with peeing in the bushes.

Um, the inconvenient location of bushes? Bushes can be dark and scary? You're in town and all the bushes are in private gardens? And what about the fact that easy access to a toilet is one of the best luxuries of campervan life? No matter where, town or country, you can always lock the door, pull the curtains and Bob's your uncle.

After discovering that there was no suitable Porta Potti available within driving distance, I dug out the only map I had of the area and had a little think. I hadn't looked at this map in years as I usually know where I'm going. It was a bit old, 1973 to be exact, and probably pinched way back when from my dad's collection. On the inside of its cover I found instructions on how to understand the weather. It was a mass of little hand-drawn symbols and diagrams drawn by Hugh, my first really serious boyfriend. Aw. What a lovely find. If my memory serves me, we were taking refuge in a pub on a wet camping trip and I was trying to make sense of the weather report on the TV so we could decide what to do next. It was a comforting remembrance.

When I looked for Benderloch it wasn't there, only a village called Ledaig and another south of it called South Ledaig. It seems that in 1973 Benderloch was an area, not a village, between Loch Etive and Loch Creran. I wondered when the transition happened and what the Ledaigers thought of becoming Benderlochers. When I got home I looked up my Ward Lock illustrated guide book, *The Highlands of Scotland*, which features little pull-out maps. Along with enough money to buy Fugue Ducato, I inherited a large part of my father's library, which in turn was his father's and his father's again, not to mention my great Aunt Emma's whose extensive library was merged with the male line. The place names in this particular 1937 relic are tiny and difficult to read without a magnifying glass, but Benderloch is there as both a village and a district, while Ledaig is entirely absent. That was a surprise. I could find no clue as to why this was.

I did, however, resolve to bring Ward Lock with me on the next trip, not for the local information therein but for the ads. Most of them are for Ward Lock's other books or places to go on holiday in England, but there's one for Bumsted's Pure Salt which caught my eye and another for Dr Collis Browne's Chlorodyne which claimed to cure flu. If only. But I digress. There were no ads for chemical toilets.

The next possibility for a new toilet was in distant Glasgow but the shopkeeper seemed unwilling to go to the bother of measuring it for me, though in fact THIS WAS THE ONE, at last. In the meantime the little green bowl from the chandlers had to do. Luckily it was perfect.

Chemical toilets have two chambers, one for depositing your business into and the other for holding the flush. The lower chamber has special chemicals which break up solid waste, if you're foolish enough to put anything solid in there. I don't, so I can't confirm this. The chemicals also neutralise smells. The upper chamber has chemicals for cleaning the bowl after use. If you get the fluids the wrong way round there can be a terrible stench, so don't. They are carefully colour-coded to avoid confusion. Blue below, pink above. There are organic fluids you can buy. I haven't tried them yet but reviews are generally good. The added bonus is you use the same stuff for upper and lower chambers, and they are said to smell nicer. However some people complained they were less efficient at breaking down 'lumps' but lumps should be kept for public toilets anyway.

It proved much simpler to use the little green chalice from the Mallaig chandlers anyway. Not useful in the middle of town because there's nowhere to dispose of your waste, it sits easily on the indoor step during use and can be emptied into ditches while masquerading as a simple washing-up bowl in the eyes of anyone driving past. You can then rinse it out with water from the tap, or a mountain stream if there is one, and your mission is accomplished. This proved so much better, I adopted it straightaway as my default plan, except for dawn and last thing at night.

I should point out that I am not polluting or endangering public health when I do this. Urine does not cause any known environmental damage except in parts of the world where large quantities of it are released onto land along with 'number twos' and grey water (household water waste) because of a lack of toilet facilities or adequate plumbing for dense populations. Not only that but urine is actually beneficial to the landscape because it is high in nitrogen, something all plants need plenty of, but low in heavy metals. The main problem is the immediate smell and also potential germs if, for instance, a small child went wandering into the ditch soon after you. This seems unlikely and if it happened would be alarming for other reasons. I've always put used toilet paper into my special bin, a simple plastic bag. Using the bowl has the added advantage of reducing the filling of the chemical toilet thus causing less pollution and lowering the frequency of the work of emptying it.

When disposing of the contents of the green washing-up bowl, be careful. Oh dear. Having stood up carefully and rearranged my clothing in a tight space, there is then the lip at the back door to negotiate, and indeed the door to open while carrying an unstable bowl full of smelly liquid. Carrying the bowl means I can't easily see this back-door lip. When the door is opened a clip at the top of the van should hold it in place. The clip is old and sometimes malfunctions. On one memorable occasion a fierce gust grasped the door and threw it back at me whacking the back of one hand and tipping over my burden. Luckily none of the contents of the bowl made it inside the van, my jeans and shoes prevented that. I hurried behind the van and stripped off the offending articles. The road was quiet, mostly. Later, I dunked the shoes in a river but they were never the same again.

So, number twos. These are a complete no-no as far as chemical toilets are concerned, though I know not everyone agrees. Despite the chemicals claiming to breakdown waste, I don't actually think they do. In any case the design of chemical toilets doesn't easily allow solid waste into the holding tank and is even more reluctant to let it back out again. The entrance hole and exit tunnel are both about two inches in diameter, the tunnel about a foot long with a bend at one end. You don't want to be fiddling about with that. This is why I've never taken the risk. It's much more sensible to plan ahead and know where the nearest flushable toilet is but, of course, emergencies do happen. Like on my first excursion to Kintyre with Vanessa Hotplate.

In a fit of guilt at my elderly mother being left at home while I soaked up the sun and wrote, I invited her to join me. I found her a BnB and settled her into it for the night. I stressed that I must write all the following morning in order to stay sane and arranged to meet her for lunch in Campbeltown, a distance of several miles. Having worked from seven in the morning until nine, I needed a flushable toilet and the only way to get one was to give up this precious time. The need was urgent and the nearest public toilet several miles away. So, in a panic, I spread a plastic bag over the toilet bowl and went to work, then sealed it inside another plastic bag and put it outside the van until I could find a suitable bin in which to lose it. The weather was hot. This was also the day I first saw the magnificent mist which sometimes rolls in off the sea in that part of the world. It began as a band of cloud which looked similar to those rolls of cotton wool that are becoming scarce now. Soon I was engulfed. This was good news because it meant the large layby I was in would not be attractive to other tourists looking for a view.

The time came to meet my mother. I packed my poo into the back, climbed into the driver's seat and turned the key. To no avail. I tried several times, I even tried jump-starting it backwards down the slight incline, but the wheels were locked. I checked my phone. There was no reception. After trying everything I could think of, I had to give up and began the six-and-a-half-mile walk to town while hitchhiking through the mist which had now engulfed me and the road.

A tricky business and dangerous.

The AA had trouble, not for the first time, with the location of Kintyre, a peninsula of some thirty miles length, but they promised to send someone within the hour and to text when they were close. Eh, no. There's no reception in my special layby, only in Campbeltown itself and I'm engulfed in mist. But all was well because the lovely man from Stag Garage in Lochgilphead, forty-four miles north, arrived in good time and worked hard to get my van up onto his lorry without causing damage, despite its locked wheels.

Meanwhile my poo was cooking in the sun and still had no home to go to. I discreetly wrapped it in yet another plastic bag and took it with me in my mother's car to the spacious bins of the BnB and we all breathed a huge sigh of relief, not least my mother who had no idea what was in my rubbish bag but rightly insisted on opening all the car windows on the short drive between my layby and her accommodation. As Vanessa headed home in the comfort of the back of another vehicle, we spent a night in the absolute pristine cleanliness and tropical temperatures of the BnB. In the morning our hosts allowed us to take mugs of tea over the road to the beach. I hid behind a boulder and sat on the golden sand watching gulls splosh into the sea in their ungainly way and berated myself for my idiocy.

The whole incident was humiliating on every level, and here I am telling you. I hang my head in shame. But I have this advice: be prepared.

The green washing-up bowl appears to be a better solution, but as regards disposal of such things the expression 'like flies on shit' isn't accidental, so you need a small spade, or at least a rock to sit on top of your 'business'. Disposal is always difficult and dog poo bags are a handy but still revolting option. An antiseptic spray and strong soap are both essentials.

A lesson in being more at ease with the basic functions of our humanity.

Say no more.

Fodder

If the last chapter hasn't put you off your dinner, I'll carry on about food.

Even in my kitchen at home, I am not a cordon bleu chef. I enjoy cooking for friends when I have time to cook properly, know what I'm cooking, have all the ingredients to hand and the house is somehow already tidy. This doesn't happen often.

But it's worse than that. For several years I had, potentially, seven other people to cater for, but often only my husband and sometimes not even him. At the beginning of our step-family set-up, I used to phone round about four in the afternoon to see who was coming in and when. I got responses like this: 'Um, yes, no, maybe. Tell you what, just make enough for me and if I'm in I'll eat it.' Such are teenagers. Oh, and it turns out twenty-somethings are like that too. Frequently there were mountains of food and no-one to eat it, or nothing at all for seven hungry mouths, which meant late evening trips to hypermarkets or expensive carry-outs. And guilt. Which is stupid. It is patently stupid to feel guilty for failing to herd cats.

Additionally, the two halves of our little family came with very different eating habits, all of which had to be accommodated. The most immediate difference was quantity. His are mostly boys, mine girls, so there was much laughter and merriment when I served up one, not two, chickens for six of us one night. Initially, not only was I veggie but I was the only veggie. The extensive meat-eating habits of his family derived partly from their grandfather being a retired manager of a large string of butchers' shops. With that and my limited intake of wine, there were murmurs I'd never fit in. However, over time, a relatively short time it must be said, I relented and ate meat again, though never much. By the end of it all, two of his, one of mine and he, himself, were veggie, or pescatarian in one case, if that's the right word. Veggie cooking is much more difficult. You have to really focus to make sure everyone's getting the requisite vitamins and protein, and once I'd given in to mince and tatties again, because it was easier, it was hard not to resent the extra work.

Then there's the mess. No-one seemed interested in cleaning up after themselves, so before I even began, the kitchen had to be cleaned and the washing-up done. If anyone else ever did it, I'd never find the whisk, though it's been in the same drawer for years along with the wooden spoons, because some clever dick had decided it would be better in with the pots, or the tins, or under the sink with the cleaning fluids that never got used.

When I served up my beautiful offering, though I must admit I flatter myself here, it was always what someone else wanted, not me, or more usually something no-one wanted. Some of this is still going on, of course, as my two daughters still come and go. Nowadays, once I've discovered some easy-to-concoct platter, I'll go on eating the same thing for days, if I can get away with it. I rarely can because someone will tell me I'm not feeding myself properly, despite salads being my speciality. I suspect it is those funny seeds mixes I put on top that no-one else likes, but nowadays I don't care.

To cut a long story short (I could go on for hours), I now believe I am suffering from a fear of cooking, a condition known as 'mageirocophobia'. Yes, there really is a word for this. Treatments recommended include cognitive behavioural therapy or medication in extreme cases. The experts disagree, however, about whether it is a good idea to force mageirocophobics to cook and thus desensitise them, or whether that will send them spinning into a psychotic state. I'd recommend not cooking unless you really feel like it. It is the perceived unavoidability of cooking for absent/present multitudes that has traumatised me. My mageirocophobia is relatively limited, really. I'm sure others are far worse and have genuine psychiatrically treatable problems. But I do, sometimes, find it hard to get down to making bacon butties for the last remaining meat-eater, even though I love them, the meat-eater that is, but also the butties. When alone I rarely cook anything which is not completely basic. I like it to be simple and quick, apart from my extravagant salads. I suspect my mageirocophobia is site specific, ie my kitchen at home, but either way I have adjusted my campervan cooking to suit.

Campervan cooking is a dream, though you may not agree. Perhaps cooking is your salve, your relaxation, your wind down, in which case you need a bigger fancier van than Vanessa Hotplate. You need better facilities, something more like Fugue which had three rings, a grill and an oven. But even in Fugue the worktop space was limited, so maybe you should consider a Winnebago.

I have a few simple rules.

Rule one is that everything should be simple.

Rule two is no frying. Rally had been subjected to regular frying with the result that the carpet stuff which covered the walls and ceiling was just ever so slightly sticky in places, and didn't smell good. Also, frying comes with a lot of fat, especially if there's meat involved, and fat on plastic plates is very difficult to get rid of and will clog the teeny little waste pipe from the sink, or even melt it if you're silly enough to put hot oil down. It's also not very good for you and will clog your arteries as quickly as it clogs drains. This is bad for staying sharp and writing beautiful words. Rule two A would need to be no cooking meat of any kind. Buy or bring pre-cooked meat if you have to. I keep a jar of roasted sunflower seeds for iron in case I get low without the meat.

Rule three is about boiling. It is very easy for condensation to linger in small spaces. It's hard enough keeping the inside of a small van dry and healthy without adding unnecessary boiling. Therefore boil only as long as is absolutely necessary, cover pots, use a whistling kettle and always have some ventilation. The problem in Vanessa is the cooker sits by the door so if you open the door for ventilation and there's a wind up the gas is liable to be blown out. Even a mild wind will slow down the cooking. As with the whole toilet carry-on, you need to be aware of what liquids are doing. Where are they going? Boiled liquids are usually attaching themselves to your windows and blocking your view and will drip down and make the cushions damp later while you're not looking. Do not trust boiling.

Rule four is have one hot meal a day, best in the evening. There are arguments for hot food and for cold. Cooking your food breaks it down before it enters your body and therefore improves digestion which in turn means more nutrients will be absorbed. Arguably you can assume more energy is available from cooked food. This is what's called being 'bioavailable'. (You may start your jokes here.) On the other hand, boiling vegetables means you lose a lot of their goodness, especially vitamins.

You can take this to extremes. Susan Reynolds of Edinburgh has had no hot food for seven years and says she feels fantastic. None of her food has been either cooked or cooled. 'The benefits include clarity, positivity, health, energy, radiance and the ability to make choices,' she says. 'Other things people have commented on include smelling good, great skin and youthfulness.' None of which is to be sniffed at.

Whatever is the truth, the temptation is to snack on cold

stuff. But, personally, I find hot food grounding. I may insist on hot food purely for comfort and because it's normal, and sometimes I need to be normal. I'm not sure why, but I know a cooked meal makes a difference to my relaxation and comfort. If I skip a day and just have snacks, albeit healthy ones, I have the sensation that something is missing, which is potentially another distraction from getting on with the job of writing.

Rule five is to clean up immediately after dinner and put everything away. This is an extension of the obvious most important campervan rule of them all which is about keeping everything tidy. Everything should be returned to its allotted place as soon as you've finished with it. Otherwise unbearable chaos ensues, not to mention breakage. This also has to do with an unforeseen sudden need to move, made impossible by a sink full of dishes. For instance, one morning I woke to find my gas bottle empty, nay, both my gas bottles empty. Like a fool I'd forgotten to refill the spare. I was anything between five and seven miles, depending on which signs you believed, from the nearest supplier of gas bottles. The road separating us was single track, busy with much larger campers than mine and extremely twisty windy. Additionally, I was badly in need of a shower. I had been extremely lackadaisical about putting things away. One slip, you see, and you're into the dark realms of pandemonium. As a result of all the resulting time-consuming activity involved in rectifying my neglect, my first cup of tea was after midday. For heaven's sake! And I was forced to eat chocolate to console myself on the way home, which brings me to ...

Rule six is about shopping. Don't go mad in a supermarket. Remember there is limited cupboard space. The last thing you want is plastic bags of grub going off in the bed next to you. Plan carefully and stick to your plan. In other words, try to avoid the temptations of eating out if you are there to write.

Stay focussed, use what you've got and avoid food wastage which is as bad for the soul as it is for the planet.

Avoid the temptation of inviting fantastic cooks along to do the job for you. They won't have read these simple rules. When my two friends joined me for the champagne escapade, they slept in a small rain-drenched tent while I shared my living quarters with the food. It was on the benches, under the table, in the clothes box, behind the cushions. Some of it even made it into the cupboards and the fridge, but not much. You get the picture. Finally, we just had to start eating.

Rule seven is obvious, ie rules were made to be broken.

To keep all those rules (excuse me while I laugh up my sleeve), I have developed certain meals. When someone suggested I do a section on campervan recipes, I confess I laughed. But here goes anyway.

Couscous and tomatoes: this is a staple dish in my meal plans. You can either use one of those packets with monosodium-glutamate-augmented 'lemon and coriander' or plain old packet couscous, and add your own seasoning, though you'll need to remember to bring some. Put the couscous in the pot, add seasoning if plain, throw in cherry tomatoes in whatever number you like (halving can help spread the flavour around), add boiling water. Return to the boil, cover, leave to sit for a couple of minutes and serve. If you're using plain couscous just cover the grains with water, put the lid back on and ... *Voila*! If you must, you can add bits of chorizo or cooked chicken to make the dish more interesting (if you haven't already polished the chicken off on the way back from the Co-op). If you're feeling really adventurous you can poach two eggs to put on top while the couscous is doing its mysterious cooking without a flame thing. Even with this embellishment, the whole thing takes about five minutes max.

Instant noodles with egg: follow the instructions for the instant noodles but crack an egg into the pot just before you serve, and stir so that it breaks up. No need to whisk beforehand as that would involve having a whisk and also washing it.

Rice takes much longer (see above on unnecessary boiling) but if you must, you can add various bits of veg, those cherry tomatoes again or herbs and spices. Pasta obviously takes less time, but still too much. At least it goes well with cherry tomatoes. Avoid cooking with cheese, for the same reasons as meat – fat and cleaning up afterwards.

All three of these tempting dishes can be topped with dukkah, dakka or duqqa, which are just different spellings for the same mixture of herbs, spices and nuts, usually hazelnuts. This mixture originates in Egypt. It is absolutely delicious sprinkled on salads or in casseroles and so on, but even better when you've forgotten you had a tub of it with you and there it is in the van ready to go on your spicy tomato couscous and poached eggs. Yum.

Oatcakes: these too are a staple part of my diet and one which I share with generations of Scots. Oatcakes are concentrated slow-release energy and full of goodies. The best ones are from Lidl. Honest. Not making this up. Oatcakes are also great because they are especially tasty when coupled with a multitude of things which often don't require spreading such as bananas. Banana in one hand, oatcake in the other, bite one then the other, repeat until finished. Cheese and oatcakes work in the same way. Jam, if it's good high-fruit low-sugar stuff, I can't resist, but again, it can be messy and requires a knife and a plate, creating unnecessary washing-up. It's sticky stuff too which, once unleashed, goes everywhere, no matter how hard you concentrate. Try, instead, oatcakes with slices of cheese and a whole apple to bite, or grapes, which are even easier.

All of the above provide extremely simple, non-messy and healthy meals.

Sometimes when I leave home I take all the fresh food that I know is unlikely to be eaten by anyone left in the house. This way I avoid going to a shop until it's an absolute necessity. Shops can be jarring commercial places which tempt you with sugary things you don't need and which will ruin your writing brain, and which come wrapped in endless amounts of plastic. So I bring what's at home and make what I can from it, then I go into shops with my blinkers on and look only for the milk. For a recent trip, I brought five apples, five bananas, two lemons, one onion, half a flower of broccoli and the giantest piece of cheddar you can buy (not quite). I ate all the remaining cake before I left the house.

Don't make the mistake of having smoked fish. I know it's tasty, nutritious, oddly comforting and is served with oatcakes in the best hotels, but the smell lingers no matter what you do. I learnt this the hard way in Rally Bedford, oh dear, and the smell hung about me for days in that small enclosed space and even, it seemed, when I'd left it. Avoid.

Cooking in the van is like cooking outside because of the proximity of the cooker to the door. In warm weather this is a good thing because you can open the door but also stay pretty invisible to the outside world. This is important if you're a woman on your own. People in campsites are usually on holiday and keen to socialise. If you don't want company, dinner time is tricky because it's when people will assume you do want company. But I'm probably just filling the tanks as quickly as I'm able for another go at the laptop, or mulling over a plot point. I'm actually happier to be disturbed when I'm writing in laybys where I often crave a bit of company and may myself be the person accosting strangers. That said, I eat outside whenever weather permits, even at home, which in soggy old Scotland is always a treat.

But back to smelly things and this time your fridge. ALWAYS clear it out. Even a sealed tub with the tiniest amount of cheese left inside can stink out the whole fridge and is almost IMPOSSIBLE to get rid of. Believe me, I know. Leave a cut lemon in there to take the smell away if you make a mistake. Fridges also need to be left open when not in use. This can be difficult to arrange, but very necessary.

On the subject of cleaning, I use mostly eco-friendly products because when you're in a beautiful spot you might as well preserve it. In my daily life at home it is so much easier to ignore the consequences of what I use, not that I want to, only it's harder to limit the damage. In the campervan I try not to do any more cleaning than is needed. Apart from anything else, I have to put all the water into the tank myself and sometimes there is no immediate source of water to replenish the tank and I could end up without any for tea, God forbid.

I have an old watering can which is the easiest way to refill the water tank without also inadvertently drenching the cupboard it sits in, which is awkward to access. The watering can is clean, don't worry. When I treat the water tank every spring I also treat the watering can. By that I mean I use a disinfecting sterilising solution which usually comes as a powder and is dissolved in water. This gets rid of all the bacteria and so on that naturally develop in unmoving water over time. You fill the water system with this solution, leave it for a few hours, then flush it out as often as you deem necessary – I would say at least four times. It's a safe and effective procedure and, depending how often you use your van, only necessary once a year. You need to make sure all the pipes are sterilised by pumping some of the sterilising solution through the taps. Obviously the simpler the system, the easier this task is. In Vanessa Hotplate I also get a workout because the water is pumped by foot.

If there is water left in your tank at the end of the trip make sure you empty it sooner rather than later and certainly before the next excursion. Always start with completely fresh water.

You're going to drink it, for heaven's sake. It has to be fresh. Campsites will have standpipes and therefore water standards to reach, but sometimes, if I'm in the wilds, I like to fill my tank from mountain streams. Choose wisely. If there are sheep or cattle close by or any human habitation, go elsewhere. You don't know what kind of diseases the water may carry. I've heard stories about giant worms in human brains as a result of drinking water close to sheep, though I think I was eight when I heard them so they may not be true. Anyway, there is nothing finer than fresh, mountain, unbottled water which you have gathered yourself. If you're worried, use water purification tablets which you can drop into your drinking water, wait twenty minutes and Bob's your uncle. I've never tried them, but they are standard mountaineer fayre. Alternately, you can boil your water and cool it, though that gives you problems with condensation.

Earlier this year I filled my watering can and tank at the site of the lengthy Battle of Glenshiel. This inglorious meeting of might took place in 1719 during the 'Little Rising' or perhaps more correctly the 'Teeny Weeny Rising' as it was a one-off which happened four years after the actual 1715 Little Rising. The Battle of Glenshiel took place only twelve years after the 'Union of the Parliaments', as it is known, when Scotland and England were further joined together following the 'Union of the Crowns' which happened a hundred years earlier. The ruling centre was emphatically in the south. Consequently, not everyone was happy about this, and strenuous efforts continue to this day to separate them again, most recently in the 2014 Referendum for Scottish Independence. In 1719, the Jacobite forces included several clans, among them the McKenzies, Camerons, Keiths, Mackinnons and MacGregors along with the most famous MacGregor of them all, Rob Roy. They were also supported by France and by three hundred Spaniards who had expected a better turnout from the Highlanders or they might have stayed at home. The government troops were also supported by some clans in the form of Clans Fraser, Ross, Sutherland, Mackay and Munro. The two sides were an almost even match, so the battle went on for a full three hours, until everyone was exhausted. The Highland Jacobites were expecting support from Lowlanders, which never came. Demoralised and exhausted they eventually abandoned the battleground and went home for tea, though they could have pre-empted my example and sat down where they were. The Spaniards had to surrender to the government as their homes were too far away and in my experience they don't drink tea anyway. Later they were freed and sent back to Spain unharmed, apart from the rigours of the Scottish jail system of the time.

A promontory of the mountain on which the battle was fought, Sgurr nan Spainteach, or Peak of the Spaniards, was named in their honour. The date was June the tenth so there's a chance the weather was hot. It seems likely that many of the soldiers who fought that day, including Rob Roy MacGregor, must surely have drunk from the very same burn from which I filled my tank. The path to it runs beside the current road and looks old, perhaps nearly three hundred years. It's a quiet and restful spot now peopled by hazel bushes and finches, so it's hard to imagine hundreds of fighting men here doing anything but refreshing themselves and relaxing.

But I have wandered from the path. There is so much interesting information to stumble upon in a van.

If all of this simple life makes me sound eccentric and a tiny bit feral, I must point out that I have to get my fun somehow. One of the great joys of my first trip in Rally Bedford was the great simplicity of my eating: I had the exact amount of food I needed and the self-control not to run off to buy chocolate and biscuits. I was magically in tune with what my body was doing and what it needed in order to do it. I'm not a control freak but I didn't enjoy having no control in my kitchen at home, and therefore over my own eating habits, for all those years, so it has been a delight to be able to reverse that lack of order.

And then, at the end of all these culinary efforts, there's my secret bottle of Cointreau.

Book Broth

Today I'm a short way along the busy A85 road from Tyndrum to Oban. I'm hungry but I've managed to not stop at the famous Green Welly shop and café back in Tyndrum, always a terrible temptation. I have all the food I need with me.

Tyndrum is the first pit stop as you head north from Glasgow and nestles at the meeting point of several valleys. Undecided tourists pause to consider their options in the canteen-like café with its simple and nutritious food. The menu is probably designed with the walkers of the West Highland Way in mind. The village is always busy with tour buses and the hotels and restaurants which cater for them. Probably a handful of people actually live here, yet it seems to thrive. The West Highland Way skirts the village to the south then passes through it, up the steep valley to the north between mountains and on towards Rannoch. The road I am on splits off to the west just beyond the last house in Tyndrum then turns south.

The road wasn't busy when I stopped in this layby, but rush hour is difficult to predict in this rural paradise. There's a rough unused field behind me, then the railway and beyond that some forestry climbs up the other side of the valley. Lochan na Bi, which means 'little loch of birches', is a little further along on the valley bottom, and here, beside the layby, are some little birch trees, their silver trunks muddied no doubt by cars that screech to a stop. The layby is not the cleanest and rubbish is plentiful, but it is too messy for me to tidy up, and this is not my chief task today. There are some looser trees, Norwegian pines, and yellow flowering broom on the other side of the road and a little opening with a gate, but they are all inaccessible beyond the busy road.

Juggernauts hurtle past. The wasp-like buzz of cars harass them, desperate to make use of the long straight beyond the layby. The weather is warm enough for me to open the back door, and because I'm on a slight bend I can see the traffic racing towards me then swerving off round the side of the van at the last minute.

I seem to have denied myself sustenance, so I tuck into oatcakes, cheese and grapes, keeping the large bar of chocolate for later, well the last few squares of it anyway. I'm also having some kind of abjection of the flesh with some wasabi peas and wondering whether they will have the unfortunate side-effect of opening up my sinuses and allowing lorry fumes in. But wasabi peas, as you may know, are full of surprises. Quite suddenly their heat hits the back of your nose and gets into your eyes, and there's nothing you can do. It's a spontaneous reminder to wake up and get on with it.

So I do. But on this occasion the getting on with it involves reading, because reading feeds me and therefore isn't a luxury. I'm careful what I read but less careful how many books I bring with me. There are staples in here, though they change. First there is *Emergency Kit: Poems for Strange Times*, a poetic survival guide to life's most painfully poetic moments. A poetry book is always the most concentrated food, I find, especially when writing fiction. Then there's an actual survival guide, *Everything that follows is based on recent, real-life experience that has been proven to work: Professional Survival Solutions*. This title is a bit long if I'm ever in a real immediate emergency, but the book includes chapters on angry animals, delivering a baby, starting a car without keys (wish I'd had that one way back when) and trapping water in a desert (not so useful in these parts but an interesting contrast). My well-thumbed bird book is by the RSPB. The delights of discovering I really did just see a golden eagle (not here) was immense. Beside the bird book is *The Cloud Collector's Handbook* (who knew there were so many kinds of clouds?), a present from a large friend who is (almost) too tall to fit in the back of my van. All of these live with the torch and tissues on the shelf above the window.

Above the other window are the maps. They bulge and flop as maps do. Without maps I am lost, but only in a personal sense. I generally know most of the roads I travel, roughly, but knowing what is beyond them, the proximity of Glen Lyon to Glen Coe for instance, is fascinating. I mention this because the laird of Glen Lyon was instrumental in the Massacre of Glencoe. He gave the insistent last-minute orders for the troops in his command to kill, in their beds, the very people they'd been carousing with for the past fortnight. Signal Rock is named for this purpose and affords views in all directions. This rock was also made famous by Robert Louis Stevenson in *Kidnapped*. David Balfour and the real but fictionalised Alan Breck Stewart hid on top of it in baking sunshine while government troops searched fruitlessly for them below. As you can see, maps orient me in time and literature as well as space. They're also handy for finding quiet little roads in which to hide teeny little campervans.

Add to that Ward Lock and Co's travel guides from the 1930s, many with pull-out maps and guides to the meaning of Gaelic place names, and the past feels very present. I also have the 1933 edition of *Scotland for the Motorist* by the AA (that's Automobile Association, not Alcoholics Anonymous) which also has Gaelic place names and a few Norse ones too. It describes the landscape with elegant simplicity declaring, for instance, that 'the Isle of Skye is the most romantic and most fascinating island on the Western coast.' It fills you in on basic local history and makes frequent references to where, for example, Sir Walter Scott or Robert Louis Stevenson wrote their great works, and other fascinating snippets of information. I like the absence of recent developments or advice about where to get dinner. I used to also carry a 1924 edition of Dorothy Wordsworth's 1805 journals which included *A Tour Made in Scotland*, complete with some of the pages still uncut. I enjoyed tracing her journey with her more famous brother and the poet Coleridge at a time when roads were scarcer and ferries more common. They seem to have had terrible weather and were 'disappointed' with Glen Coe. So I left them at home next time.

Beside these are one copy each of my novels, *Mavis's Shoe* and *Rue End Street*, to remind me what I'm there to do and to offer myself encouragement. There are two more under the bench in case anyone wants to buy one.

To back all this up there's usually some nonfiction above the windows, probably something to do with my writing project, but not necessarily. Having something enriching is just as important. And for a complete rest to the creative right-hand side of my brain, I have a Sudoku book for exercising the more scientific, and therefore in my case less developed, left side.

But now I need to put down my pen and read.

Highways And Bylaws

Andy Strangeway is the aptly named Yorkshireman who made it his business to sleep on all one-hundred-and-sixty-two Scottish islands with an acreage of over forty hectares. This is quite a feat and also an indicator of single-minded determination. Admirable in anybody's book. He was also the person who campaigned successfully for the removal of the glaring yellow signs in many Scottish laybys a few years back which sported the words NO OVERNIGHT PARKING.

I have long deplored these signs, just as I deplore all signs which tell us all, including freshly arrived tourists, to NOT do something which only a tiny minority of us ever do. I'm thinking of a café on a Highland road that best remain nameless which has NO signs all over it. No parking here, no sitting there, no touching this, no distracting the waitress, toilets are for customers only, and no, you can't have your teapot refilled with hot water. NO. This seems very unfriendly and also rather stupid from a business point of view.

However the online debate over laybys is a heated one. Many people, like me, were delighted with Strangeway's victory. A large and more vociferous band were horrified. One cited their experience of stopping in a layby and finding evidence of someone's chemical toilet having being emptied close by. I find this hard to believe but if true I join this arguer in their abhorrence. What a revolting thing to find and shocking in its chemical disregard for the environment. Why would anyone do that?

Frankly, most people don't. The vast majority of people also take their litter home or put it in the bins provided for that purpose. I suspect people in the countryside drop less litter per capita than people in the city, though obviously I can't prove this. I think we are less horrified by litter in the city because we often don't have much choice. In recent years, cities seem to have fewer public litter bins because of the fear they may conceal bombs. There's also the issue of packaging. Goods are commonly wrapped in several layers, a practice which provides so much more litter to blow into your hedge and get stuck there.

Unlike England and Wales, there is no national law of trespass in Scotland. Being able to stop your campervan and sleep or even make your tea is a matter for local bylaws and land ownership. It's down to whether landlords or local authorities appreciate campers stopping on their land. Land ownership is also the latest hot potato in Scottish political discussion, so this may change. The best advice, wherever you are, is to ask.

Or is it? It's your choice, but I think, rather, it depends where you are and what time of day it is. I usually stop late in the evening, preferably at twilight so I can still see what I'm doing, but also because by then you are less likely to be noticed, or to annoy other drivers by slowing down to examine likely spots. I get in the back and close the curtains so no-one has to watch me eat, never a pretty sight, and no-one will know I'm on my own. Obviously personal safety is a concern. This is my discreet way of going about things, but it may not be the best plan for you. If it's not, you can limit the likelihood of being asked to move on by finding out first if parking overnight is allowed.

There is a handy website which you'll find in the bibliography which gives information and links to relevant pages, council by council in Scotland, on what is provided and what is or isn't allowed. Shetland and the Western Isles come out well in this. Shetland 'doesn't discourage' wild camping and the Western Isles goes further by offering a leaflet with lists of campsites, public toilets and recycling points. The Western Isles also make a polite request not to park on the machair, which includes sand dunes and sandy low-lying arable or grazing land used by crofters, as this is an environmentally delicate area. Other parts of the country, for instance Moray, ban all sleeping and cooking in campervans anywhere outside designated parks which on a short survey seem to be comprehensively expensive. Dundee has the same ban. You can stay in Port Errol in Aberdeenshire for three nights for nothing, but the harbour trustees suggest a donation of a tenner a night towards the care and maintenance of the historic harbour, which seems fair. Fort William offers advice on which car parks to use in that vicinity and does not charge, or not beyond the usual 'pay and display' in car parks. In Hawick in the Borders there are 'dedicated spaces where sleeping, camping and cooking are permitted' for one night from Easter until the end of September. 'There are toilets, a fresh water tap and volunteers on hand during the day to welcome visitors and give them information on the town.' Fabulous. This is part of a two-year trial, which after one year was said to be going well. South Ayrshire are planning a similar initiative. These are just a few examples of the information available to show you the range of responses you might encounter. It's best to check the website for up-to-date information.

During the Scottish Independence Referendum, I went on a visit to Aberdeen to count their postal votes. I followed the advice of this helpful website and asked the council where I could stay for two weeks for the purposes of this work. They were extremely helpful and suggested I park for free on the Esplanade by the long and beautiful beach. This, of course, is wild parking in a city and comes with a different kind of 'wild' with which to contend. On my second night there I encountered a man nearby who resembled Popeye in stature, behaviour and especially, rather wonderfully, in his gravelly voice. However, he was behaving oddly (being over-friendly, talking to himself and staggering) and I felt the need of a circuitous route back to the van. This was most likely unnecessary, but why take a risk? Risk-taking ruffles your sense of calm and wastes energy otherwise available for writing beautiful words. Other inconveniences on the Esplanade included noise, unavailability of water supply and the lack of toilet disposal facilities. Grey water waste, the stuff from the sink, can be put straight down roadside drains but doing so may draw enquiring eyes.

There is a very different story to tell in France where most cities, small towns and even some villages have special campervan spaces within their municipal car parks. They often supply toilets or chemical toilet disposal points and even electricity, and are sometimes free, yes, even the electricity. However, this free supply of electricity appears to be going out of fashion and is being replaced by special electricity tokens which have to be bought from the local mayor. Motorhomes now use extraordinary amounts of electricity, so this is understandable, but the *mairie* (town hall or city hall) is often shut at the time you are most likely to stop. However, even taking that into account, the French show a better understanding of the needs of campervan and motorhome travellers than the Brits.

In France there are businesses which supply facilities for campervans in their private car parks because they know you will come and visit their factory shop or museum, maybe buy something, or perhaps pay for a tour of their workshops. Some people will, others won't, but there's still a likelihood you'll spend something in their town or tell your friends about their facilities. This is sound business sense but also makes human sense. How much further can you travel (and how much more often) if you don't have to worry about campsites being open or harassment from local police. There are sites in Scotland and France which are open all year round, but these are in the minority. Come on Scotland! You can do better.

We need more initiatives like Hawick's, but perhaps we also need to learn to see campervans and motorhomes as more than just nuisances on the road that have the potential to leave waste behind them. The small community design organisation who borrowed my van also invited me along for a week of their month-long tenure. They were called 'Lateral North' and their purpose was to facilitate brainstorming workshops in local communities to help people think laterally and envision their future. I came along to help out on these workshops, to write some stuff of my own and also to give creative writing workshops on a futuristic theme. We travelled from Helmsdale, a coastal village in Sutherland in the north east of Scotland, to the island of Shapinsay in Orkney, then back to Thurso and Tongue, both on the north coast of the Scottish mainland. Next we turned south to the peninsula of Applecross on the west coast, north again to Lairg, and thence back to Helmsdale and the Timespan Museum and Arts Centre there to deliver our findings to a conference.

We did this in early March when there was snow everywhere, the roads were treacherous with ice and there was often a horizontal wind. The scenery was stunningly beautiful, not least on the vast open wildernesses of Sutherland, the coves of Durness, and the famous Bealach na Ba road over the mountain in Applecross to the village on the coast. Impassable on the way in due to snow and ice, this precipitous mountain pass was clear enough on the way back for us to drive between six-foot snowdrifts amid swirling mist.

We had tea whenever we needed it and also access to a toilet. My companion was about half my age and we barely knew each other. Between that and the sub-zero temperatures, it made sense to stay overnight with local people instead of in the van. We conducted most of our sessions in community halls and similar venues, the exception being at Applecross Primary School where we fitted all nine of the pupils inside the van. We also held occasional meetings with grown-ups in there, once even in Palace Road in Kirkwall right opposite the magnificent St Magnus Cathedral.

I'm surprised more businesses don't use campervans in this way, especially in the more remote parts of Scotland. They seem ideal for the purpose, with all the necessary facilities in one including overnight accommodation and an interview room. I will admit that Romahomes are really too little, especially for tall people. You might have to touch knees or toes with the people on the opposite bench in order to be comfortable, or you could stagger them, though that might feel more intimate than you'd like to be with your bank manager. Your van wouldn't need to be much bigger, however, for this to be practical. What might be required is a change of attitude and a few more basic wintertime facilities like hook-ups.

This would also work in big cities like London where people frequently have to travel considerable distances to do business. Often they meet in hotels and restaurants and lack quick access to all the documentation and so on they'd have at hand in an office. In a campervan they could have a drinks cabinet and provide three-course meals to entertain customers who need a little more persuasion. My friends' hired motorhome would have accommodated two meetings simultaneously and had a shower to freshen up in and an ironing board to make the best impression. We are into the realms of motorhomes here, and they bring with them problems of size and manoeuvrability in city streets. They also come with a complete lack of cool, which Vanessa, Vera, Rally and Fugue all trump without effort.

Laybys By Day

Floating Narrator

I am the floating narrator of our lives.
From Glasgow
to Manchester,
Aberdeen,
Edinburgh,
I weave a spider's web of stories,
meeting in unlikely railway stations,
the sides of roads,
my vagabond, disparate family,
spread to the many corners of this
multi-faceted, hexa-deca-penta-non-agonal world,
fractually blinded by the beams of our reflected headlamps.

I am surprised, despite the glare,
by my yearning for home,
though I am already there.
I am the yearning of us all for home.
I bring our stories there
and pass them on.
Home is wherever we are.

There was a period when nine of the inhabitants of my house
seemed to be more on the road than off it. (I include one of the

cats, Bambam the itinerant tom, who eventually abandoned us for the family at number fourteen.)

At that time I thought that, as the woman of the house, I had the function of glue: I had to hold everyone together. Obviously, ultimately, I wasn't very good at it, or perhaps it wasn't what people wanted, but I did function in many ways as a kind of hands-off coordinator. I mean the mapping kind of coordinator rather than the manager of a busy team. Then I rediscovered campervans and joined the throng of homeless people inhabiting my home part time. About the same time, I also discovered laybys and then the concept of floating narrators, which I'll explain.

This chapter is about the benefits of cutting loose. I'll start with a little literary theory, specifically about floating narrators. Please bear with me. I didn't find this an easy concept to grasp, but quite exciting once I had.

Neither of my published novels have a floating narrator. They are both first-person narratives. You could say it was just 'me, me, me' all the time because first-person narratives are written entirely from one person's point of view: the story as told by them. The advantage of this is you get right inside the narrator's experience. The downside is also you get right inside the narrator's experience and it can get quite claustrophobic in there for both reader and writer. For the writer it is restricting because you can only really tell one story, or only one full story, though you can still have fun letting the reader understand something the narrator can't yet see. But what about the goings-on of all those other characters? With only one narrator you can't delve into their stories in any great depth.

With a floating narrator you can have any number of standpoints and a greater exploration of subplots too, all of which can involve complexities not possible with a single voice. This is, in part, the 'he said-she said' type of writing, but it's more than just third person. Even in third-person stories the narrator tends to take one vantage point, as if the narrator is an invisible being sitting on the shoulder of one of the characters. This still restricts what the reader knows, and even though we get to experience other people too, our understanding of them is usually less complex. The reader's vision is necessarily skewed. We are invited to be biased. With a floating narrator, that disembodied observer-cum-reporter moves around different vantage points, as if the same disembodied reporter is hopping from shoulder to shoulder between the characters, or even sometimes just floating above them all, which I think is the most fun. In theory this should make it easier to let the reader decide the rights and wrongs of the story for themselves, or at least to feel as if they have, which is perhaps more important. It's certainly a good way to draw the reader into becoming actively involved in your story.

In practice this shoulder-hopping is extremely tricky to do, the transition from one shoulder to the other being the most difficult part because there is a danger of interrupting the reader's absorption in the story and, therefore, of losing them. The best floating narrator novels are so smoothly written that the reader is completely unaware of any transition.

Before I knew this, I wrote a whole novel of one hundred and fifty thousand words, all of it in the first person. The trouble was, each chapter was 'written' by a different first person, so at every new chapter the reader had to pause and completely re-orientate themselves. To their great credit, several friends read the whole of this monstrosity, for the most part not wandering off between chapters for something better to read, for which I will always be grateful. Certain other people's novels manage this multiple narrator business far better, for instance Cormac McCarthy's *No Country For Old Men*. But this was my first-ever book and I lacked McCarthy's skill to make it work, and anyway, I did the first person thing because I thought it would help me get inside the head of each character and, having done so, I could then 'translate' all one hundred and fifty thousand words into the third person, and ... Bingo! There would be my novel. You may now laugh, especially any writers reading this. Having finished the initial draft, I quickly learnt the error of my ways and wrote a new novel with a clear beginning, middle and end, and a first person narrative to make it all easier for everyone.

I mention this because it seems to bear some relation to my habit of hanging out in laybys. I may have given the impression so far that laybys are for sleeping in, whereas in fact they are quite specifically for writing. Occasionally I use them to read, once in a while to clean up the tea leaves after forgetting to put the teapot away at the last stop, or even for checking the map. But mostly I believe laybys were put there for writing.

They are good for writing, whatever the weather, and in fact whatever the level of traffic, depending on how urgently you need to get down to it. Laybys are always there waiting for you when your house is full of noisy people wanting to watch TV, eat your last scrap of food, or argue with you, again, over whose fault it is the bathroom's in a mess. Therefore, these laybys don't need to be far from home. I have a favourite about forty minutes' drive away on a single track road with a dead end. It has no mobile reception too and once you're gone, you're gone. Having this certainty that, no matter what else happens, I can always go there and write, takes the pressure off me even when I'm at home. I know my salvation is out there. I know I am not trapped. All I need is the laptop, water for tea and my tiny gas heater.

My mind is scattered with a thousand other laybys and as many layby experiences. The encounters I have with other people in laybys are always more intense and memorable, and if you get uncomfortably stuck with anyone you can just move on, though this has never happened. Like the floating narrator, I get a bird's eye view of the world but one with snapshots of places and lives. I swoop down on a layby, quickly examine the world around it, get in the back and write, perhaps about my surroundings, perhaps not. It is the sense of detached involvement that it gives me, coupled with a feeling of forward motion, which feeds my concentration. Being able to move at a moment's notice somehow keeps my fingers moving on the keyboard too.

Today I'm in Calder Glen near Lochwinnoch, not far from Glasgow. My layby was probably a small quarry in days gone by, so there is naked rock behind me and more to one side shrouded in a tangle of little birch trees. It's a bite out of an outcrop on the side of a hill. The road runs at a slight incline for three miles, two behind me and one more to the end of the road, which traverses the hill about halfway up. Below it the fields run steeply into a gully at the bottom, where the River Calder rushes and tumbles towards the town. The rise on the other side is at a similarly precipitous angle and I can hear a waterfall running down it, rushing over rocks hidden in hazel bushes. The hill is green and undulates over the crevices of hidden burns. A line crosses them and links with two trees further up the valley and a square of disused field. Eight untamed miles of mountain and moor stretch from my layby to Largs on the Clyde coast. Within this area there are traces of no less than twenty airplane crash sites, an exceptionally high number, which all occurred between 1938 and 1958. Some of them remained undiscovered for up to a week, which is a bit gruesome. People blamed the mists which gather here, also the mineral deposits in the area that they believed created some kind of magnetic field which interfered with the primitive navigation technology of the day. They said the hills were like a new Bermuda Triangle, or perhaps more correctly a Cunninghame Curve. There used to be barite mines in this glen but barites aren't magnetic so the theory is likely to be local myth. My money's on the mist. Two of the unfortunate crash sites are within view of my layby, but I can't see any debris, even with the binoculars.

An hour ago, here in the layby, I heard some high-pitched squealing. I went out to investigate and saw two young buzzards turning circles round each other. Buzzards are actually a fairly common sight in most parts of Scotland but I've never seen two together before, only singletons. Dark against the blue sky and with their distinctive white markings under long straight wings, they are oddly similar to the planes which fell all those years ago. They seemed to be making use of warm updraughts, which is their habit, turning on miniature whirlwinds, higher and higher, then swooping back down and starting upwards again. It's possible they were flirting, or maybe just playing, but whatever they were up to it looked fun. They progressed gradually southwards until a hill obscured my view.

I turned back to the van and there above it hung a pure black raven. Unlike buzzards, ravens are social creatures, intelligent too, and this one suddenly fell from the deep-blue sky and vanished over the green curve of the field. Almost as quickly, it reappeared and climbed with great speed and grace until it was almost above my head. This is what ravens do, muck about and throw themselves around mid-flight. They usually do it in pairs. I've seen pairs of them coordinate themselves, dancing so close I can't help wondering whether they ever bump into each other, and what the raven equivalent of stepping on each other's toes would be. They're extremely fast and pull out of these crazy dances as swiftly as they fall into them. Perhaps this lone raven was practising her moves, or maybe it just feels good to shake yourself out of the sky.

They're nosy creatures too. Once upon a time, when I reached the top of Ben Lomond, Scotland's most southerly

Munro at a height of 3196 feet, two ravens were there to greet me. One hovered, like the buzzards, in the updraught that rushed up the crags to the north and east, while its companion landed six feet away from me. Sleek and shiny blue-black creatures, they squinted at my companion and me with disconcerting inquisitiveness and seemed reluctant to leave. Today's raven, however, appeared oblivious to my presence and continued its high jinks for some time, gradually moving further from view.

This is what I love about laybys, these small opportune encounters. Ten minutes later a friend and her husband happened by and, recognising the van, stopped for a chat. Luck, fluke, random occurrences are what laybys bring me. Also two clegs whose company was less endearing. These are orange-coloured horseflies. Cleg, the Scottish word for them, seems to capture more readily their liking for horse manure and for stabbing defenceless humans.

Earlier this year, in desperation and after failing miserably to write in the quiet of a good friend's house, I stopped in a layby just east of Connel Bridge near Oban, a biggish town on the west coast of Scotland. It was a shallow layby so I was very close to the road. The traffic was heavy and almost constant, making the van shake with every vehicle that passed. I got in the back, made tea and wrote a section of this book. While I was at it, a car stopped and three Oriental-looking people got out, two women and a man. None of them spoke. They also behaved as if I wasn't there, even standing very close to my van and between my large side window and the view across the water, which wasn't necessary and can't have been easy as the verge was narrow and featured a sharp drop towards the sea. After a few minutes, they moved back near to their car and stood for a while in a row in silence. One of the women got back into their car. The other woman hugged the man while he, unflinching, hands in pockets, continued to gaze at the view. Thirty long seconds passed. She unwound her arms from his neck. He stood a moment longer. They got back into the car without looking at each other. The car U-turned and they drove back the way they had come. A story played out in my mind of a holiday long planned, a clumsy confession of some sort, the pain of hearing it, and a woman who was not to be forgiven. They all wished the holiday was over and could not properly see the people around them or the amazing views they were looking at.

The traffic continued to growl past my window, inaudible to me as it rocked the van. I felt as though I was on a train journey and someone else was driving. I quickly took note of what I'd just seen and their imagined story, then continued with my work.

It's only the noise in your head that will disturb you. If you can train yourself to ignore the traffic or the crowd, or compartmentalise them, or accommodate what disturbs you by writing it down, as I did, you can actually live in a peaceful little bubble all of your own and get some writing done or painting or whatever you are doing. On the way back from France once, we parked in a service station amongst the lorries. We were twenty feet from the motorway. I thought I'd never sleep so I listened to the traffic rumbling past, the lorry doors opening and closing, and the wind in the railings of the van roof, then I told myself not to wake up if I heard them. I slept soundly all night. I was completely amazed that this little experiment had worked. It seems that, asleep or awake, screening works. It helps if what you're trying to do won't give you peace until you've done it.

Laybys are a little pocket in time and space for you to inhabit without commitment, a kind of one-night-stand of camper-writing. I can stay (almost) as long as I want, or leave on a whim. I can write part of a novel or a tiny little poem, snippets or screeds, laptop or notebook, but whatever it is I'm ten times more likely to be fully focussed. The physical freedom laybys and campervans grant me is paralleled by the mental freedom I often magically find in such places. It's also simultaneously limited and not limited, protected by the existence of wheels but a comfortable place where I can be sure of being internally still enough to work, and a fast track to the Zone (when we are working at our optimum level with minimal effort). So, as long as there's a suitable layby, which is a pretty broad category, I can write.

The added bonus is the problem of being off grid. Yes, problem as bonus. I can explain, but first a little more literary stuff. I need to tell you about OuLiPo, otherwise known as *Ouvroir de Littérature Potentielle*, which translates from the French as 'workshop of potential literature'. I suppose in English that would make it WoPoLi. Anyway, OuLiPo was started in 1960 in France by a group of writers and mathematicians and it endures to this day. Possibly one of the most interesting and unusual collaborations of thought, the principle of the movement is to release literary potential by using restrictions, often mathematical ones: expansion through constraint. I believe there's a similar theory in theatre called 'The Theatre of the Poor'. The idea there is the smaller the budget the more inventive you have to be. Both stem from necessity being the mother of invention.

The easiest OuLiPo writing exercise is the snowball poem in which the first line has one word, the second two, the third three and so on, but there are much more complicated and mathematical challenges you can take on, such as excluding all words that contain the letter 'A'. See how long you can keep that up!

My all-time favourite, which I learnt in a creative writing workshop, is about opposites. You take a short paragraph and change each individual word into its opposite, or the closest you can find to an opposite. The first time I did this I was hysterical with laughter and couldn't speak for five minutes. This was a little embarrassing as I had to read my piece to the rest of the workshop. Luckily most of the other students had the same problem. I could feel my brain morph. It was like having your thoughts tickled. Try it and see for yourself.

If I do this exercise involving opposites with the quote from Susan Sontag at the beginning of this book, you'll see how it also has poetic possibilities:

'Can I love someone … and still think/fly?'
becomes:
'Can't you hate everyone … or never sleep/fall?'

It kind of doesn't make sense but it also sort of does, in the way that poetry can often be found between the meanings of words and in unusual juxtapositions of words. It shakes up preconceived notions and opens possibilities. Try it and see what makes an opposite for you. It's not an exact science.

So, problem as bonus. I usually write on a laptop, and use the paper notebook mostly, but not exclusively, for notes. Work written by hand feels different, as if it's coming from a different, possibly deeper, part of me. Poetry has to be by hand, at least for a first draft. Unexpectedly, quite large parts of this book were written by hand, but this is not my norm for prose.

My current laptop began life with over seven hours of battery time. It now does only four at the most. This means I have to get focussed with my freedom to write and not waste it. When the battery finally runs down I'm forced to stop. Then I plug it into an 'inverter' which transforms power from the twelve-volt leisure battery in my van into something I can use. I then sit back and wait or, better still, go exploring in the surrounding hills or along the beach, or head to town for supplies or an invigorating swim. When I come back, the laptop battery and I are both recharged and ready for the second session of the day. The limitations of the laptop battery are very focussing, and limitations are often another fast track to the Zone.

In addition to the laybys themselves, there is the road in between them which, if you have your technology working correctly, will recharge the leisure battery and therefore the laptop without you doing much at all. At the same time, and in the way of the piano lesson and the Mars bar, sometimes in order to concentrate you have to distract yourself first. In this case I do it with the driving and perhaps the admiration of the view. The answers to knotty problems miraculously appear or I inadvertently come up with new ideas, and, of course, I can stop any time and scribble a reminder to myself in that notebook.

Please note that the notebook is always roughly A5, lined and with a hard cover. A ribbon bookmark is an added bonus. All these attributes mean it can be whipped out of a handbag at the drop of a raven, perched on a knee and scribbled in with lucidity and immediacy, capturing the moment. But, above all, notebooks provide the comfort of reliable availability (unlike electronic devices which run out of juice or crash).

So, with the help of laybys and notebooks, I can float around the countryside picking up stories, reflecting on my strange family life, musing on the wonders of the universe and generally rising above all of this to choose the next words to put down: a floating narrator of my life, the universe and everything, and of course my books.

This is somewhat akin to the popular theory of 'combinatorial creativity'. Yes, what a mouthful, but don't panic. I can explain. Fundamentally, it says that creative people simply cross-pollinate between ideas, experiences and disciplines. The idea is you link your different thoughts and experiences in a variety of combinations and come up with apparently new ones. Therefore the more experiences we have, the more there is at our disposal for varied and interesting new connections between them and thereby new ideas. The late Steve Jobs, the Apple entrepreneur, added that people who come up with ideas consistently have often 'had more experiences or they have thought more about their experiences than other people.' Obviously the more experiences you have and the more fully you experience them the more you have to play with and the more you can mix and match them into new concoctions. Albert Einstein is said to have had a 'delay-oriented' form of problem-solving. When given an hour and a tricky problem, he'd think for fifty-five minutes and form the solution in the last five. In other words he'd be searching his mind for what he knew, putting thoughts and understandings together with other thoughts and understandings in any number of combinations, then choosing which ones were best.

I like to think I do something similar in laybys. I collect experiences but I also have the peace to sit still and make those mind connections.

A related idea, this one borrowed from Buddhism, is observation. I don't just mean trying to figure out what the other people in the layby are up to, though that close scrutiny of human behaviour is all part of writing stories. I mean observation as a tool for making sense of the emotional rollercoaster called life. Like the floating narrator, simple observation is a way of being aware of, but simultaneously detached from, whatever is happening. This can either be outside myself or within my personal life and feelings. The idea is to foster uninvolvement, in other words to let thoughts, feelings or even physical sensations arise within me and simply watch them. I try not to fight against them because that's what gives them power and detracts from their true nature. I try not to wonder why I feel like that, particularly. In that moment, my aim is to just observe.

Of course, I might also need to act, for instance if I'm terrified because I've encountered a madman with a knife. (This has never happened.) In this case it would probably be best if I ran away very fast or, failing that, focussed my attention on negotiating my way out of the situation. Fear, like all feelings, has a function and exists to keep us safe and to alert us to the need to act. Likewise, if grief overwhelms me, as it did many times after my marriage collapsed, I might need to go somewhere private to let the tears fall and be with those feelings without having to explain anything to anyone else. It's important to stay safe, but to leave dissection for later, to not deny what is happening around me or in me, but also to not become overly involved with it. To let it pass of its own natural accord, which it will because it always does. Life goes on. I try to see the moment in a detached way, almost as if I was writing someone else's story. I'm being my own floating narrator, hoping to rise and see bigger pictures, to observe, take notes, and let it inform my writing.

In this way, I don't deny any feelings, but neither do they get to wreck lives, or even good storylines. Of course, this is big talk. It's a habit Buddhist masters (and mistresses) spend years cultivating. There is also a special meditation you can do to help you on your way. It's called 'tonglen' and it involves inviting the full sensation of your emotions into your awareness as you breathe in, then immediately after, on the out breath, you shift your conscious thought to a sense of your own wisdom and strength. In with the full extent of your fear and its awful consequences, out with your great bravery and wisdom, in with your greatest fear, out with peaceful wisdom, in, out, until you've shaken it all out. Tonglen is a little more complicated than that but it's very powerful and extremely good in a crisis.

It's also a handy trick when trying to write about difficult material. I think my job, as a writer, is to tell the truth as I see it. Other writers will no doubt see and do things differently, but it seems to me that if I flinch from the truth, I render my work meaningless or at least waste my time and possibly yours. Like everyone else, I have precious little time to waste. Looking at terrible realities in the controlled spirit of tonglen is a good way to face difficult things.

Martin Stepek, while researching the atrocities visited upon his Polish ancestors in labour camps during the First and Second World Wars, used a similar mindfulness technique in order to appreciate the full horror of their experiences. It enabled him to contain his own distress at their suffering. In this way he managed to carry on writing his book *For There Is Hope* and to stay sane and happy in the process. This technique allowed him to become fully immersed in their experiences and then withdraw himself to safety, in and out. *In* horror, *out* peace. In this way all experiences can be observed, understood, learned from, assimilated and written about, without causing damage to yourself or indeed anyone else.

Forgive me for so much talk of Buddhism but those guys just get so much right. If the idea of tonglen makes you nervous you can stick with the Buddhist concept of impermanence, the idea that *this too shall pass*. Everything changes, and I mean every last thing, even the great grand mountains of Assynt are changing every day. All situations are evolving and nothing stays the same. I know some people may be alarmed by this. Worrying about change and the unknown is natural and part of being human, but personally I find reassurance in this notion of fluidity. As a way of dealing with seemingly intransigent situations, the idea that it won't be long before the difficulties have evaporated or lost their meaning or sting, gives me courage and hope.

Here in this layby, a farmer's quad bike passed by on the road a short while ago with two sheepdogs on the back, their black-and-white hair pulled back along their bodies as they faced into the wind. Ten minutes later they appeared, dogs and man on foot on the opposite hillside, rounding up the sheep. This is no mean task. They covered an area roughly a mile and a half long and two thirds of a mile deep into and up onto the hillside between Lairdside Hill and Hannah Law on Mistylaw Muir (lovely names). The sheep were spread the length and breadth of this area and the team worked tirelessly to gather them in and move them to a sheepfold at the top of the hill. I watched the whole proceedings through my binoculars, including the unfortunate moment when five sheep broke loose and headed downwards instead of up. I saw the man ponder a few seconds, glancing between the five and the other fifty or so. Then he abandoned the rebels to their freedom rather than lose the coherence of the rest. Ten minutes later, the flock were gone from the pen and over the brow, and heading I know not where.

I mention this because it somehow mirrors my efforts in this van today, herding my thoughts into something coherent, losing a few on the way and hoping they end up in greener pastures. But also because this place is within commuting distance of my home and has no interruptions other than watching wildlife, and farmers obviously.

My good old mum has the great wisdom of an unrepentant atheist brought up in the Presbyterian Church. She has absolutely no truck with Buddhism but has an easy grasp on the idea of impermanence. You could say she understands the power of waiting. If she hears about some poor soul taking their own life she'll say, 'If only he'd waited. Things would have changed. Everything would have been different if he just hadn't given in to that black moment but waited for it to pass.' Of course, this is easy to say, and those left behind will never know what drives other people to suicide. But even the darkest of dark moments pass and new dawns happen because they must.

In campervans, as in life and in writing, I've learnt the trick is to keep moving, experience all to the full, stay focussed, don't flinch at the unpleasant stuff, and don't get embroiled in it either. So don't just wait for the new dawn, get in a campervan and drive towards the sunrise.

Of course, if you take that literally, you'll always be driving east.

Part Two

Inner

The Universe

'The universe is made of stories, not atoms.'
Muriel Rukeyser, American poet and activist

On a dark night in the west of Scotland, I set off across the Cowal peninsula all by myself in a very small campervan. The kind of super-dark darkness I find there is something I don't get in my own back garden in central Glasgow, or indeed in the outskirts where I was brought up or in any other city in which I've lived. It's a strangely mummifying darkness which on this occasion also comes with a resounding silence, something else I never get in my own patch.

If I hadn't left home at nine in the evening, which theoretically is better late than never, I wouldn't have experienced it at all. As it is I'm not drowned in this darkness until I've crossed the great water of the Clyde Estuary from Gourock to Hunter's Quay near Dunoon, driven four miles north and then west, and the last of the neon streetlights have dwindled far behind me.

At the turn-off for inner, deeper Cowal, which is easily missed even in clear daylight, I'm reminded that the phone signal fades and dies as you head towards Portavadie. I'm hoping not to meet my maker on this occasion but to find instead a quiet spot to spend the night.

The phone whistles a few space-cadet-style notes then dies. I turn the van round and retrace the few hundred yards to the junction and connection, and return the call. I am on my own in a tiny van, should any of the various beasts in my mind come to life: wolves, snakes, yeti spirits, madmen and rapists. So I am grateful that someone knows exactly where I am, what time I will have been there and where heading. My friend and I joke about the ghosts of long-lost warriors of the peat bog peeking through my curtains as I undress; she reminds me that cinemas, traffic and jobs will all be waiting for me when I come back and that, in the event of panic, I can take the long drive home via the mountains at two in the morning. 'Panic, schmanic,' I tell her. We say our goodbyes and once more I turn away from electric lamps and traffic and head into the dark.

Like a thick blanket the forest wraps itself around me. I am in no hurry. I can stop when I like, but it's late and I'm tired. This is the first trip in a while and although I know the road I don't know how well the van will function. Stopping sooner seems better than later. My mind travels ahead. There are no cars coming to meet me, no beams slicing the night but my own. I pick a spot I haven't tried before, relax into the short drive and look forward to the melting of my everyday tensions.

There is a reservoir, held back by the appropriately named Tarsan Dam, providing storage and flow regulation for Striven hydroelectric power station. A small car park allows hydro workers to pull off and affords the public a viewing area from which to gaze down the sweep of the dam and also out across the surface of the loch. But in the pitch-dark all I can see is the gravel in my headlights, the safety barrier looming out at me, the grassy verge, and a curving comma-like puddle. With no bench visible in the back of the van as a gauge, I can't tell how flat I am, so I shift about until I feel like I can't be bothered anymore, then turn off the engine and the lights.

It is like being muffled by soft velvety black fur; there is no sound whatsoever. Stupidly I have no torch in the front cab so I wait in vain for my eyes to become at least a little accustomed to the super-dark dark, then gather my bag and phone. The cab light doesn't work, so this isn't easy and I don't want to do it twice. I open the door and step out, noting a slop-sound of puddle. My heart is thumping. The darkness is now heavy, weighing in on me, making my breathing labour. I close the door and the noise rings out, alerting every living creature for miles that isn't already awakened to my existence. I sense heads turning, eyes piercing the night.

I watch for the ground I can't see, and fumble along the side of the van to the back door, poke the tiny key at the lock and pray I don't drop it. But it's ok. It's in and it turns and I open the door and hurry inside, and as I turn to close myself safely in I see a wedge of sky, soft with stars, still as death, ice-white above me, in the angle of the door. I am so electrified by this brief vision of heaven I shut the door and plump down wheezy on the bench inside. There is no immediate way of making sense of this panic I feel, so I look through the windows for the dark outline of bushes or hills and assume I'm scared of maniacs lurking. I close the curtains against them as quickly as I'm able.

I am in fact utterly terrified. Have I, as feared, just met my maker? I have no wherewithal whatsoever to even pinch myself and check it hurts. I am vaguely aware of this panic not being attached to any concrete source, not even maniacs in bushes. In reality, whatever that is, there is absolutely nothing to fear; I know this. I know I am probably in the safest place in the whole world but, just in case, I quickly pin the curtains tighter with bulldog clips to keep whatever monster morphs into being from engulfing me. I light my little battery lamp so I can examine the evidence, then quickly turn it off again in case I need my eyes to stay adjusted to the dark. Moreover, I wonder whether it is an act of blasphemy, punishable by who-knows-what, to disturb the darkness. And I don't want to draw attention. Wolves, I was told in countless children's stories, are attracted by light.

I try to be sensible. There is no-one out there and what exactly are these things I should be scared of anyway? I pull them out one by one and examine them, ticking them off the list of concrete reasons to be vigilant that might justify risking the journey from the back door of the van to the front cab in order to move elsewhere, somewhere lacking this unfathomable danger. Those wolves: there are none in Scotland, only talk of reintroducing them, which hasn't happened yet, as far as I know, or has it? Yeti don't exist, or do they? Not in Cowal, surely. Snakes aren't that interested in campervans because, despite my accidentally cycling over a viper in France, I know they're only deadly when provoked. Even madmen and rapists are more likely to look for prey in streets with half-decent light.

Finally I have to admit it: I am scared of the sky.

Ridiculous. I laugh out loud, the act of a mad woman.

I'm reminded of Chief Vitalstatistix in the *Asterix* stories who is afraid the sky will fall on his head. A likeable buffoon with a historically semi-accurate origin to his fear, he is the mouthpiece for the Gaulish chiefs who were asked by Alexander the Great for their greatest fear. Of course! Not so daft after all. I am in good company.

Except I'm not afraid of the sky falling, I don't think. That's not it. So what exactly am I afraid of?

I hear a car approaching in the distance and am surprised that, instead of fearing abduction, I am comforted by this banal sound, the ordinary world infiltrating my overactive imagination. The car's headlights worm through the remaining gaps in the curtains, stroking the walls and table but halt against a pile of blankets. Why have they stopped? A second slice of light moves round and I realise there are two cars on the single-track road. One has stopped to let the other through. I breathe a sigh of relief. Their combined light allows me a glimpse of table and bench, cooker, sink, plastic shopping bags and books lined up above the windows: normal van life, the reason I am here. I keep still, not wanting to attract any human attention. After all they could be the madmen or rapists, so I feign sleep (don't rock the van) and wait until they are gone.

In their sudden absence, the darkness is complete once more and I decide there will be no more cars on that lonely road for the rest of the night. As it happens, I'm wrong. Just as I've dared to reopen the back door, a distant flicker of light in the silence tells me there are more. I close it and wait with eyes shut for it to pass.

Then I bravely stand, give myself a shake and reopen the door a crack.

The whole icy sky gazes back at me through an inch-wide gap. I have to close the door, breathe, and argue with myself before I can open it again. I allow myself to stay inside, to keep hold of the handle and open it a little and a little more, checking the dark shapes of the bushes for wolves I know are not there, until the doorway is fully wide and I can fill it with myself and square up to the world.

The Milky Way is wispy candy floss above my head, bluey-white and stretching out across the world, a glistening cloud, and I see how it is a mass of lights and at its centre there is no space between the lights, only more light of different textures.

I move only my eyes to begin with, and without hurry, then my head, nothing more, in case I disturb anything, attract attention, bring its might crashing down on me, wake God from his slumber or disturb the entire universe. It seems best to be cautious. I decide to wait until I've stemmed this ridiculous fear, and to hold myself there for as long as it takes. Sure enough, time passes and I am neither devoured nor vaporised. Neither do I go mad and tear my hair out or see visions. I look for constellations I can recognise, Ursas Major and Minor, the North Star, Orion and his Belt. The longer I look, the more can be seen, shimmering glittering light the nature of which and whose distance from that spot cannot even be imagined. Nothing of this sort can be truly imagined.

But heightened feelings of this kind can't be sustained for ever, as the old Buddhist idea of impermanence asserts, and my heart rate slows enough for me to realise I'm cold from standing still, and tired. I have no-one to share my awe with so it's time for bed. But as I turn inside I see this same Milky Way and the vast firmament with which I have so recently reached a quiet truce stretching in all the other directions too. Obvious, really. But I'm terrified all over again and rush back to the safety of a bench behind a closed door.

This is all, of course, completely illogical. But I am entirely helpless and this is the closest I've ever been to the God I don't believe in. I am lost. I stare at the curtains for twenty minutes debating whether I'll ever make peace between the firmament and myself, then get into my sleeping bag with a hot-water bottle and weave an invisible safety bubble around me, keeping incomprehensible notions emphatically beyond the curtains. I flick through my impenetrable book about the local history of a place I've never been to, until the battery in my wind-up lamp makes even this impossible and I close my eyes and sleep with starlight on the brain.

I did not write this down at the time or the following morning or even a week later. No words have ever come to me to adequately describe exactly what I saw and felt, so please forgive this clumsy picture. The following morning I packed up and moved on, pleased that I had wrestled my own fears to the ground, sort of, and not run away. But the feeling of being with God or the entire universe, and the spine-bristling fear and wonder that came with it, never left me. Instead, these sensations coloured the coming days and weeks, haunting reminders of my own etherealness perhaps. The sense of losing all notions of time and space or any other measuring apparatus for my world stayed with me, along with the apparent lack of logic to my terror, and the feeling of being utterly blessed and spectacularly lucky for being where I was at that time to witness this secret world of unspeakable beauty.

Under the rich blue sky of morning, alone in my little van, I wondered how it would have seemed had I not been by myself. The company of another might have dulled the experience; I can't imagine it could have been further sharpened. But the truth is that witnessing this with my other half might have bonded us closer together at a time when he and I were drifting like satellites around a planet of truth (otherwise known as the elephant in the room) but rarely in proximity to each other.

Zen And The Art

Initially, vans were undoubtedly for escape and adventure, something I hoped I could share with my husband and family. We were still living together, along with my two teenagers and usually some of his four, plus two cats and two little goldfish whose survival in this chaos has always astounded me. Diversion was imperative.

I likened the van to the pressure valve on a slow-cooker. It quickly evolved from that into a mobile office for me, somewhere I knew I could write, even if the weather was unreasonable, metaphorically or otherwise.

I brought the first van home in a blaze of disco lights. The wiring was all wrong, a bit haywire you might say. I indicated left and the right hand bulb came on, the brakes activated the reversing lights and so on and naturally every car that passed me on the motorway home flashed its headlights in annoyance or alarm or as a warning. Of course, until I pulled into a service station followed by one of the headlight flashers, I had no way of knowing what my own lights were up to. The rest of the journey was embarrassing at least, life-threatening at worst and all shades of discomfort in between.

It seems to me that if you want to be a solo traveller in a campervan you need to be comfortable with a bit of discomfort, unless you are a mechanic or a general handyman, or rich enough to buy a brand new van when the water pump breaks down. I am none of these things and I don't own campervans for the joy of fixing them, though I do get immense satisfaction when I do. If I have a series of trips free of practical hassle, I feel blessed and usually celebrate my good fortune with a wee swig of Cointreau.

(Note to reader: I don't swig and scribble at the same time. Writing is its own reward.)

Finding solutions to little practical problems, like looping a piece of string found on the beach to tie my door open on a warm but windy day, makes me feel grown up and secure. Even better when I attached a proper door-holder eighteen months later. Surely if I can show such practical ingenuity I can also write clever books? If I can fix the cracks in my van, I must have some chance with my personal life.

Writing is not something done best with hordes of young people in proximity, not by me anyway and especially not if the young people are my own, the kind who need fed, watered and spoken to about the mess in the bathroom. Writing is almost always best done alone. The great beauty of all but one of my four campers has been the lack of space for more than one other person and the absence of a bathroom over which to fight. There is often no mobile reception in the remote areas I favour and if there is I can usually arrange for there to be none by stepping on the gas. With no internet connection, there is no temptation to surf, make new virtual/trivial friends on social media, or pay bills. Lacking the necessary will or power to create the right conditions at home, I tempt myself to beautiful places in which I am then my own captive audience and have no alternative but to write.

Writing in the van has become so much my habit I sometimes forget there are other things to do in it, like invite your friends in and have a (very small) party. As well as this element of focus, there is the joy of unconnected spaces where you can wander off on foot or bike into the wilderness. There are the questionable pleasures of being alone with yourself in a small space for prolonged periods, regardless of whether you write or not. This takes practice and courage, but being alone, like writing, brings its own rewards.

In Buddhism there is the notion of 'Beginner's Mind'. Often experienced by newcomers to meditation, it is a state of sudden bliss and euphoria in which many of the fundamental popular truths of life, the universe and everything, feel close to hand, exciting and easy to achieve. The Zen teacher, Shunryu Suzuki, said this about the right approach to Zen: 'In the beginner's mind there are many possibilities, in the expert's mind there are few.' The beginner is at least as valid as the expert. The idea is to keep your mind as fresh and open to your task, whatever it is (or simply to the present moment) as if you were a complete beginner. It's a state of complete openness, of not knowing, and of freedom from preconceived perceptions. It is devoid of any boundaries to possibility and is a state not only without fear but also generally pretty full of joy. He recommends being in this state all the time. Sounds good to me. If a little hard to achieve.

On my first van trip I experienced something like Beginner's Mind. Here is how it worked.

Choosing a remote campsite in Kintyre, an area I'd long wanted to explore, I stopped in the supermarket in Tarbert, planned all the meals in the coming few days, bought healthy fresh food to last me and absolutely no chocolate. I prefer to get my supplies in the places I travel to so that local people get at least some benefit from my being there. On arrival at my chosen site, I plugged myself into the national grid for the first time in a camper, got inside and began to write through the evening. The following morning I wrote again and continued into the afternoon until my brain got tired and I needed a walk. Walk I did, down to the beach, a mile or so along it, and back again. My work so far was on a novel. On my return, I had another look to check progress and keep it fresh in my mind, then wrote some poetry, took notes, made contact briefly with home and went to bed.

This was the shape of my days for the following four, writing morning, noon and night with breaks only for strolls to clear cobwebs, to reassure family I was still hale and hearty, and to eat. Previous to this, I had no idea I was capable of being so focussed or of producing so many words or ideas in a single day, or indeed of being alone for so long and staying happy. I survived and prospered. Even my food was perfect in every way, providing me with a healthy balanced diet every day including the drive home and running out upon my deliverance into the arms of family and the kitchen.

On the last full day I was as high as a kite, a combination of a sense of achievement, a pure diet and the fact that the campsite was perched on a rise close to a long sandy beach and an area which had been designated as one of 'special scientific interest'. The weather came and went, from and to great distances, and was therefore visible swirling in or beaming out for miles and miles across the machair to my right, the golf course to the left, the farm fields and gentle hills behind me and the sea out in front. Golden eagles were nesting in a cliff not far off and that day, by some good chance, I saw one glide over the hills. Like a buzzard it spiralled upwards on the draughts but with far greater stillness and majesty. It was indeed golden, and giant with a likely wingspan of over six feet, and therefore not light. How does it stay up there? The beach that day had been peopled with scores of black-and-white oystercatchers all moving in unison as if they were line dancing, but squealing blue murder through their long bright orange beaks. Bobbing wagtails lived up to their name and lingered in the camouflage of the sand and rocks. In the morning I had read that the squabbling seagulls who'd been fighting over the crusts from the next-door motorhome, can live for fifteen years, which at that time was longer than either of my daughters. Kintyre was my new astounding paradise.

After so much labour, uplifting wonder and health, I decided to break my no sweets vow and thus risk fogging up my brain. I went to the campsite shop for supplies. This shop was only open for one hour a day so you had to remember when and be vigilant for signs of life. I went into the shop and grinned at the two people who were there, the man behind the counter and his customer who were chatting. As soon as I could I insinuated myself into their conversation, then took over completely. The machinations of my day, the weather, the birds, all of these and a multitude of other minutiae were all spellbinding, but only to me. Not that I let that stop me. After several minutes of trying to raise smiles, I finally noticed their blank faces, quickly chose my chocolate (comfort food now, not treat) and scurried back to my van.

I have since learned that the owner of that campsite is neither helpful nor friendly and has sold up and moved on, so it wasn't just me, but I arrived back at the van shaken by my own behaviour. I quickly realised I had been so starved of human company, even though I hadn't missed it, that I had become unsocialised. That first van had fantastic all-round visibility which suddenly ceased to be a good thing. I wanted to hide. Once I'd recovered some perspective, I realised this sense of exposure was similar to the sense of vulnerability many people experience following time on Buddhist retreats. It meant I had reached some depth of immersion in my work and I had left the normal everyday world behind in order to get there. Talking nineteen to the dozen to complete strangers was simply an unfortunate side effect of something unusually good in the writing experience, what I would call 'the Zone'.

People in all walks of life can experience the Zone. This is one of the most beautiful aspects of being human. The Zone is when we are working at our optimum level with minimal effort, when the conscious mind can take a break and let the rest of you get on with it. It's when the chatter in your head quiets down and you are so involved in the task at hand you are unaware of yourself. You become the task. Your inner censor is gone and something elemental, something fundamental and overarchingly essential slips through onto the page. I have long asserted that the nature of the task is not important but the beauty, precision and depth of application most emphatically is. I can therefore admire almost any task if performed in this way from within the Zone including the work of shop assistants, plasterers, organisers, software engineers, as well as artists of all kind, who are only the most obvious example of Zone inhabitants. The Zone is a beautiful place to witness in others and a mesmerising place to be in yourself.

And then, just as you become aware of being in the Zone, and are therefore also conscious of the self again, the Zone evaporates, usually leaving no clue as to how to get back there. Or something simple happens, like your daughter sticks her head round the door to offer you tea, and the Zone is gone. Research shows it takes a full twenty minutes to return to the Zone after even the tiniest most innocuous conversation.

The Zone is a close relation of Beginner's Mind and both are similar to a drug in that they both create the desire to have these states of being at all times. I would argue that unless you are the Buddha himself, or perhaps Shunryu Suzuki or Thich Nhat Hanh, both of whom I've read but never met, then it is just not possible to sustain such flights of applied creativity indefinitely. Sorry. That's the bad news. I probably should have warned you about that. What usually happens, however, is that the perfection of the Zone and Beginner's Mind haunts us, driving us to strive for something long gone that returns only for brief periods of absolute ecstasy. Oddly, it is the ecstasy inspired by its longed-for re-adventure that often kills it, the awareness that it is Happening Again. It can also be like a tiny label somewhere on our clothes that itches, especially when we're hot and bothered, the source of which we can never find nor satisfy, a constant reminder that our writing experience could be better. This is the point at which many aspiring writers get so frustrated they give up. But as writers or artists we need to take control and not get downhearted. We must see the Zone and Beginner's Mind as teasing cousins who occasionally deign to bring a party round to our house, or indeed our campervan, and towards whom we can but extend the invitation and promise the kind of conditions they best enjoy. In other words, we need to find ways to make our way back to these blissful states without getting too upset when it doesn't happen. The best and most productive creatives just know better how to do it. I've been figuratively trying to make my way back to that first Kintyre trip ever since I was first there.

Another way of putting this is I need to make my inner child feel happy and safe to make sure she comes out to play. For those of you not aware of the inner child concept, it's a theory of the counselling world which basically states that the child we once were is still within us as adults. Gosh. We still need to play or act out, and we have patterns of behaviour that stem from what happened to us as children. I'm not entirely comfortable with separating my inner world into characters but it's a handy framework for understanding your muse. In this context, as with all children, it's important to be consistent and dependable, which translates into keeping promises to yourself to turn up at the desk when you say you will. Writing is often extremely hard work. I think this is true of most creative endeavours. Writers and artists need encouragement and support. Amongst the moments of fun when our inner thoughts surprise us, we often struggle alone in dark rooms (or damp campervans) for days on end trying to sort plot points or bring characters together with no other guidance but our own. It's easy to lose perspective or any sense of judgement about what works and what doesn't. We may be dealing with difficult material or big issues like life, death, rape, murder and betrayal. Inner children therefore also need encouragement, if they're going to face all this. They need gentle cosseting, a system of rewards and respect for their physical and emotional requirements. This can all be done by your inner adult, the one who drives the van, watches out for danger and makes sure there's food.

Before I started writing in earnest, I painted, not very well but with some enthusiasm and with an exhilarating connection to my own life. I had two small children and a husband. I painted during nap times and occasional hours of precious solitude. My painting often depicted emotional representations of life as a young mother in a less than idyllic marriage. As my daughters grew, the naps shortened and with them my painting time until I would put the little ones down to sleep, race full of eagerness and hope to the easel, only to be interrupted ten minutes later by complaints from the bedroom. The actual physical discomfort this caused me was extraordinary not to mention the mental and emotional torment. I felt nauseous, as if I was pumped full of adrenalin but with no concrete way to fly or fight, and no obvious reason for the fright I felt either. I therefore gave up completely for several years in order to avoid that agony.

My 'addiction' to writing is far more serious and untreatable. The possibility of stopping altogether is simply not for contemplating, but luckily my children are older and can tolerate long periods of being ignored, even several days on end. My inner child is something else but she can be fooled into greater happiness and hope simply by getting into the front cab of the camper and leaning on the steering wheel. However, fooling only works if there's a genuine promise to do what makes her far happier: take her to one of several secret locations within an hour's drive of my home and allow her to do what she loves best, tap away at a keyboard at the table in the back of the van. Best of all is bringing her to a remote and beautiful spot for a few days of undivided attention.

Owning a small campervan is the only way I can facilitate that depth of happiness and productivity with any certainty, and without breaking the bank.

Visions

The term 'wild camping' is a tricky one, sparking different interpretations according to the credentials of the user. People in tents, especially wet cold people who've survived a night on the side of a mountain, will probably guffaw at the idea of campervanning being called camping at all. It's partly terminology. After all, 'wild-campervanning' is a bit of a mouthful. But although these adventurers haven't spent a night in Vanessa before her draughts were fixed, I tend to agree. Pitchup.com is a website where you can view and book thousands of campsites of all kinds. It offers a rough definition of wild camping which includes as location anything from pathless wildernesses to campsites in wild areas which have facilities. The latter is the best of both worlds. For people who have never camped before, or been to the countryside, this will definitely feel wild, but it's not, I'm afraid. Not really.

The dictionary definition of 'wild' is 'in its natural state; not tamed or cultivated; uncivilised; lacking control; disorderly; or furious.' The last three made me smile, and I suppose, therefore, it depends how the campsite is run and what campers get up to in campsites. But in all seriousness, I use the term 'wild camping' loosely to mean spending a night in the campervan but not in a campsite. It means bringing my facilities with me, if I have them, and making do with what I've got. Obviously the best places to do this are wild areas away from other people who might be bothered by my presence. I'm in a vehicle so I can't leave the road and trek out across the moor, so I'm limited to car parks and laybys, which, arguably, are not that wild either.

Wild camping for me also means a lack of electric light, so here are some simple truths about eyesight which are worth knowing if you intend to wild camp and you're not confident about your campervan's internal lighting system, or if you're planning a life of drunken piracy, as we'll see.

When you are on the seashore in western Kintyre at six in the evening on the twenty-first of June in the baking sunshine staring west at nothing in particular as the rays of the sun bounce off every tiny wavelet on the sea, your pupils shrink to pinpricks (almost) in order to block out as much light as possible. This is a simple muscular reaction. When you go inside your campervan to make another cocktail (or tea if you're me) you find your beloved campervan is suddenly dingy and uninviting and you can't see the cocktail shaker (or teaspoon) even though it's right where you left it in the cupboard over the sink. If you have patience and stand for five minutes, your pupils dilate again, the reverse muscular reaction to when you were outside, allowing more light to reach the receptors at the back of your eyes.

But this is not all. When you were outside, the light waves were also affecting the pigment at the back of your eyes and deactivating the pigment molecules, or 'bleaching' them as it is known by experts. In other words they are reducing their sensitivity to colour. An electrochemical process lets your brain know what has happened and it receives instructions accordingly. Later, when you come out of the light and enter the dark interior of your cupboard, the chemicals tell your brain to reduce the bleaching effect by reactivating the pigment molecules.

Other things at the back of your eyes are the cones and rods you may have been lucky enough to hear about in a science class at school. Cones and rods are cells, each with special and distinct properties. Cones are good with colour, like the pigment molecules, but chiefly in bright light and are less good in the dark. They need light to function well. Conversely, the rods specialise in black and white, and are particularly handy if the lights are out. In fact, the most important chemical involved in all this is Rhodopsin which is found in the rods. Rhodopsin is your friend. People with night blindness commonly lack vitamin A which is helpful to Rhodopsin. If you want to see in the dark, try eating food with plenty of vitamin A such as cantaloupe melons, spinach, seaweed and, of course carrots, amongst other things. Old wives' tales are so often true. Good on ya, old wives.

So when light is limited, for instance as you stare into the back of your cupboard, the eye connects the rods with the cones using an electric coupling and this triggers the colour-loving cones to function at a lower light level than they prefer. The longer you linger over the sink and peer into the cupboard, the clearer and more colourful and attractive the cocktail shaker becomes.

The entire process takes some considerable time, much longer than the dilation of your pupils, usually about twenty to thirty minutes from staring at the Atlantic on the sunniest day of the year to fiddling in the almost complete darkness of your campervan's cupboard. This is impractical, being much longer than most people are prepared to wait for their cocktails or tea.

The solution is one favoured by pirates, the eyepatch. You can scan the horizon with one eye then swap it to the other eye as you dip below decks to give orders or find the rum. The darkened eye is always ready to see in the comparative dark so you won't risk being ambushed by the crew while you linger on the doorstep waiting for your eyes to do their magic. You simply switch the eye patch from side to side as required.

Indeed this process of ocular change can even be

pleasurable. My friend walked into a basement bar in Palm Springs in California after a day of installing wind turbines in the desert, as you do. The seemingly complete darkness he experienced was a balm on his tired eyes and he had to indulge this pleasure and stand at the door for several minutes before the room took shape in front of him and he could find his way to the bar. Apparently the very cold beer there made it worth the wait. After a few more minutes he realised the lights had in fact been up full the whole time.

I mention all this because light or rather lack of it is a recurrent problem in a little old campervan with limited battery capabilities in the long dark autumn evenings of Scotland when the summer campervanning bug refuses to leave me. This information is particularly useful when the electrics fail, the torch batteries are dead and the candle I always keep for such occasions has no wick. Knowing all I have to do is keep my eyes open and wait is a great comfort, and in tune with the slo-mo nature of most campervan trips, though not usually my working ones. But taking time to smell the roses, or see in the dark, is definitely vital.

I also think seeing clearly is a major component of writing. Take care of your eyes and don't wind up seeing double, unless it's metaphorical double-sightedness which might make for something poetic. I spent three blocks of eight days working twelve hours every day to redraft my first book, *Mavis's Shoe*. By the end of each day, and indeed earlier and earlier in each day, my sight became increasingly doubled and then blurred and was accompanied by daily headaches. The cause was not just sheer time at the figurative wheel; it was a new monitor screen which resonated at the wrong frequency for my brain. Its XXL size meant I could see two documents at once side by side with ease. It also maximised the onslaught of the brain-killing waves which were killing my brainwaves, so to speak. My work slowed accordingly. I dug out all my old reading glasses, even the giant tartan ones and the ones without rims. Nothing worked. I spent late evenings in a dark room resting all those rods, cones, pigment molecules and irises, not to mention my overworked synapses.

After the event, I returned to my lowly laptop and discovered I could work for long periods perfectly comfortably. I only discovered the truth much later at a book event where I met a marine-zoologist-cum-science-fiction-writer who explained where I had gone wrong. Being something of a polymath, perhaps his mind's eye was used to seeing double.

Obviously there are people who don't use technology more complicated than pencil and paper to write their great works, and others whose sight is either absent or so totally restricted that they're forced to use other methods. On a recent visit to the Royal Blind School in Edinburgh I spent an hour with a small group of blind or partially sighted young people between the ages of twelve and seventeen. Together we read a section of *Mavis's Shoe*, half of them using large font printouts, the others Braille. It was a totally fascinating experience and the most engaged and engaging group of young people I've ever been lucky enough to meet. Losing one of your senses can surely augment the others; their talents have been hard won. Interestingly, two of this little group are keen writers, including one who has already written two novel-length pieces. They use digital and other technology developed specifically for their needs. Clearly lack of physical sight has not adversely affected the inner ability to envision or their determination to put what is 'seen' into words.

Which brings me to the other kind of seeing, that which goes on inside us, the ideas, the mental pictures, the internal sensory experience which informs our writing. These are the 'visions' I once told my father I had. He didn't understand and laughed at me, thinking I was having some kind of religious experience. Of course, he wasn't entirely off the mark.

There are times when it seems that something 'spiritual' or otherworldly is going on when storylines or characters seem to present themselves of their own volition.

Lenny Gillespie, the heroine of *Mavis's Shoe*, was one such visitation. I had written half of the first chapter and I was deep in imagining what being bombed must feel like when a strident little voice, complete with bad English, rang through my head. 'For those of you that don't know … ,' she said, and went on to tell me in a sassy nine-year-old voice exactly what it was like to be bombed. She wanted to be called Lenny, which I let her away with on the stipulation that she become a girl and stop trying to be a boy, which she also tried to insist upon. A lively relationship developed between us in which we tussled over storylines or she'd go off in a huff if I lost focus and spent too long with other characters. In my mind's eye I can see exactly how she looks but I can't draw well enough to put her on paper in anything other than words. Her opening gambit to me became the opening sentence of the book. She is of course not a ghost, but her appearance amid the real events of the Clydebank Blitz and its aftermath, gave her a spectre-like quality as I was writing her story. Perhaps she is an expression of my own inner child, but that would be admitting too much.

Places, sounds and smells presented themselves in similar fashion. The book was written in a period when I had six months off work. By pure fluke of circumstance, no-one needed anything from me for most of my day. It was a quiet, focussed time and place in which to allow whatever stories might occur to me to arise and be noticed. How lucky was I? And being naturally opportunist when it comes to writing time, I exploited this to the full. I have not always been so lucky since, until I discovered campervans, the ultimate writer's opportunity.

I'm at the end of a quiet valley today, half-hidden from

the road by trees. It's exceptionally green here and has been raining most of the morning. I can hear birds in the trees calling one another, but I can't see them and don't know what they are. The thickness of the foliage, mostly sycamore and bramble, seems to deaden any sound other than rain on leaves and the roof of the van. There is no phone reception. This is ideal. If I need it I can drive a couple of miles back towards civilisation. By disappearing in a small campervan I minimise the influence of the human world. I may appear to be communing with nature, but really I'm communing with myself. I'm looking inward for whatever arises, whatever I can facilitate or conjure up. This is everything which is hardest to find in the hubbub of home life, the stuff that doesn't arise when there's washing to do, phone calls to make, jobs to go to and people with whom I must converse.

This involves metaphorically and actually closing my eyes and looking at colours and shapes I can't paint, faces that don't exist, places I wish I could go to or am grateful I can't, smells I'd forgotten or only just remembered, tastes and temperatures for underwater swimmers, ways of falling over, what it feels like to be a bird and what you'd see from a hundred feet up, how men feel in circumstances only men find themselves in, how I'd live in a world with no sound, how a tall/short/skinny/fat/daft/clever/serious/funny person might live in a world without sound, what I find admirable or despicable, who to forgive and who to hang, how the world might be if the sky was orange and the trees blue, which words resonate and suit the rhythm of my prose, and which create a deliciously uncomfortable dissonance. You can't do any of these things with Bob Dylan playing in the room next door or when it's nearly dinner time and everyone's hungry but incapable (allegedly), or you have to finish a paragraph in time to make an 'important phone call' before closing time.

Alone in a campervan, dinner is when I need it,

conversations are usually reassuring hand gestures to other humans who come to share my layby, and 'important' is what's going on in the creative chamber in my head. Work and play merge into a simple sense of real life, as in everything I experience seems vital and part of a coherent whole that goes well beyond the physical body I inhabit. I am undisturbed by piped music or other people's priorities, so I can follow the logical sequence of my own imagining without it being watered down. I deliberately render the nuts and bolts of physical survival as unimposing as possible. They are, as they should be, the infrastructure for the more important business of facilitating the freedom of my imagination and the shaping of that imagination onto the page.

Therefore, my current van, Vanessa Romahome Hotplate, has large windows for seeing the outside world but is itself very small. I fill it with necessities which include all those hand-picked books that may or may not be relevant to my topic. They're just as likely to be there to sustain either my concentration or my flights of fancy. There's usually a range of footwear. I like cosy slippers even in a small carpeted space. Walking boots are handy for rugged terrains. Clothes will be functional. Commonly inhabiting a city world where clean perfectly ironed clothes are a cultural requirement, being a little tatty and having muck on my jeans, as long as it's not food or champagne, is very liberating. I'm not obliged to be present. I usually bring one silly piece of clothing on the grounds that dressing, too, is a creative endeavour, but I rarely use a halter-neck floral party dress. I will have my laptop and a battery (or even batteries plural as in Fugue Ducato) from which to recharge it. There will be tea-making facilities and a variety of teas, china mugs, plastic crockery, super-strength binoculars, a sleeping bag and cushions, as well as the built-in facilities of a small cooker and a sink. I like it when the engine works, though occasionally it doesn't. I need the compact plastic toilet under the bench. I have favourite laybys I like to go to in this palace of convenience and creativity, preferred areas and destinations I know will be friendly where local people will not mind if I park by the beach, stay overnight or indeed if I'm two nights in the same place. I hole up with minimalist grub, though plenty of it, a sound system that's rarely used because it's not part of the place and because I'd miss the sound of rain on the roof, and of course, my notebook and a variety of pens in case they all run out of ink at the same time.

It's not complicated. All basic requirements are covered. It works.

By freeing myself from the constraints of my 'normal' everyday city life and giving myself an infinite choice of bedroom locations, I also change the view from my desk on a daily basis. (At one time this prompted a series of photos on Facebook mostly entitled 'view from today's office'.) I physically and mentally vary my experience of the physical world thereby keeping my inner life fresh. By shifting at whim I attempt to foster or maintain an absence of the 'white noise' of daily concerns which are arbitrary or even destructive to the gathering and writing down of ideas. Such white noise is like a slip of fine gauze between me and what I am straining inwardly to see. It waters down colour, fades definition and often confuses the senses so badly as to make me doubt my own perception. We are all subject to the tyranny of mass communal thinking, the great 'We' as in 'we all watch the latest hit TV programme' or 'we all have dinner at six', neither of which is true, obviously, but which make the person who never watches TV and has dinner at nine feel uncomfortable and excluded.

My campervan life is the antidote to all that. I can be as odd as I like and no-one will ever bother me. It is anti-homogenisation and a fine way to keep your inner eyes peeled.

Autophilia

'Courage is a love affair with the unknown.'
Osho, Indian mystic and spiritual teacher

Finding myself alone in the world was scary. It happened suddenly, too, which made it all the worse. And I hadn't intended being alone. I didn't want it. I wanted to stay in the safety of coupledom and never face uncomfortable truths. But there was no choice. Without warning, the bed was too big, and so was the world. Even the campervan didn't fit anymore.

Ordinarily I quite like being on my own. There are lots of things you can't do if someone else is there. I don't mean anything illegal or immoral. It's just different, more like a way of being really. But sometimes it isn't fun at all. In fact, it can be quite overwhelming.

For some people being alone at any time is downright frightening. As I found on that starry starry night in Cowal, solitude leaves room for all those indistinct fears to be conjured out of the void into starkly imaginable monsters. Learning to be brave is something we do from the beginning of life. We see this in the plethora of kids' books which address the subject: the *Funnybones* series by Janet and Allan Ahlberg or *Can't You Sleep Little Bear?* by Martin Waddell with illustrations by Barbara Firth, two of my favourites.

Then there are people who like being scared. They set themselves death-defying challenges so that they can feel fully alive. Perhaps Winston Churchill understood this when he said 'Nothing in life is so exhilarating as to be shot at without result.'

In my view, and assuming you are not campervanning through a war zone, a modicum of fear can be helpful to the creative process. I don't keep a van so I can face my fears and get exhilarated. The times I've had to face death in the van have not been remotely pleasant, like the time I came to a particularly tight bend in Cowal, going not too fast but not too slow either. I skidded on what felt like oil but was probably only grit, the wheels locked and instead of following the road to the left I went straight on towards the black-and-white stripes of a crash barrier. Fortunately there was no oncoming traffic and with equal good luck I did eventually manage to rein Vanessa in. The green bushes swayed in the safety of the far side of the barrier. Time stood still. No physical harm was done, unless you include my heart rate, which soared. Grit is not my van's friend. I have had several such moments, two of which took me over a junction onto a main road. This is neither fun nor sustainable, but it certainly made me sharpen my wits and get the tyres seen to.

Muriel Spark would argue for 'nightly composing [one]self to thoughts of death' and that 'there is no other practice which so intensifies life.' I, on the other hand, have a van to make my inner life and my creative process as alive as possible, not to face physical death.

Unbounded fear can also curtail both our physical freedom and our liberty to roam imaginatively, so it's worth containing. In fact, I think of freedom and security as opposite ends of a continuum. Maximum security, in other words imprisonment, sits at one end, and total freedom, in which nothing can be assumed, is at the other. Fear naturally increases for most of us at either end. We are usually most comfortable somewhere in the middle where we have some control but not too much. But if we can let go of our perceived need for any excess of security and give ourselves over to increased freedom, there is a lot of fun to be had, not to mention inspiration.

I'm sometimes aware of this on Westport beach in Kintyre, which is a walk of about three miles on soft golden sand, completely open to the Atlantic. If you like a bit of exposure it will take you to Machrihanish village at the other end, and obviously three miles back again to your campervan in the car park. If I've forgotten to bring fresh water, food or money (and who takes money to the beach?) and only realise my mistake as I approach the other end (which I never expect to do), I panic. The greater the distance between me and sustenance, the less present I am to the gannets plummeting into the sea for their own dinners, the cloud shadows rushing towards me across the sand, or the thoughts I might have about the next plot point. Instead, an unhealthy fear drama plays out across my mind partly based on the 1958 film *Ice Cold in Alex* but with dive-bombing curlews, angry seagulls and sudden Atlantic storms. I imagine torrential rain making its way through my imagined soon-tattered and completely inadequate coat. The presence of a simple sandwich prevents this.

Susan Jeffries talks about containing fear and using it to advantage in *Feel the Fear and Do It Anyway*. She suggests we build our freedom gradually and never take ourselves beyond a tolerable amount of fear, but instead challenge it incrementally. Too much and you'll be put off altogether, not enough and you may be stuck in a small world. When I'm solo campervanning, I am constantly aware of this conundrum and its perpetually shifting balance. If I'm not in the mood for a twenty-mile valley with no phone signal, why increase anxiety by braving it out? If I'm already stressed it might be easier to go to a proper campsite, hook up to the national grid and avoid the further tension caused by trying to find an appropriate spot to wild camp. But then I wouldn't be lost in the wilderness, and closer to the stars and myself. Truthfully, wild camping is almost always worth it in terms of expansiveness and adventure, but only as long as you can relax sufficiently.

A useful trick at the end of any day is the one under the stars in Cowal when I wrapped myself in an invisible safety blanket, switched off the sky-god and went to sleep. This is hard to do if your anxiety scales too great a height, in which case you need to return to somewhere you feel safer or perhaps just abandon campervanning for the day and rejoin the human race.

I recently pushed my bike through the Falkirk Tunnel on the Union Canal. The waterway itself runs from Edinburgh to Falkirk in Scotland's central belt. It also links to the Forth and Clyde Canal at the famous Falkirk Wheel, a technologically astounding rotating boat lift. The wheel runs on next to no electricity and replaces eleven canal locks which used to take a full day to mount. It's quite a climb so if you're as unfit as I am you'll be pushing your bike part of the way up the hill as well as through the tunnel at the top.

At two thousand and seventy feet long this is as good a place as any to test your fear tolerance. Known locally quite simply as 'the Dark Tunnel' it is in fact perfectly adequately lit, but not brightly, leaving plenty of room for your imagination to run riot. The canal is inky black and sits on the other side of a fence which looks flimsy but actually isn't. A braver person than I was in the lead, thankfully, while I brought up the rear in a state of near hysteria, controlling my ineffable panic by singing long-forgotten melodies and cracking unusually funny jokes (not my norm). Ultimately this fear was fun, but it might have turned to blind panic. Shortly after we'd emerged from the tunnel and were high-fiving and feeling pretty clever as we once more raced along beside the canal, we encountered the Avon Aqueduct. At eight hundred and ten feet long it is only a little bit of a thing compared to the tunnel, but it's still the UK's second longest aqueduct. It's also eighty-five feet high which feels massive and you get to look down on very large trees. So I got to face my fear of heights as well. Fantastic. More life-enhancing terror and also more singing and jokes. It felt good to face down fear twice in the space of an hour and to have made contact with parts of myself I didn't know I had. Surely music and laughter are good uses for adrenalin.

For some people, remote and beautiful spots are just too frightening, especially if they're on their own. I once took a seven-year-old London boy to the remote island of Berneray in the Western Isles and frightened the bejesus out of him, though not on purpose, I hasten to add. 'Where are all the houses?' he asked in bewilderment. 'And the trees, and the shops?' At that time, Berneray had a population of one hundred and thirty-four people. It recently swelled to one hundred and thirty-eight. Its acreage is a mere two thousand, four hundred and ninety-six acres, but every square inch is beautiful, especially the long white beach. It has single-track roads over gentle hills, almost no traffic and very few houses. The boy's fear was a fear of the unfamiliar. His world had taken on an unknown shape. Once he knew what to do with all the space, dipped his toes in the water and had discovered sweets in the tiny local shop, he was very happy indeed, as long as an adult was within half an arm's reach. His fear was too great to be much use to him and probably spoilt the fun he could have had. Perhaps the memory of his time there may have meant something over time. In the right quantities, unfamiliar things and the tension they create, are muse fodder.

But we have new things to fear.

I'm writing this next to Cashlie power station in Glen Lyon in Breadalbane. To get here I had to pass Meggernie, a beautiful white fairy-tale castle thought to date from the sixteenth century. Rather gruesomely, it is said to be haunted by the upper torso of a young woman who was murdered there, while her lower torso haunts the nearby graveyard. I didn't know this at the time which is probably just as well. The castle occupies the centre of the glen but is too far back from my parking spot to be visible. The countryside is remote and beautiful with a narrow single-track road running roughly alongside the river.

I arrived here via Loch Tay. From Killin I drove a few miles east then turned left at Edramucky on the shore and headed up the side of Ben Lawers. Strictly speaking the name of this mountain means 'noisy mountain' because it takes its name from a burn which runs down the mountainside to an ancient church further along Loch Tay. If you're lucky, as I was, you'll find yourself ascending into the clouds which move across, hover, chuck rain at you, then move on, magically revealing rocky summits, more thundering burns and the great castle-like retaining dam of Lochan na Lairaige, which hangs in the clouds. Lairaige, incidentally, means 'a sheep pen', specifically one on the way to the slaughterhouse, but this one in particular is probably submerged in the reservoir.

I filled my water tank from one of the loch's tributaries and checked the map. There were clusters of 'shielings' in various places around the hillsides. Further on I came to a little green corrugated iron shack with a layby and another burn rushing down a glen towards it. On a first glance you'd think Coire Riadhailt, the great scoop of hillside which I then walked into thanks to a break in the weather, had never been touched, but I'd checked the map before leaving the van and found lots more shielings marked a short distance in. They were tiny rough huts, only walls left now and barely big enough to lie down in, which were scattered amongst the grass by a river. I could almost hear the voices of the women and children playing and chattering there while they watched their cattle in summer. The long thick grass on the lower slopes and the contrasting heather high up confirmed this. Animals must have grazed here, perhaps food was grown too.

Incongruously, and to my greatest amazement, two miniature control reservoirs and the openings of two connecting tunnels were also close by. Part of the post-war hydroelectric scheme, they carried water from this and other surrounding valleys through the mountain, Creag an Lochain, and into Lochan na Lairaige, the one with the castle-like retaining dam, on the other side. This is an old game of mine, trying to figure out what came before by reading the signs in the landscape. Weirdly, I had just finished reading *The Hydro Boys*, about the lives of those who built these massive developments. History felt spookily alive.

The mists lifted and I returned in sunshine via the clearest of burns which hastened back towards the road. Here it joined the greater river, Allt Bail a Mhuilinn, meaning 'river of the town of the mill'. I didn't see a mill or evidence of one, but the forward momentum of the river as it plummeted downwards, white waters over white stones in a wide and bright valley, made sense of the name. This is, perhaps, the most beautiful mountain pass and glen in Scotland. Empty of obvious signs of current human settlement or even much in the way of previous, yet there seemed somehow to be a strong presence of many souls from older times. The road was tiny and hugged one precipitous side of the valley, descending in little curves with few places to pass oncoming cars. I had to concentrate and not be distracted by speculating over piles of stones and green patches amidst heather. There was a peculiar sense of great space but it was difficult to have any sense of scale, there being nothing but the natural world which consisted mainly of thousands of loose boulders, rocks and pebbles, their sizes all not discernible from a distance. The river split and spread itself across the valley floor and grass stretched up the ascents until heather took over once more.

It was odd, after such breathtakingly quiet grandeur, to suddenly find myself in human habitation once more in the village of Bridge of Balgie where the road and valley join Glen Lyon.

The junction is about halfway along the glen. Decisions, decisions. It was a question of bravery. Right for more civilisation, a rich and beautiful valley and a teashop; left for wilderness and a dead end. I chose left and was immediately rewarded.

This little road eventually peters out into a dirt track at huge Loch Lyon. This is another reservoir, the main holding one for this section of the Breadalbane hydroelectric system. It's fed by several underground tunnels from the surrounding hills. The track runs alongside it and stops with only four miles over the mountains to get to the A82 trunk road, busy with traffic heading for the west coast.

I didn't drive the whole thirty-four miles to this finishing point but followed the road seven miles from Bridge of Balgie as it meandered through mixed woods and fields and scrub, undulating over a landscape rich with variation and ever-changing views. I passed, eventually, that photographers' delight, a herd of unafraid hairy hielan' moos hanging out together on the road. Yes, on, not by, and therefore the cause of some delay.

Now I am by the small dam at Cashlie in a tiny car park. In front of me, swooping downwards, is the steep concrete slope of the dam's retaining wall. Unless a light is left on inside the power station over the road to ward off burglars, there will be no electric light outside the van tonight. The nearest house is on the other side of the glen, hidden from me in trees, but from a distance it looked empty when I passed along the road. The nearest human company is in a bright-blue tent quarter of a mile along the loch, which is oddly reassuring, though they're probably fast asleep already, if they've any sense. There is a fierce wind blowing so the trees are turned inside out. A few sheep shuffled past five minutes ago looking as if they knew exactly where they were going, the wool on their backs parted by gusts.

Tonight I'm going to stay here and confront some more demons. It will be dark and I'll be alone. This may be aggravating for my loved ones because there is no mobile reception with which to reassure them of my safety, and the last place I found any was Bridge of Balgie. Unless I wind up having total heebie-jeebies, this is too far back, but I always make sure I know the distance I need to travel for human contact.

There is an official word for this new fear: nomophobia. No Mobile anxiety. This is a distress which I don't believe I have as a habit but which occasionally raises its head if I'm feeling lonely. A road such as this one would be a nightmare if I were feeling sad or unloved. Arguably this would not be nomophobia but more likely monophobia, the fear of solitude or being left alone. Or perhaps autophobia which is not a fear of cars but actually a fear of being isolated. It can also, interestingly, be a fear of oneself. Well. Perhaps I go too deep. These fears are probably a bit older than nomophobia, but perhaps not very old given we didn't have street lights or live in cities until comparatively recently in the wider perspective of human development.

Obviously, nomophobia and monophobia are closely related. Conversely there could be nomophilia, autophilia and monophilia, all of which have afflicted me at one time or another. They are, respectively, the love of not having mobile contact, the love of being isolated, and the love of being alone or, perhaps, of being single. Surely everyone catches these bugs occasionally.

I'm glad I'm in a positive frame of mind today and ready to experience a modicum of fear.

But fear is a feeling entirely dependent on perception. There is nothing to be afraid of here. Absolutely nothing, not even the violent winds or the wildcats which wouldn't be able to get into the van anyway. By contrast, last night I chose a junction on a quiet road. There was some traffic but not much. I watched a group of people descend the nearby hill and listened as their voices rang out across the stillness of the fields. There was no wind. The day was bright, the grass full of flowers. I chose that spot because I felt vulnerable. I wasn't scared of sleeping alone in a camper with a dodgy lock. It was a more general anxiety caused by the unwanted attentions of a man I knew, someone who didn't drive and was fifty miles away. I didn't feel physically threatened by him but his constant emails hadn't stopped when I'd specifically asked to be left in peace. His latest missive had arrived that morning. He had no way of knowing my whereabouts, but I was unsettled. Illogical though it was, I needed to be in the public eye, or even just close to other people and with good phone reception, just in case. It was a feeling, a bodily rendition of my imagination. I think if you have fear of any kind you have to accommodate it, whether you're confronting it or not. It made no sense to ignore my discomfort or try to confront other types of fear, so I played safe. Making my presence obvious felt like a kindness to myself.

There's a fantastic poem by Fleur Adcock called 'Things' in which all her worst moments 'stand icily about the bed' in the middle of the night 'looking worse and worse and worse'. This is how fear can be, a gathering of awful possibilities when you feel least able to defend yourself.

Sometimes it is the fear itself that I fear. Fear is so unpleasant a feeling that anticipating it can cause panic. I worked as a counsellor for a number of years and often heard people say they were scared of being scared, anxious about being anxious, upset about being upset: all dreadful ensnaring spirals. The only way to deal with these maelstroms is to grab something solid and pull yourself out. In other words, either physically move somewhere that feels safer or consciously rearrange the contents of your head to make the fear dissolve. Examining your fears one by one at home, or in the safety of a counselling room if you need to, you'll soon realise how unlikely or unfounded they are. But examining them closely by yourself as they clutter up your campervan may only give those fears extra power, or even make new fears develop from old. Another way is distracting yourself with physical activity, but that may be impractical or exhaust you when what you really need is sleep.

A third way I learned from a children's book about Buddhism. There was a guided meditation in which kids were invited to visualise hanging their worries on a 'worry tree' by an imaginary gate before entering a garden beyond and beginning the meditation (or going to sleep). They put their worries to one side to be dealt with later. Of course, arriving back after the meditation or sleep, the children find their fears have either diminished or vanished altogether. Knowing that this is likely to happen is often enough to make it come about naturally.

Beware, also, of the phone call to 'civilisation'. One night recently my equilibrium was disturbed when, seeking reassurance, I called a friend who turned out to be a few sheets to the wind and speaking truths best kept to himself. I finished the call then drove three miles down the beautiful western side of Loch Awe, as I'd previously planned. This is a long leafy road with almost nothing man-made on it, very beautiful I'm sure, and on a brave more settled day I might have continued. But the call had ruffled me and caused nomophobia to kick in. I turned and came back to a busier spot on the eastern side of the loch. The sunset and early morning view were spectacular from this other road's height, though if I'd known juggernauts were going to shake me awake at five in the morning I might have gone elsewhere.

It's worth noting how, from the comfort of my warm sleeping bag, I considered the possibility of being smashed to pieces as they rollicked past, but concluded it was a risk worth taking, such was my comfort, and went back to sleep. It's all relative, isn't it?

And speaking of relatives, I try not to fall into the trap of succumbing to their fears as well as my own. As Robert Louis Stevenson said, 'Keep your fears to yourself, but share your courage with others.' This is a very caring outlook. Many of my family members are also writers. We have some artists and musicians too. When I've shared my concerns about the weird guy in the campervan next door, or the violent storm approaching my Tupperware box on wheels, these loving people either ridicule my overactive imagination which, coming from a family of vivid imaginers is a bit rich, or they express their love by suggesting I panic and leave immediately. I'm not sure withholding your fears in order to avoid having them ridiculed or magnified is what RLS meant, but his advice holds water. Your anxiety feeds that of others, which in turn feeds yours. You get caught in a whirlwind of fright just when you were seeking the sunshine of their love.

'If the wind hits you sideways you'll be blown right off the road, over the dry-stane dyke and into the valley below. Of course your entrails will be picked over by ravens, so it's very environmentally friendly, not to mention deeply in tune with the universe,' said another sarcastic friend when I phoned her from a similarly remote spot on a previous trip. From the darkness of my van, I imagined her lounging on a reassuring and deeply cushioned sofa by the telly. In truth, the laughter her own joke caused her was weirdly comforting.

Or, you can brave it out and tell everyone how great the solitude of the mountain was, how exciting the wind, how beautiful the sky, how cosy your tiny bunk, how interesting the odd man in the next camper is, how inspiring the resounding silence and how you wrote a story which derived from a mad dream you had last night in the light of a starlit sky with the trees turned inside out like white ghosts. In time your bravery will be real, but it can never be real if you don't go there and survive, and aim to thrive, as you inevitably will.

And besides, cities are far more dangerous than wide open spaces. You may remember the case of Matthew Brooks, a twenty-two-year-old police officer, and his underage girlfriend, Naomi Mills. They disappeared in 2003 from their homes in Worcester and tried to be invisible in the Highlands. The authorities began their search and reports soon poured in of sightings of the couple in Orkney (north), Skye (west), Stonehaven (east) and finally Tongue (north again). It didn't take long. They were actually more visible, not less, in these sparsely populated areas.

For solo campers, this makes you safe. Additionally, if you can raise your level of courage, wide open spaces with no mobile reception can act as a natural shield from worries which don't need to be your own and troubles about which you can do nothing from a distance. Nomophilia is potentially so much more fun than its phobic cousin.

Relatives quite often don't get what I'm up to anyway. Here is a brief but typical conversation with my still bemused mum a full six years after my first solo camper trip:

> Mum: 'Come on, you don't really work morning, noon and night when you go away in the van. You're just having yourself a holiday.'
> Me: 'Actually, no I'm not, and yes, I do.'

A quote attributed to Ralph Waldo Emerson states: 'Whatever course you decide upon, there is always someone to tell you that you are wrong. There are always difficulties arising which tempt you to believe that your critics are right.

To map out a course of action and follow it to an end requires courage.'

He wasn't a campervanner, but he could have been.

What's also required, in my humble opinion, is a simple acceptance that others may be nonplussed or possibly jealous of what you're doing. Notice how short the conversation with my mum was. I know there's no point in defending myself. In fact, sometimes, defending myself makes me doubt. I write because I'm a writer. It's what I do. I do more of it in a campervan. Somehow that argument seems flimsy in the face of empty kitchens and dinners from the freezer. I go off in the campervan because it's what I do. And because it works. Solo campervanning facilitates my writing, and has become an integral part of it. It's not a holiday, even when it looks so much like one and often brings so much pleasure. But few people want to take me at my word on this.

The antidote to the Fleur Adcock poem is 'Cow' by Selima Hill. It describes that need to be dozy, ditzy and free in order to feel fully alive and to create. It's what I'm aiming for when I leave home in the van and evokes all those reasons for leaving behind the 'lobsters and warm telephones'.

> I want to feel free to feel calm.
> I want to be a cow who never knows
> the kind of love you 'fall in love with' with;

It's possible this is my favourite poem ever. I urge you to read the full version.

You can do this getting brave and free in the wild fields of life gradually. Try a caravan site first, and work gradually away from big fancy ones to small and basic, and from central to more isolated and with less facilities. I have a couple of favourite ones I occasionally stay in to charge up batteries and water tanks and in which I find it very easy to work. By far the best is Killiegruer on the west coast of the Kintyre peninsula. It has all the basic facilities in a discreet inoffensive block out of view of where I park. The beach is as close as I dare put my vehicle to it, usually about six feet. The view is up, down and across the vast expanse of sea off the coast of Kintyre. On a clear day you can see the islands of Jura, Islay and Gigha to the west and north, and to the south Ireland. The campsite is open from March to September and I've been there in all weathers during that time. I never tire of this place because, like gazing into an open fire, it is much more interesting and mesmerising than the telly. The mood of the sky changes constantly, and the light feels somehow magnified in the grand space of the south of Kintyre, the dark shades of heavy cloud and the burning rays of sunshine never clashing but instead complimenting and augmenting each other. Dear, dear! It's hard not to wax lyrical when confronted with such profound expansive beauty as you find on this shoreline. Anne, the campsite owner, is always cheerful, pragmatic (always good when campervanning) and welcoming. The place is unpretentious and friendly and a great place to lose your fear of open spaces.

From caravan sites, you can graduate to laybys with phone reception and finally to the west of Loch Awe or Glen Lyon or Assynt and their ilk where phone reception have you none.

Not being in a designated zone of some kind can cause some people alarm in itself. If you try a city 'day retreat' first you'll realise quite quickly what there is to be worried about in cities and therefore how rejuvenating and safe wild places are by contrast. You'll remind yourself what life without those habitual stressors is like. Ideally to do this you need a city spot with no nosy neighbours, for instance with a derelict building behind you, or you can always close the curtains on one side. Across the road there should be a park so you have some greenery to keep you going. These are ideal factors but you may be a person who finds solitude in crowds, for instance in the giant car park at your local superstore with people to watch instead of trees. The difference between writing in a campervan and writing in a café, which is the obvious closest comparison, is tea. In a camper you can drink as much of it as you like without forking out wads of cash. You can pick your nose and scratch your bum, if it helps, without anyone looking askance, yet you still get to people-watch. And you can have a little nap if the writing gets too tough. I have snoozed beside busy roads in Glasgow when the need has arisen.

What you don't want to do is attract attention. One day I parked down near Glasgow Green, which is a large park in the eastern end of central Glasgow. The park was originally an area of swampy land which was gifted to a local bishop and the people of Glasgow in 1450. It has served many practical purposes since, not least the beginnings of local football giants, Rangers FC, the bleaching and drying of linen and the building of the Templeton carpet factory. I stopped on the park's northern edge with a derelict building behind me. Perfect.

Then along came some neds, or 'chavs' as they're known in England, though chav is actually an old word for Traveller. We have learnt to fear young guys in hoodies, especially in red track suits, a primal warning sign to leave well alone. They made a few faces, nudged each other, pointed a few fingers, realised I was boring, nodded and passed by. Then there were the other suits, grey or, well, grey again, who eyed up the van and worried about the kind of lateral thinker I might be and whether I'm there to infiltrate their boxed-in world. No thanks. Perhaps they were considering which bylaw I might be breaking, but ultimately they needed their thirty-minute lunch break for better things, and kept going.

The truth is I've only been asked to move on once and that by a church minister.

I was researching a particular view for my novel *Rue End*

Street which is partly set on the Clyde and its Estuary. I had missed a turning and was searching for the next opportunity to stop. As I pulled into a large empty car park beside a church, I saw, too late, a sign telling me it was private parking for churchgoers. It was a Tuesday so I decided to risk it. I bounced across the puddle-filled potholes and stopped slap-bang in the middle. It was close enough to the viewpoint I was looking for, had trees on both sides and a clear view out to sea. Perfect. I took a few photos, made some tea and was reaching for the binoculars when a shadow passed the window and a man appeared at my door.

Was I going to be here long? I told him I realised it was private but I was doing some research. He eyed me sceptically and didn't ask. I promised I'd leave as soon as I finished my tea. Again he eyed me with suspicion. I returned no arguments, only reassurance, and he wandered slowly away.

I could have said, 'I am a lost soul; please save me.' I wasn't, but could have been.

In fact I already knew about the other kind of fear, the stuff coming my way, the trepidation inspired by me in others. Or rather the anxiety caused by the appearance of an old campervan, as opposed to the respectability of a new one, or by a lone traveller, albeit a female one, as opposed to the safe normality of a couple. All these things make me an unknown quantity. In Ayrshire in particular there is a fear of campervans stemming from the area's popularity with Travellers in the past. Travellers are no longer in evidence but all the car parks the length of the Ayrshire coast have height bars low enough to prevent any of my vans from entering. This is a shame. I once planned a small beach party at Seamill near West Kilbride using my first van as a mobile kitchen and toilet facility, neither of which are available there. Luckily I visited shortly beforehand and was reminded of the existence of the height bars. Ayrshire is my nearest coast and parts of

it are stunningly beautiful with views west to Arran and Goat
Fell or south to Ailsa Craig, a seabound volcanic plug known
locally as 'Paddy's Milestone'. I could make good use of an
Ayrshire car park.

The council responsible for this coast had promised me
the barriers were coming down, their reason being to allow
vehicles for disabled people, which are often high, to get in.
When I spoke to their representative, I pointed out that they
were perhaps missing a trick tourism-wise and might want to
take a tip out of the Frenchman's *livre* and encourage campers
into their area by supplying designated campervan spaces
with hook-ups in all towns. We had a long and pleasant chat
during which he told me his parents were in fact setting off
for France the following day in their campervan. Yay! I wished
them well and looked forward to many happy writing hours
by the sea.

I visited Seamill Beach by car and observed the bent height
barrier. Your days are numbered, I said rather smugly. When I
visited again only two months later I found the height barrier
had indeed been removed, but a brand new one was gleaming
in its place. I contacted the nice council man again and it
transpires the Seamill dunes are privately owned and therefore
the council have no jurisdiction. All their other height barriers
have now been removed. But Seamill is the most popular
beach. We must hope this person also visits France in a
campervan, and soon.

I have no desire to make anyone feel uncomfortable. Apart
from anything else, other people feeling anxious would
make me anxious too. Anxiety is nagging fear and as long as
you're listening to nagging you're not listening to your muse.
Anxiety is counter-productive. Muses do not come out to play
when anxiety is about. So I am vigilant about how I appear
to others. I often hide away and never spend more than two
nights in the same wild camping spot, especially if it is in view

of houses. I know I'm harmless and that not only do I leave no mess but I also frequently remove rubbish left by others, though I did draw the line at that rotten fish in its unsealed plastic bag floating in a sea of green bushes on the edge of a small secluded car park which shall remain nameless. Poo! Other people don't know how nice I am. (But I'm not that nice.)

Timing is also of the essence here. When staying overnight, I aim to turn up late and leave by lunch time, meanwhile opening my curtains as soon as is decent in the morning and nonchalantly tapping away at the keyboard as if I've been doing it since dawn, which sometimes I have.

The night in Cashlie by the small dam with its dinky power station has passed. In the cold morning, there is no-one to disturb me, only chaffinches to spot and sheep whose constant wandering up the road, back again and up it once more whilst nudging each other as if there was a great hurry, was distracting and fun. The wind had fallen during the evening and was followed by the patter of rain on the roof, then a resounding silence at five in the morning, by far the most productive time of day. But instead I rolled over, or rather rolled round, there being very little space, and slept on for two more hours, completely forgetting that I was either meant to be scared witless of the absolute silence and the dark, or be inspired to fill it with words. You see, I forgot to be scared, and yet I survived. I forgot the night before when I was making up the bed. I forgot again in the morning. So I slept long and woke refreshed with no fear whatsoever.

Be brave!

Mindfulness Meditation

Because I've talked about Buddhism quite a lot, I feel I must give you a rough guide to mindfulness meditation. First a definition of mindfulness itself. The best I've come across is by Thich Nhat Hanh, a Buddhist teacher from Vietnam who runs a retreat centre in France called Plum Village. He's also a prolific writer.

> 'Mindfulness is the energy of being aware and awake to the present moment. It is the continuous practice of touching life deeply in every moment of daily life. To be mindful is to be truly alive, present and at one with those around you and with what you are doing.'

That sounds pretty straightforward, doesn't it? Simple really. Hmm.

The word 'mindfulness' is a translation from the Pali word 'sati'. It's not a direct translation because we simply don't have that word in English. Included in the original meaning is memory, recognition, wakefulness, intentness, lucidity of mind, conscience and self-possession. The verb equivalent also includes the idea of remembering and witnessing. Mindfulness is just the closest the English language can come to the meaning of sati.

Mindfulness is the aim, but I'm guessing very few people achieve this, not in every moment. To be conscious in this way every minute of your waking day seems like a pretty tall order.

Mindfulness meditation is a tool for honing up your everyday capacity for mindfulness. I've been doing this meditation on and off for years. If I was more disciplined I'd do it more often than I do because it's always beneficial. Even when it feels like it's not working, it still makes a difference.

Although I'm giving you this written guide, I suggest you also find someone to help you and support you in practising its simple techniques, especially in the beginning in case you have any questions. The support I've had from Buddhist organisations, books and talks has been invaluable. The practice does seem very simple, and in fact it is very simple, but it can also feel extremely difficult and challenging. Try it and you'll soon see why.

Mindfulness is the meditation I favour most. There are others designed to promote loving kindness and positive thought, but I think positive thought is less effective when not coupled with the focus of mindfulness, so I'm offering you the following as a platform from which to proceed.

Blaise Pascal, an early inventor of calculators, said: 'All men's miseries derive from not being able to sit in a quiet room alone.' Even the physical sitting still for a short period of time can be difficult. You need to be comfortable in a way which relaxes you but which also keeps you alert. You therefore want your body to do as little work as possible without falling asleep. So no lying down. Unless what you really want is to sleep. In my experience.

If you can manage a lotus position, where both feet are up on your thighs, then do, but don't worry if you can't. I can't. I can't even begin to. In fact it feels downright dangerous in my present state of unfitness. The main thing is that your back is straight, as if the bones of the spine are stacked up one on top of the other. Your head should be balanced on top in such a way that your back does as little work as possible, all the vertebrae lined up perfectly. I tie a scarf round my upper hips and tuck my hands into it so that my shoulders are not carrying the weight of my arms and pulling me forward. I use a little green meditation stool that a friend made for me so that I'm kneeling but my backside is supported and my weight isn't on my feet, but you can also use an ordinary chair. Tilt it slightly forwards, perhaps by putting a rolled-up blanket or some books under the back legs so that your back will naturally straighten. Another way is sitting astride a pile of cushions.

Then you have to inhabit your body and make sure it is relaxed. That probably sounds a bit fancy, but it's not really. Just start by focussing your attention on the top of your head and working your way down to your feet, or vice versa. It doesn't matter which way you do it. Then bring your attention back to your breathing. This is when the real meditation starts.

It comes in four stages:

1. Focus your attention on your breath while counting from one to ten. Try and count at the exact moment you stop breathing IN and start breathing OUT. Repeat for five minutes.

2. Again focus your attention on your breath while counting from one to ten, but this time count at the exact moment you stop breathing OUT and start breathing IN. Repeat for five minutes.

3. Stop counting. Just focus on your breath in whatever way works. No rules here. Just observe what your breath does in your body. Five minutes.

4. Focus on the tiny bit at your nose where the air enters and leaves your body. Five minutes.

That's it. Start with five minutes per section and increase this as you get the hang of it. Either guess the time or keep a watch handy. Don't fuss about being too exact but do make sure you do at least five minutes of each stage. You can also download meditation programmes, such as *Insight Timer* or *Meditation Helper*, that will ring a singing bowl at the required interval so you know when to move on to the next section. Singing bowls are actually bells which sit on their base instead of being hung, kind of upside-down bells, and they can be quite small or very large. When struck with a wooden implement they produce a long lingering and very beautiful sound which is made of one central note with two harmonic overtones, if you listen very carefully. There are computer apps, which will also ring a singing bowl for you at random times throughout your day in order to point out to you how unfocussed you are and give you a chance to remedy your ways. Some meditators use this to focus briefly on their breath, three in and three out, like an instant escape route to mindfulness. I have a singing bell as the text alert on my phone so sometimes I just stop what I'm doing for the duration of the bell and listen. Then I look at the text, or ignore it if going back to whatever I was doing would be more mindful.

If, while meditating, you discover you have counted up to thirty-seven, as I have done, do not be alarmed! Do not chastise yourself in any way. Just go back to one and start again. Likewise if you lose count or mentally wander off to think about dinner or that attractive person who just started at work, just keep coming back. Over and over. I have found that this mindfulness meditation, which involves effort on my part to control my thinking, is actually a fast track to being able to be in the moment and get lost in my imagination, though obviously not while I'm actually meditating. It is the ultimate way 'to be here now'.

To quote the transcendentalists whose meditation is very similar: 'Neural imaging patterns and EEG research show that transcendental meditation practice produces a unique state of restful alertness, which can be seen in the decreased activity in the thalamus (the area of the brain that relays input to all other parts of the brain) and increased activity in the frontal and parietal cortices (two areas involved in attention).' They also say that after meditation '... the emotional response to the world is more balanced and appropriate.'

'Being here now' can be described thus: 'With the removal or minimisation of cognitive stimuli and generally increasing awareness, meditation can therefore influence both the quality (accuracy) and quantity (detection) of perception.' This was Joseph Tloczynski, an American psychologist.

As well as all this clear thinking, other research has shown that stress shuts off the part of our brain associated with compassion. Meditation turns this part back on. I do believe that fostering compassion is an important part of writing characters of depth. I have to care about all my characters, even the baddest of bad guys, and I have to feel for them, even as I torment them for the sake of a good story.

Mindful meditation, if you do it well enough and over a long period, also makes you need less sleep, which means more time to get lost and write. It will also improve your blood circulation, lower your heart rate and boost your immune system.

Meditation can feel akin to a power nap, but I don't know if there's any neurological connection. Both involve stepping out of what I'm doing for a short period. Both therefore involve a deliberate letting go of immediate stress and a turning inward. I would even argue that if I take my mind out of my actual surroundings for as little as a minute or for the time it takes the ring of the singing bowl to fade, I break the unhealthy spiral of anxiety, despair, anger, yearning and all the other things which take me away from the present and generally cause me harm.

Try closing your eyes and thinking about your breathing for one minute. Do it now. Do it whenever. It's a tiny but extremely effective way of taking back control of those unhelpful fleeting thoughts and therefore of potentially letting yourself roam free in the wilderness in search of metaphorical peacocks.

Storm Clouds

I'd been itching to get away for ages, but couldn't because of a heavy workload and other commitments. I was so tired it took me a whole day to pack up the van and go. These preparations included a trip to Ikea for storage. The wooden shelf in the Luton (the bit above the cab) had finally collapsed, so I bought three foldable boxes, two turquoise and one orange, at a cost of £7.50 in total, less than the cost of this book. I put them above the red-and-white polka dotty bar at the edge of the Luton where they clashed, but they resonated with the seat covers and also echoed the sunset colours in Kintyre when I arrived.

Before I left, I bought new wool for knitting because I knew my brain was only half-working and knitting would calm my jaggedy-edged thoughts. Could have done with a bit of mindfulness. I was sad to be leaving alone again. I like alone but I was sad that although I was recently back in touch with my husband after a year's separation, we were only drifting, our contact sporadic. It was eight in the evening before I finally left the house. I needed to knit, but really what I needed was meditation. The great thing about mindfulness is you can find it in anything at any time. It's instant. Knitting was becoming a form of mindfulness meditation.

The roads were quiet. It was Saturday night and everyone was somewhere. Most would have been drinking, not driving. It was the perfect time to travel. So, exhausted though I was, I drove through the long beautiful summer evening. It was shortly after midsummer in Scotland which meant darkness barely came at all. I chose for my final stop a layby somewhere beyond Ardrishaig on the western shore of Loch Fyne. The layby was on the landward side of the road, the sea reached out on the other side towards the shores of the Cowal peninsula, a dark smudge on the vague horizon.

I got in the back of the van and immediately started knitting to wind down. Then, having knitted, I read *Way of the Wanderers* by Jess Smith, about Traveller history. Then I slept, but not particularly well. Cars passed occasionally and close, and I was woken by a walker tramping past in the wee small hours, so I allowed myself a lie-in the following morning. The van was warm, the sun beating down on the plastic roof. It was deliciously snoozy. I began my day with a breakfast of tea, toasted tattie scones and a bit more knitting, then tiptoed back to the cab past the evidence of that layby's alternative use as a toilet, amazed I had managed to get into the van in the previous evening's twilight with clean shoes. Clearly the gods were with me.

After a quick stop at the Tarbert Co-op for lunch supplies, I changed into shorts in a layby then continued to Westport on the Kintyre coast to meet some friends. Westport is the most popular beach in Kintyre, the one surfers like. It's reasonably close to Campbeltown and has ideal sand dunes for camping and picnics, a large almost flat car park for brewing up tea in campervans, and a chemical toilet which is, in terms of cleanliness, nothing like the ones you get at festivals and even has toilet paper. Because the beach itself is long, you can get a good steam up or linger in a stroll, whichever you please. My friends and I had a brisk walk for about an hour and a half along the shoreline in brilliant sunshine and a breeze, then ate lunch in my van.

It is an unmitigated pleasure to provide lunch to van guests. I'm not an enthusiastic caterer at home, but supplying good food in this small intimate space makes me very happy indeed. That day we had oatcakes and two cheeses, salad and a choice of teas. No-one, to my knowledge, was sick, everyone ate plenty and they were very complimentary about my van, which pleases and endears them to me all the more. Additionally, these friends are a couple and it's always great to be near their warmth.

Too soon they went off to play golf on one of Kintyre's oddly eccentric courses where, I'm told, the challenge is second guessing the strong side winds. I remained in the van and knitted, then went to the beach and read. No writing happening at all. Throughout all this time I was listening to and watching the people round about me. Sometimes I think the title of Naomi Mitchison's wartime memoir, which was largely written in Carradale on the other side of the Kintyre peninsula, could be applied to me: *Among You Taking Notes*. Watching the activities of others is one of the chief pleasures of layby life, or as in this case, beach and car-park life.

Then everyone was packing up to go home though it had just gone five in the afternoon. Only a few kids were left by the shore and a straggle of walkers lingered in the distance. Westport beach is a stretch of golden sands normally peopled by a variety of seabirds, dog-walkers and surfers. I even found a sixty-year-old surfer here one New Year's Day. The beach faces roughly west with nothing between you and America but the tumultuous ocean, or indeed the placid glassy ocean if you're lucky, as I often am. The light is always amazing, perhaps because there is so much of it. On a clear day the cliffs of the north of Ireland show themselves to the south, likewise the island of Jura with its distinctive Paps to the northwest and in the north the wind turbines of Gigha, with space aplenty between all of these and a vast sky over-reaching. You hear the wind, high or low. There is no need for any kind of music here and the company of noisy oystercatchers means I never need the radio and its spoken word either.

But itchy feet always get me, coupled that day with a bout of nomophobia. Westport had no signal, so off I went to Campbeltown for gas, petrol, food supplies and to make a couple of phone calls. Finally I turned to Machrihanish and beyond it to the little two-car parking spot where I'd encountered the van full of surfers and where I can reverse the van in, close the front curtains and gaze out the back door all the way up the west coast of Kintyre. It's popular with seals too. At Peninver, on the east coast of Kintyre, I once counted fifty-three seals in one sitting. They used to arrive in Machrihanish in impressive numbers too, but nowadays seem to come only in twos or threes. When not bobbing in the water like lost leather footballs, they lounge like giant smiles in the sunshine on the rocks. This position never looks that relaxing, feet and head higher than the belly. In fact I often think seals look awkward when they're out of the water. If you've ever watched them scrambling up a rock to get into their smiley position you'll know what I mean. They have to wriggle. Having more substantial flippers would help. But they seem happy and are also playful and vocal and like music. I always mean to bring a tin whistle, even though I can't play one.

It is also a place I've seen many kinds of seabirds and ducks including shelducks which are easy to spot with their striking black, white and amber markings. Swans congregate here too and shags which live on the water and occasionally pose on rocks with their wings outstretched. They appear to be drying their wing feathers but rumour has it they are actually crushing their dinner inside their chests when they do this. It's also fun to spot gannets nearby folding their wings and hurtling from a great height into the water to catch fish. There are gulls of every description, the common, the herring and the black-backed or black-headed. Black-backs are the neds of the seabird kingdom and go around attacking other birds and pinching their grub. When the day is quiet, you can hear the little sandpipers if you tread carefully on the beach, and you can hear those oystercatchers almost any time, even in a high wind.

All these birds used to congregate in great numbers, but for some reason not that day and not any day for a couple of years now. I'm an amateur when it comes to birdwatching, but the tiny Machrihanish Seabird and Wildlife Observatory, manned by the ever-helpful and enthusiastic Eddie Maguire, is just around the corner. This is where I once, briefly, saw a charm of goldfinches. Charm is the collective noun for a gathering of goldfinches though I'd say they were more of a cloud, or like fireworks but much more exciting.

I stopped in this spectacular spot at tea time, so I ate my packet couscous with extra cherry tomatoes and followed it up with strawberries, a few super crunchy crisps and some decaff Earl Grey. My face was burnt and the wind too cold to sit out, but I tried anyway and knitted a few rows, then washed up and knitted some more inside. This was my first complete day off from writing and writing-related things in ages. Although writing is a pleasure, and generally leads me back to sanity when I've wandered, sometimes it's hard to switch off. This is arguably the diametrical opposite of 'being here now' and those close to me can testify that the writing part of me rarely shuts down completely. It's who I am. It's what I do. What do you want me to do? Sigh. I'm sure it's very annoying. It certainly can be for me, and then I need that inner writer to just stop, please, for a day. That day it did. Thank you. Zzzzzzzzzz …

The next morning I was up early and refreshed. However, feeling heavily influenced by the Jess Smith book, I was uncomfortably aware that my van was a bit tatty, and also that a woman on her own in a van is an oddity. Another lone woman walked past early as I sat outside drinking tea. Just the two of us at the beginning of the day, we had to say hello. I initiated our greetings but could see she was uncomfortable. I was uncomfortable too. *What does she see when she glances over here?* I wondered. *Do I look like a Traveller?* I was wearing cut-off jeans and my hair was fashionably 'just-out-of-bed' because I was, um, just out of bed. I was definitely a bit tatty, something often levelled at Travellers, albeit unfairly.

A while later a car came past with a sign on its roof and for a second I thought it might be the police come to move me on. In fact it was a taxi, but the paranoia was there. The Martyn Bennett track 'Move' rang through my head. Martyn Bennett was a young musician with extraordinary talent and originality who specialised in fusing music from different cultures with his native Scottish folk. His life was cut short by cancer and 'Move' is the opening track on *Grit*, his last album. In this imaginative project he fused recordings of Travellers' songs with a plethora of fabulous sounds. 'Move' features the voice of Sheila Stewart who comes from a family of famous songster Travellers. She is singing lines from 'Moving on Song' by Ewan McColl, a famous socialist and songwriter. 'Go! Move! Shift!' she sings.

I felt the Travellers' vulnerability, which colours swathes of Jess Smith's book, and was reminded of the vulnerability of all minorities when faced with the might of the majority, and of all the people who do things considered 'odd' by enough others and whose pleasure in doing them is so often dampened. In extreme cases some are even being bullied out of existence.

I realise, of course, that what I'm doing in my van is not that odd, and that I can step out of all this at any moment and be respectably mainstream again and therefore relatively invisible and safe. It's extremely temporary. But it is the lot of many writers, not to mention counsellors and ex-counsellors of which I am one, to empathise with and even slightly drown in the experiences of others. This happens even when we're apparently off duty. It's a useful and sometimes inconvenient truth that writers, and no doubt other artists, often and in some minor way, live the experiences of the people we encounter, in our heads and hearts at least. It's the prerequisite for writing believable stories and portraying life as it is.

I've long been wary of reading fiction when I'm writing, in case I get lost in another writer's voice. One evening when I was working on my first novel, I read a chapter by Margaret Atwood. The following morning her style and phrasing appeared in my writing. Ms Atwood had inadvertently taken over. I therefore introduced a ban on reading fiction until the first draft was finished, so that I could retain the voice of Lenny Gillespie, my central character and narrator. Luckily this draft took me less than six months. This might seem a long time but the yearning was eased by reading loads of nonfiction for my research.

Of course, nonfiction writers have distinct voices too, perhaps especially affecting when I'm writing nonfiction myself. As well as *Way of the Wanderers*, I'd been reading Andy Wightman's *The Poor Had No Lawyers* and David Kynaston's inaccurately named *Austerity Britain*. Their three voices had joined forces, infiltrated my thinking and my sense of myself, and my book. No harm to these three writers or Margaret Atwood, all of whom are excellent in their own way, but they are not me. I wonder if the business of taking on written voices is similar to picking up spoken accents – people with a musical ear are more likely to take on (mostly accidentally) the local accent when they move to a new area. I seem to do this without realising. If I'm in London long enough people don't even realise I'm Scottish. Now I do it in my writing.

This time it seemed to run deeper. Reading about Travellers while wandering around in my van had made me self-conscious.

My trip, habits and personal cultural identity are not Tinker, but I could have been misconceived as one. I was there escaping the trappings of my everyday consumer life in Glasgow, and I was conscious, as always, that my presence worries people. I was being odd, not conforming. Women don't usually travel alone in campervans, perhaps with good reason.

The sum total of all this was I became anxious, lost the metaphorical and actual plot, and the sleeping muse slept on.

Occasionally, while in campsites, I've worried that my obviously 'working', that's to say writing, makes me a party pooper. Famously, on my first trip to Killiegruer a cheery man came and asked me with a smile if I was ok or if I was there to 'top myself'. Good opening line, sir. Straight to the point and an indication of the general public's view of people who travel solo. Clearly this friendly man had no idea what fun I was having. Unfortunately he seemed unable to grasp it either, despite my protestations. Being alone, in his world, equated to misery, and I was bucking a trend.

Jess Smith's book preyed on my mind and made me feel I had no right to spend a night here and there in quiet laybys. I sensed I was being frowned upon by other people, though in Kintyre probably erroneously. Kintyre always feels extraordinarily welcoming. But even as a traveller in a more generic sense, I was more self-conscious than usual.

I reminded myself I was there with three specific missions: to write, to repair the damage done by city life in Britain, and to root myself in the real world. Perhaps on this occasion my sense of dispossession was exaggerated by the new contact with my husband, by not getting a job I'd applied for which would have removed all financial worry, and by failing to do any actual words-on-page writing, even though I had deliberately not written the day before. Just writing alone would have lifted me above all these worldly concerns. Writing has often saved me from these torments.

I must stress, also, that there is nothing inherently 'odd' about what Travellers do or more correctly, in most cases, did. People have been doing it for centuries, living in the open air and surviving off their considerable wits. The odd part is that the rest of us find someone else living this lifestyle so threatening.

In anticipation, alone in my campervan, I felt the discomfort of being misunderstood. I was a little off-kilter. That spiralling anxiety-about-anxiety is perhaps what so many people fear about travelling alone. There was no-one to ground me in good sense.

Suddenly I wanted to write a short letter to the local newspaper, the *Campbeltown Courier*, stating who I was and why I was there – a 'letter from a tourist'. I know the *Courier* is sympathetic because one spring they ran an article about how excited they were that the tourists would soon be arriving.

Dear *Campbeltown Courier*,

You may have seen this van (photo enclosed) in various locations around Kintyre. I love this area and come every year, usually several times, to enjoy the scenery and wildlife and to write. While I love solitude, I also love people and some of the great joys of my solo travels are the encounters I have had with strangers in laybys in far-flung locations. As a writer who believes the world is made of stories I therefore invite you to stop for tea and a chat. My van is small and easy to identify, with butterflies all over the outside. Within, a warm welcome awaits.

I forgot to mention the butterflies on the outside of Vanessa. That was me, I'm afraid, and they're gone now. Their purpose was to cover some messy repairs.

Obviously, I didn't send this letter. Paranoia prevented me.

The woman who reluctantly said hello that morning passed again. I wished I could have spoken with her and that my confidence had not taken this sudden dip.

Painful though this emotional state was, in some hazy part of my mind I knew that ultimately it would be more grist for the mill. Everything in life is worth experiencing to the full and, if you have a mind to, you can use it later either in your work or your life.

The reliability of hot water and ample supplies of toilet paper at the Machrihanish public toilets lifted my spirits a little, as did the antics of three gulls after the same crab. I wanted to yell 'There are plenty more crabs in the sea.'

I headed off to the wild and beautiful bay of the Gauldrons to meet my lovely friends again. The Gauldrons (as in cauldrons) is a circular bay like a giant bubbling witch's tureen with a great scoop of cliffs around it and a roaring soundtrack to match. Whenever I come here the beach-scape has changed, the sand either blasted away by gales and the rocks beneath exposed, or vice versa. On this occasion, there were bluffs of pebbles which scrunched under my feet and collapsed towards the incoming waves, and these same waves made beautiful music by knocking the stones against each other. The Gauldrons is also home to golden eagles and feral goats, though the goats are breeding more quickly than the gardens of Machrihanish can cope with and a local man has taken to herding them back round the cliffs every day.

En route there, I checked my emails on my phone and found one of those unwanted messages again. This upset me greatly. Why did I check my emails? What was the point? With my equilibrium now in complete disarray I crossed the rocky field and went to meet my friends. Eventually I told them about this upsetting email and, through our discussion, two other similar incidents from my past returned to memory, both of which I must have somehow blanked. A chill gripped my stomach. Being single at this (late) age has made me the focus of attention from a few men, mostly married. Realising again my very real vulnerability in this respect threw me completely. I bid my good friends farewell and noticing storm clouds gathering out to sea in the west I hurried back to the safety of the van.

On my arrival, I found the driver's wing mirror lying on the ground. The passenger one was folded against the window but not damaged. The awful significance of this will only be fully understood by people used to driving vans and other large vehicles with limited rear vision. You are completely dependent on wing mirrors. Without them you're forced to stick your head out the window and craning round backwards means not looking where you're going for longer than is safe.

I had parked in a field, positioning myself next to my friends' car. There had been sheep, only sheep: silly fluffy things with wee lambs and no horns. When I came back there were cows, big stupid swaying beasts presumably with itchy backs. A couple picnicking by a car not far off informed me they'd only been there fifteen minutes and hadn't seen the cows doing their worst. They said something similar had happened to their own car once. These other cows had also put a dent in theirs. I was silently pleased that this had not been my van's fate. The cows had then licked their car all over. I eyeballed the car in front of which the couple sat. It was a very shiny car. The wife's theory was that the cows had seen their own reflection in their (previous) car. They really liked what they saw, she said: themselves only ten times bigger, magnified in the car's curves. They liked it so much they licked it all over.

Really?

The wifey liked to talk. I had a job getting away. Her stories seemed a tad daft and there I was with yet another van problem just when I'd been thanking my lucky stars that at least the van was in full working order.

I drove straight to the garage in Campbeltown with whom I was already familiar from previous trips in Vera Bedford. In the lovely local accent, the friendly proprietor phoned several places of his ken for a new mirror, but came up blank. My garage in Glasgow was closing that day for a week. I was bereft of help.

The weather had turned chilly as the storm clouds moved closer so, as I drove off in search of sanctuary from all this practical angst, I tried to wind up the window, but to no avail. The glass leant towards me and refused to follow its allocated alignment. It was stuck. This was enough, really enough. It meant I'd have to park well away from people. It meant I couldn't even take refuge by returning home because I couldn't park the van in a Glasgow street and reasonably expect all to be well in the morning.

I left a phone message for a friend who'd fixed some odds and ends in the van for me, more to calm myself down than anything else. In an earlier life he had been a scrappie so he was always a good person for practical help. As I drove slowly northwest towards Westport, the sky continued to darken and a heavy band of cloud sat over the sea beyond the muddy farmland. My friend called me back as I approached the small village of Kilkenzie, first home of my beloved editor for *Mavis's Shoe*. I pulled into a small car park next to a tiny portakabin of indistinguishable purpose. Over the phone my friend gave me tricks that meant I could at least wind the window up using two (but preferably more) hands, and talked me through it as I did so. This was a relief but not being able to wind it down limited my rear visibility to zilch.

Without intending to I then related the story of the unwanted emails and the various unsolicited attentions I had suffered in the previous year of being single. His dismay was comforting. In the midst of all this and through watery eyes, I realised, now the window was up, that I'd been licked. Not me, but my window, in fact all my windows. This was a tonic, and we laughed as I traced with my finger the great swooping mud-streaked saliva lines of the giant tongues of cows. It looked very like wallpaper. They'd barely spared an inch.

Cheered at last, I thanked him and continued on my way to Westport for more knitting, tea and a whole packet of Jaffa cakes, eyeing up the newly bought Cointreau for later.

I cleaned the van windows. I never travel without window-cleaning equipment. How else can I see those spectacular views? So I got to work.

Later, and it's amazing how slowly the human brain works when distracted by painful memories, I asked myself why cows might like licking vehicles. My white plastic van does not reflect cows to ten times their size, or indeed at all, because yes, the sides of it were smeary too. Neither do the old plastic windows. I can only conclude that, in a field of relentless green, the smoothish surfaces of vans and cars have novelty value for bovines. Perhaps my van was salty from sea spray too. Whatever, this shed a whole new light on wanting to be Selima Hill's cow …

The incident had raised my sense of alarm, but was also, strangely, a little cathartic.

Be Here Now

The following morning I was still feeling unsettled and decided to move. Sometimes moving helps me collect my thoughts, though at other times it's just a new form of distraction. It's often not clear which of the two it is. Having wheels to move means this dichotomy is intensified. It can go either way. But at that moment, movement seemed like the only thing I could do.

The storm which had threatened the day before had not materialised but a sea mist now engulfed the Westport dunes, hanging like a bad mood. I packed everything away and wandered back south to the comparative metropolis of Campbeltown and down Long Row which is a narrow street with long rows of successful small businesses. The temptation was to shop in the Nickel 'n' Dime on Kinloch Road overlooking the harbour, but I knew this would not calm me. So I turned west for Machrihanish once more and my favourite home-from-home, the two-car parking spot beyond the end of the village with its views up the west coast. I needed the uplifting spaciousness of the sea and the comfort of familiarity. But the mist was there too. I tried tea, knitting and watching seals but none of these things were a match for my overwhelming restlessness and unease.

But here is what I was missing, what I wasn't doing. Here is the truth: wherever I was, I needed to BE HERE NOW. I needed to be properly present in my surroundings and task. And I absolutely wasn't, though I'd managed to fool myself I was.

Oh dear.

All at once, I thought of Lenny, the heroine of *Mavis's Shoe*, as if she had just tapped me on the shoulder. Whenever I was lost when writing her story, I would put down my pen (actually my key tapping fingers) and ask myself where she was. I'd wonder how she was, what she was thinking and feeling. This invariably got me going again. It was the central driving force of the narrative, a fact that was easy to forget in all the action.

There was no Lenny in this instance, only me trying to write a book about campervanning, and not just about me and my experiences. I am not asking you, dear reader, to follow the emotional ups and downs of my innermost emotional life for its own sake. I do so only to elucidate the trials and tribulations of writing, of going solo, and of solo campervanning with a pen or laptop. Even for this book of mostly nonfiction I still have a narrator and that narrator is a particular part of me. But that same part of me was more concerned with my husband, my two daughters, the organisation who didn't give me the job I was after (my own fault), my newly released book and how it was faring, my friend's aunt (who unexpectedly bought me dinner and who I didn't feel I'd thanked enough), and Mr Stalker. I was more concerned with this punchbowl of disturbing thoughts than anything right in front of me.

I was vaguely aware of my shortcomings in this respect and sat head down for a solid hour, knitting frantically until my arms ached.

When I finally lifted my eyes the mist had rolled northwards at last and the sun was bathing the rocks below. 'Go, move, shift,' whispered a voice in my mind. 'Yer work's a' done.' Another line from the same song. So I set off, yet again, from my magnificent spot at the southern end of Kintyre, to which I had so recently strayed. I paused only to answer emails once

I had reception (but not that one) and to collect water and use the 'facilities' at Machrihanish, before heading north, possibly even for home which was several hours away.

Instantly I was amazed by the beauty of the drive along the Campbeltown road across the area of rich farmland called 'The Laggan'. A giant field of feathery barley waved and undulated in the breeze. It was indeed golden. Elsewhere all was a lush, rich fecund green. A-four-by-four startled me from this awe by overtaking. I needed that rear view. Then I turned onto a quieter road for safety, traversed the Backs Burn and cut across the machair by the airport. I love this road. Known locally as the Moss Road, it winds and twists, and skirts a roadside cottage nestling on a sudden slope with only stones painted white for protection. There are hedges which limit your view so you feel low down, near the earth. This feels good. Shortly before the tiny airport, with its enormous runway, there's another house. There was a small field in front with Clydesdales in it, including foals – so beautiful with their shaggy legs like flares from the 1970s. Ahead of me some kind of emergency vehicle with high-vis stripes had stopped on the one-track road to chat with a woman pushing a pram. I kept a distance to indicate there was no hurry, then waved to the woman as I passed.

The little road joins the trunk road from the south of the peninsula to the north. I trundled over the crown of a hill which normally affords the first clear view of the sea. I was nervous about my lack of rear vision, but now wondered where the sea had gone. The van was bathed in sunshine but mist still covered the sea. The islands had disappeared, there was no horizon and all I could see were the familiar grassy sand dunes, hay-coloured in the sun, and then an eerie shapeless nothing, as if the edge of the earth had drawn closer and we were in danger of falling off. It was an astonishing sight. I gasped and slowed to take this in, but with no rear view mirror I had no idea what was behind me and had to press on.

A little further on there's a sign for a place called Tangy, which I assume is a delicious place to be. Just before it, there's a T-shaped layby. It's part of the old main road which meanders from side to side across the new one. This layby was another favourite of mine and sits above some small cliffs usually affording a grand view in all directions and plenty of birds to watch, especially shags and gannets. I wanted to stop there and take in what was happening to the sea and sky, but just before I reached it, my eyes fell on the water below. The colour was something I'd never seen before and honestly can't describe. It was linked in some mysterious way to the mist further out which inexplicably reflected this blue. I gasped again. I should have stopped at the T-shaped layby in the name of safety with all this gasping, but it was occupied and I really didn't want company. I continued to gulp for air at this extraordinary vision which I still can't find words for. It was so fleeting. I pulled into the parking area at the foot of Tangy.

What I saw, at sea, was stunning. I was stunned. For once this word meant something. I blinked and absorbed what was in front of me. It felt like more than seeing, but I don't know what it was and none of the words I have can describe it. My sense of heart-stopping wonder was similar to my night-sky experience in Cowal. This was beauty and therefore pleasure, surely, but there was also something deeply disturbing about it that I couldn't place or articulate. Perhaps it was the atmosphere of secrecy brought on by the mist which made me feel like I'd inadvertently glimpsed beyond a secret doorway which someone had forgotten to close, a door to something magnificent and sacrosanct. A weird combination of exquisite pleasure and abject terror. You see how ridiculous it is to try and describe it? Nothing had actually happened. There was no ghostly tall ship, no woman drowning, no battle between two dolphins. Just clarity and colour and light. I sat with my mouth open and gawped.

Then I checked my phone, all of two seconds, and when I returned, the splendour was less, still splendid but somehow normal, and the irresistible wonder had also passed, the invisible door closed.

'BE HERE NOW,' the world had shouted at me.

I sat bolt upright. I silently pleaded with the world to rewind, give me back that feeling, that siren-like magic.

I chucked the phone on the dashboard, turned the key and hurried along the road past layby after layby full of holiday people and locals parked to fish off the rocks until, at last, at what seemed a massive distance, I reached an empty layby close to a beach. I parked, jumped out to check I was in right then parked again. It was ten feet at the most from the busy road in the area. No matter. I got out the folding chair and set it down behind the van. Then I sat. Being, here, now.

It was utterly magnificent. The sea was almost flat calm but not quite. The swell rolled over the hidden rocks and shooshed. So I shooshed too. I shooshed the noise in my head. I shooshed the noise in my body that fussed and fiddled and wanted the best spot and the quietest. Sit and be, I told myself, on my red stripy chair. Sit. Sit still. Be still.

Be. Here. Now.

The birds I'd thought were missing reappeared: a laughing gull argued with some oystercatchers; five little brown birds streaked by and swooped along the beach, too fast for my binoculars. LBJs my mother calls them, Little Brown Jobs, because there are so many similar species and they're impossible to distinguish from one another. A large family gathering of eider ducks arrived, last seen at my beloved Machrihanish stop several miles down the coast. Quite a day out, surely, for them. This is the joy of binoculars. You get right up close. It is a kind of spying. And the great thing about watching seabirds is they're not hiding in trees, teasing you with beautiful songs, but right out in the open for you to see. A lone gull near the shore was standing in the seaweed with water up to his bum, perhaps enjoying the hot/cold sensation as the waves lapped in and out.

I, on the other hand, covered myself in suncream then covered up altogether. Despite the mist and various lingering clouds, the sun was hot and there were plenty of surfaces from which it could magnify its effect. Then I wrote about being, here, now. A gull-like cry from the south echoed against the cliffs to the north and west. A herring gull headed towards the cliffs then drifted back, hovering, still on the warm updraught. A peewit raised the alarm as several lorries, vans and cars roared past. A plane buzzed in the distant heights, flying straight out to sea and America. A ferry crossed to Islay probably twenty miles north of me, shimmery in the heat haze, but its engine noise arrived at my stripy chair loud and clear. A wagtail bobbed and bounced across the pebbled beach. The sea changed colour as the mist thinned out, reflecting the pale blue sky, then the clouds, then blue sky again.

I thought *I may finally be here now*. After those days of worry.

A bird I'd never seen before landed on a stem of grass. It bounced a few seconds then fluttered off. The shadow of a seagull crossing the rocks alerted me to its presence. A lamb and ewe were calling to each other in the field behind. The eider family came inshore amongst the rocks and seaweed, paddled about then drifted back out to sea. There were eleven of them, all different sizes. Bands of wind began to come in, darkening the sea.

The engine noise throbbed louder. Now I could see the ferry more clearly, the red and yellow of CalMac, the main ferry company, on its side. The oystercatchers were arguing again. The lone gull floated lazily in the water but occasionally stopped to poke at something in the shallows.

I went inside the van for relief from the heat. There were birds on the roof, one of which was silhouetted on the skylight. Birds of a feather. I thought of signs I could stick on the back of my van:

Cow took wing mirror – limited visibility.
Mavis's Shoe and *Rue End Street* on sale here.
Free tea to cyclists and walkers.
Be here now.

(Un)fortunately I had no printer or marker pens. But I could get them. It wasn't important to examine the practicalities or sense of this idea at that moment; I could think it through later. The birds flew off the roof so I opened both skylights and tied the van door open for a through draught. I stayed inside and watched the light, like oil on the water, and cooled myself down.

Then I went back out to my chair and watched a heron struggle by, awkward but determined in its flight. Its beautiful long neck was pulled in and it lurched about trying to keep its large self airborne. They're so much more elegant when stalking fish. But then I saw that there were several gulls in tow who swooped and lunged and I realised the heron had a fish hanging in its mouth. The gulls gave chase, harassing it from all sides while the heron dodged right and left before finally dipping behind a rock followed by a cloud of grey and white. My heart beat fast for a long moment. I stood for a better view but saw nothing, heard only the occasional squeal of the gulls as they rose and fell, first one, then others. Probably half a second later, you know how time stands still, the heron rose, flapping its giant wings, its long neck receding again as it gained the sky. Unharmed, it seems, and no longer impeded by gull or fish, it continued on its way. All in a day's work.

The duck family were going south again, maybe down to the bay beyond Machrihanish. The oystercatchers lifted like dust from a cushion but screaming blue murder at each other, then landed again further down the beach. All facing to sea, they were many replicas from the same cast.

The shooshing sea was more insistent then, but there was no need. My heart had slowed and I watched dark bands of wind on the surface move closer to each other and merge, the sunlight pushing through the fuzz of cloud, burning it off like drops of water on a hot stove.

This was all that mattered and even that didn't matter. I felt calm and sustained, and as if I belonged, as if I'd arrived home. I was at last free and unburdened.

Fertile Swamp

If I can't go off in the van for any reason, I have to find other ways to get down to the task of writing. One method is to get up before dawn (and anyone who might be at home), make tea and bring the laptop back to bed. It usually works. As long as I actually do it and don't just roll over and go back to sleep when the alarm goes, I'll plough through loads of work. It's an odd mixture of hard work and indulgence, but writing can be hard work, so why not be comfy?

On one occasion I'd been in bed most of the day wrestling with certain literary problems with this book (I'm aware this sounds weird) and with some success. It had been a tough day. I was also longing for the following Thursday, three days away, when I could go off in the van and give my book the focus it deserved without the demands of home life. I'd even found someone to look after the cat, paid for it and everything. Yay! Then a call came from the garage to say they couldn't sort the electrical problem (which they'd created a month earlier) until next week. This was the same electrical problem that eventually resulted in me going to the Clachtoll campsite in Assynt. However: no electrics = no laptop charge = no writing in van = no trip. This is how I saw it. The following Thursday was the only gap in commitments I had. My world fell apart.

I barked at my daughters, paced up and down the hall, and seethed in my helplessness. It was an ugly sight. I made calls to everyone with entries under 'campervan' or 'motorhome' on Yell.com, but to no avail. At the time I lived in an old house which often required attention. Again, I was looking at spending yet more of my valuable writing time FIXING STUFF.

Drat and double drat.

I was inconsolable. I am ashamed of how much this shook me and I have no idea why this practical turn of events had quite such breathtaking power. But I knew I had to get out.

Dear God

Please …

So I took my van to the new super-duper car wash round the corner so that whoever was going to fix this electrical problem would think I was a clean citizen of this world and therefore worthy of their help. The car wash was oddly soothing, as if it was me having the bubble bath and not the van. My mind began to clear along with the windscreen, and I remembered a couple of fleeting ideas I'd had for the chapter I was writing, or trying to, and scribbled them into the notebook. I had brought with me Rebecca Solnit's book *A Field Guide to Getting Lost*, which seemed a promising title. I so wanted to get lost, physically and metaphorically, but somehow getting lost takes more concentration than I had that day. On the second page I found this: 'Leave the door open for the unknown, the door into the dark. That's where the most important things come from, where you yourself came from, and where you will go.'

Ah, so that's what I was doing. That's why I often get uptight when I'm about to go on a campervan trip. I'm going into the dark of the unknown, the dark of my very existence, the dark of all our existences; and it's where I came from and where I'll return to. My birth and my death, also yours and everybody else's. Well, that was alright then. That I could accept. Freaking out in the face of such enormity was perfectly understandable (but I went home at full speed to apologise to my daughters).

Rebecca Solnit's door to the unknown is reminiscent of the door I imagined I was accidentally peeking through on the road in Kintyre when I saw the indescribable sea. The electrifying night-sky I glimpsed through my actual campervan back door in Cowal was like that too, as if I'd been let in on the secret of existence. Trying to get into the Zone often has that sense of seeking out and opening a door to something clandestine which is only there for the initiated.

But I think there are two doors, one which is the cultivation of an inner openness to all experience, and a second which is more elusive, not to mention evasive. Some people might describe it as contacting God. The first can be worked on, but the second feels like it has some magic attached to it. It seems you can't consciously search and find it but only stumble upon it like a tree root hidden under leaves in a forest. Like the wardrobe entrance to Narnia, it just happens when you're busy with something else. It brings new meaning to John Lennon's statement that 'Life is what happens when you're busy making plans.'

Similarly, while writing can undoubtedly be demanding work, sometimes great phrases or ideas arrive by accident. The trick is to notice and recognise their worth despite their being thrown up from a dark swamp.

One day I was standing on the beach at Ronachan, place of seals, where the A83 first hits the coast in Kintyre. It was a windless day with a flat silvery sea of pastel marine. Peachy light shimmered where the haze allowed the sunlight through. No-one else was in the car park so I had the beach, fort and rocks all to myself, and the sea stretched out like glass all the way to Islay and Jura. Making sure you arrive physically and emotionally is the most deliberate you can be about transcending that door or finding the secret root in the forest and being able to appreciate its wonder. You can only facilitate. While I was at Ronachan, I wrote a piece about being properly awake in the wilderness, by which I mean the wild-ness of the natural world which is quietly going on around us all the time. The original version was written for an experimental collaborative collection between a number of writers, some visual artists and a few musicians. The project was published as *Triangle* in 2008.

If I stand here long enough I'll be like that boulder with
the sand sucked round it. Perhaps the seaweed will stick to
me like waxy hair, like Thompson and Thomson in *Tintin
on the Moon*. I could stand too long, fall from exhaustion
and die as my head hits the boulder I want to be like.

If I carry a small rock to the edge of that drop, tie a
rope between it and my neck, and jump with the rock
cradled in my arms, a deafening splash will race
across these still waters in ripples and sound waves,
sending shocks of seagulls shrieking into the air.
But I have no wish to disturb the peace.

If I step beyond the sea-line that creeps and bulges its way
up the sand, I could slide the water over me like an old silk
dress and swim towards the opposite shore and, calculating
I'll have fifteen minutes on a good day before
my blood freezes over and my strength is gone, I'll still be in
the Gulf Stream when I sink, my body breaking up
between here and Scapa Flow.

If I watch the gannet swoop and dive, a fish bucking in
its mouth as it takes to the air, I will know the careless trade
of life and be thankful for my choices
as I tiptoe home for tea.

Death and danger are everywhere. You can drown in a cup of tea, for goodness' sake. Large quantities of water featuring dangerous currents and extreme cold are life-threatening if you don't understand them. I'm keen on staying alive but, as Muriel Spark pointed out, in considering death it is sometimes easier to see through that door to the mysteries of life. The sea had been mesmerisingly beautiful or profound or something else which words feel inadequate to cover. I sometimes think I could become so absorbed that I'd forget myself completely and only return to consciousness to find I'm out there on the Gulf Stream floating and sinking, bobbing and turning and sinking again to the bottom with my eyes wide open and full of wonder at all the strange fishes under there.

I'm fooling, of course, but perhaps I'd better get back to shallower water.

Sometimes we talk about the need for immersion in a project, or even submersion. There is something about being completely swamped by a piece of work which is quite delicious. I don't just mean the Zone. I mean when I'm so involved in a project that I'm fully engrossed even when I'm not actively working on it, as in tapping keys. Akin to sleeping on a problem, a piece of work may be sitting in my awareness for swathes of my day. I will appear 'distracted' and may have the same conversation more than once simply because I wasn't fully there when I had it the first time, or even the second. I often feel lost, or bereft even, if there is a project I want to get back to but can't for whatever reason, like eating, sleeping or being polite to the window cleaner. I can't concentrate on what's going on around me. I lose things, like the special ring my daughters gave me for my first Christmas without my husband. I've mentioned the almost physical pain I felt while trying to paint when my kids were wee and how I gave up in the end. I can't give up writing because writing is what I do, so this same pain, which I still experience when taken from my work, simply has to be endured.

Flannery O'Connor, the American writer, put it best: 'Writing a novel is a terrible experience, during which the hair falls out and the teeth decay. I'm always irritated by people who imply that writing fiction is an escape from reality. It is a plunge into reality and it's very shocking to the system.' A dunk in the sea off Kintyre.

My kids joke that I have early dementia, but I know I have a book to write.

They aren't entirely wrong. Not that I have dementia, but there is something alarming and dangerous about this state of mind, which causes considerable brain overload akin to a temporary madness. I have ideas in the middle of a conversation with the guy who wants to fix the roof and suddenly I'm an empty shell staring blankly at him while I try desperately to store these ideas in my head. It seems rude to say, 'Hang on 'til I write down this thing which is nothing to do with what you've been saying for the last five minutes.' Or I worry I'll forget something vitally important like emptying the cat litter for five days or not walking into the ocean. The people I care about prey on my mind: bereaved friends, daughters moving house, my elderly mother, sick friends or just happy friends who want my company. When I'm submerged, all those little phone calls or get-togethers that would mean a lot to them, all have to wait.

While visiting the lovely Kames Hotel in Cowal recently, I saw a ghost. Or I saw a man in a green-and-white check shirt sitting in the otherwise empty bar as I passed through looking for the manager. He smiled at me. The thought passed through my mind that he wasn't really there and when I turned back and looked again, sure enough he wasn't. A friend later suggested I needed a psychiatrist. I think my friend needs an imagination. And I'd say two things. First, we don't know for sure whether ghosts exist and though it seems unlikely, I've heard too many stories in the counselling room after bereavements (and experienced some myself) that mean I can't rule ghosts out altogether. Secondly, in my distracted writing state, it can sometimes be hard to differentiate between what I'm imagining and what I'm physically seeing. There was another man in the Kames Hotel in a different room which I had passed through to get to the bar. He was wearing a similar shirt but in black and white. I wondered if I was confused. But when I went back and looked at this other very real man, he was most definitely there having his coffee and cake at the window. He was different in every aspect apart from the checks on his shirt, that's to say weight, colouring and demeanour.

This was scary. Was I losing my marbles? I scampered up to my room to consider. Then, having retreated, it was too late to go back to the bar and check. The night before, people had been talking about a local man who had recently passed away. I had no way of knowing what he looked like and it would have been insensitive now to ask. And I'd have looked foolish. Clearly there had just been a man in the bar who had moved fast, and silently, and probably through a trap door, surely.

Perhaps he was a ghost with a story to tell. Then again, he might not have been important at all. Equally, he could have been a new central character appearing from the swamp of my imagination. He was green, after all ...

Being open to my imagination made it difficult to tell what had really happened. When it came down to it, I realised it didn't matter what I'd seen, whether he was real, a ghost or a figment of my imagination. I was also sure I wasn't the first person to pass through a metaphysical doorway in a bar. All that mattered was getting back in the van, going to the sea, opening the actual back door and writing. The man accompanied me for the rest of the day in my thoughts. I asked him what he was doing there but he just maintained his enigmatic smile.

All of this makes me a complete pain in the backside to

live with or be near at certain stages of writing. I must register my gratitude to all the friends and family who put up with me on a daily basis and who probably sigh with relief when I go. Really we'd all be better off if I'd just go away in the campervan and leave everyone in peace.

Parallel Process

I've noticed that life doesn't move forward in an orderly fashion. Obviously it begins with birth and ends with death, but everything in between seems to run in circles and at tangents and is rarely what you expect. This is also my experience of writing books, especially this one.

I began writing it in the van. Having started, I then decided I wanted to write *all* of it in the van. This seemed like a good thing to be able to say at some future event or on the back cover. Then, to my great inconvenience, I discovered that I couldn't write it anywhere else. When I'm sitting at the fold-down table with the kettle whistling and a green hillside beyond the window, great washes of memories and ideas come flooding in. Family, elderly cats, the weather, day jobs, van repairs and so on have kept me at home, and this has meant the book has taken much longer to write than I'd originally anticipated. I also thought I ought to visit new parts of Scotland in order to make the book more interesting instead of writing about places I already knew were fantastic, which is a tiny bit counterintuitive. Whatever, off I went on my next trip, north instead of west.

Often after a trip I realise the mood of the excursion has mirrored the process of the writing. If I understand what's happening at the time, I can take some control of it, perhaps by letting go of control, but often I'm too engrossed in trying to make the trip work to notice.

The concept of 'parallel process' in the title of this chapter comes from the counselling world. It means when client and counsellor are dealing with, or 'processing', similar emotional material. Counsellors are human too and suffer losses, have hang-ups and get angry just like everyone else. Sometimes, necessarily, these coincide with the losses, hang-ups and anger of their clients. As long as the counsellor makes sure there is no actual or damaging crossover during the counselling session, in other words she or he doesn't start acting out on the client, both parties can learn from each other and benefit. The counsellor can use their understanding of their own issues to benefit the client and the client's experience will further the understanding of the counsellor. This is parallel process. Most counsellors engage an 'external supervisor' to help them keep a check on such things, which keeps both client and counsellor safe.

What is the relevance here? There is only one of me, and no-one with whom to be parallel. This is true, but I have a split personality while I'm in the van. I'm a writer but I'm always someone else too, perhaps the writer's minder, or a recluse, a mourner, a layabout or an escapee. In fact we are all many more people than just a writer, accountant or parent, for example, and I much prefer the Gaelic way of putting it: 'There is a writer in me.' There is also a dancer, an organiser, a driver, a mother and many other versions of me as well. As you'd expect with a room full of people, sometimes those different personas don't get on, or they work beside each other but don't pay much attention to what their neighbour is saying.

During the trip to Loch Cluanie, where I encountered the French Canadians in their Ducato, I thought my inner colleagues were barely speaking. It turned out they were secretly working in perfect harmony, feeding each other with their various trials and tribulations, but I didn't realise this until later.

I set off early one summer evening, as I often do to avoid heavy traffic and take advantage of the long evenings. It was delightful to have the open road to myself, especially one that's usually chocka. I was already in that alone place as soon as I hit the road, and as I drove, my mind wandered through this book searching for the best place to start in the morning, like my gran laying out the breakfast table the night before. Crianlarich and Tyndrum flashed past and I climbed the hill, came over the top into the long slow descent towards Bridge of Orchy, then on across the grand expanse of Rannoch Moor, through Glencoe with its steep descents, caves and tourists lingering in car parks, and on towards Fort William and the Great Glen. As darkness began to fall, I started looking for a quiet spot to stop for the night.

It's better to do this earlier in the evening, especially if you don't know the road well or have never examined it before from the point of view of discreet overnight parking places. Darkness falls surprisingly quickly and with it your peace of mind.

Loch Cluanie means 'meadow loch', according to the Ward Lock guide to Scottish place names which would suggest this deserted glen was once populated and farmed and not just peopled by sheep or deer. Perhaps the old steadings are now submerged beneath the reservoir itself or maybe they were 'cleared' a whole century earlier than the hydroelectric scheme was built.

I parked just off the road that runs along the glen. There hadn't been another car for several miles when I stopped. The silence seemed absolute and oddly permanent until the wee small hours when I began to be disturbed by occasional cars. The road was only a few feet away. As daylight seeped through the curtains, more cars arrived and departed at regular and increasingly frequent intervals, then in blocks with no intervals, then, once full daylight had arrived, in weirdly regular patterns. The first batch was fifteen or so sports cars identical in shape but in a variety of colours; then a few of the giantest lorries you ever did see; another block of sports cars, again identical in shape but all different hues; a general mix of cars, vans and the lorries; twenty motorbikes, mostly black; another mixed batch; twenty identical sports cars, and so on. Proportionally to its size the road was as busy as the M8, the busy motorway that runs across Scotland's central belt.

The little car park filled and emptied with reassuring regularity too, each group of visitors providing something to satisfy my curiosity and my need to create stories about everything I see. Some arrived for breakfast or lunch, rooting about in boots for thermoses and plastic plates, while others took a quick snapshot and left, sometimes without even getting out of their vehicles.

Meanwhile, I gazed at the cupboard in which my laptop hid and trembled. You'll have noticed I often have difficulty getting started.

I decided to keep notes, a journal of the journey so that I might find something of interest from which to pluck gems later. Journaling is not something that comes naturally to me because it feels like writing letters to myself. So I can't really see the point. Most people would disagree with this, I know. Uncharacteristically, however, I was soon absorbed in my notebook, scribbling down total drivel, but having a lot of fun.

Then, to ease my overexcited mind, I tried something practical. This is the Mars bar principle I learnt from my piano teacher along with playing my scales. Variety is the spice of life and diversity of occupation is also a great tool for writers to help them stay mentally fresh. I set about fixing odds and ends in the van.

In the not too distant past I had spent a couple of days at the Wigtown Book Festival. I parked in a field full of vehicles, reassured by the presence of two other campervans. When I returned from the last event of the day, my little white van was completely alone, gleaming brightly in the dark. The following day, in a field full of sunshine, I realised how scruffy it looked. A previous owner had pierced the sides in several places while attaching shelves inside above the windows. There was also a multitude of unsightly cracks in the bodywork, though none structurally serious. I had brought some fibreglass fixing stuff which I then applied to these holes using a plastic fork. It was a warm day. The stuff was utterly unwieldy, impossible to flatten, and a fleshy pink. It also dried with alarming rapidity into peaks which refused to go down. The field was surrounded by houses and gradually filling up with cars. I felt not a little foolish.

A few months later, somehow forgetting the inside of Vanessa Hotplate was already covered in butterflies (this was before her designer revamp), I ordered a pack of brightly coloured sticky-on butterflies to cover these flesh-coloured blobs and spent a happy half-hour by Loch Cluanie choosing the brightest and positioning them over the damage. Vanessa was transformed. Sadly this didn't last because they faded before the end of the summer.

These practical distractions facilitated another couple of hours of writing drivel until suddenly the road-buzz became intolerable. But where to go next? It pays to have a reasonably firm plan in any endeavour, one that can be adapted if need be, and an obvious forward direction. Novel writing is the same. Campervan writing is not exempt. My plan was a bit vague, a tad hippy-dippy, like the new appearance of my van. I was going where the mood took me, which meant nowhere. I was in danger of being a *lepidoptera papilionoidea*, a butterfly flitting about willy-nilly. This may seem like it's ok and is all part of the fun but, in reality, floating in such uncertainty is a pretty uncomfortable, albeit necessary, part of writing.

It's probably a stage in most creative ventures. Except I was talking about that van trip, wasn't I? Sometimes the journey and the writing intermingle in my head, all things parallel.

In a practical sense, the anxiety of not knowing where the next safe stopping point is or where a water supply can be found can distract from the very important business of getting words down. Van trips and writing, but especially writing can involve a sense of disorientation which can be quite nauseous. Most people think it's just fun all the way. I'm afraid not. Like any job that is challenging there are moments of dizzying doubt and confusion, often followed by tentative moves towards resolution, a smidgeon of progress and delight, then more doubt and confusion as I move on to the next decision. I sometimes think writing is just a series of decisions, some of which have terrible consequences for my characters or plotline. It's the *soupçon* of pleasure that makes the whole recipe work.

The prospect was north along this busy road in a slow vehicle amidst racing traffic. Hmm. I needed a quiet road. The problem with Scotland is the mountains. You have to get round them, rarely over and never through (apart from 'the Dark Tunnel' on the Union Canal). There is usually only one road for everyone, from push-bikes to little campervans to juggernauts. I phoned my husband. We had, again, just started talking. He told me about the beautiful, winding, partly single-track road from Shiel Bridge to Glenelg, where he had been the year before and where there were fantastic views to be found. Beautiful, winding, good views and single-track? That'd do me. I had a rough plan for that night at least. It was a start.

Being married to an engineer meant we had many conversations about the pros and cons of planning creative projects, or whether just getting started and meandering was enough. Obviously as a scientist he favoured rigorous planning, and I do know writers whose plans for ninety-thousand-word novels run to thirty-thousand words in themselves. I also know an engineer who writes. This other engineer plans everything about his novel or short story, and I mean everything, in his head before putting any words down at all. I know writers who just start writing whatever comes into their heads and carry on from there, and I've read many writers whose work suggests there was no effort at all involved in the writing. These people usually turn out to have worked the hardest at their plan and also the execution of their project. That's exactly how they make it appear so easy.

Basically, everyone works differently.

I plan things like character, setting, themes and colours, and I'll plan scenes, usually by having an image or idea to work them around. I do this mostly in my head and only a little on paper. Putting things on paper often kills the process of exploration going on in my head. The trick for me is to catch thoughts as they pass, like those butterflies, and store them in short phrases or sentences. In any brainstorming session, I don't risk interrupting my thoughts to store them until I have worked the idea through in some depth. I use the notebook lightly and often, and keep to the subject or subjects. I mark notes with 'SHORT STORY' or 'CAMPERVAN' or whatever so they are easy to find again when I'm lost for inspiration. These are more likely to be ideas rather than any serious planning.

To many people, this gazing into space and putting almost nothing on the page probably looks like no planning at all. Planning, for most folk, means plot if it's fiction or chapter headings if it's nonfiction. At this dreaming stage, I may or may not have more than the bare bones of the plot.

I once observed my visual artist brother build up a drawing using a combination of pencils, pastels and watercolours. He laid down blocks of colour then more layers, gradually adding in detail. What at first appeared to be an abstract piece began to take on the known shapes of the real world. It became obvious that he had seen in his mind how the detail would fit in before he laid down even the first section of colour wash. I had seen him paint many times, and often been his subject, but I had never really witnessed so closely this channel between what was in his head and what arrived on the paper. This was not a photographically realistic painting in which arguably you are copying directly from reality. He was employing artists' tricks to set mood, tone and emphasis, to bring certain objects to the fore and push others back, and to draw attention to one object at the expense of others. I was amazed to see the final image suddenly shine out as the final touches were laid down.

This was long before I started writing, although I was already keeping notebooks, but I made a mental note of this. Now that I write lengthy pieces like novels I see that this is often how I plan, with washes and themes, gradually building up the final picture. Much later, I reach a point where I need to get stuff down so that I can test whether it works. For instance, I might put my two part-rounded characters into a situation and see how they behave. As with friends who have never met, you can't really know whether the chemistry between them will work until you try it. Of course, like any new relationship, they may take time to get to know each other. Often I write a fun scene for them then lose it for the finished novel because it was only a 'getting acquainted' exercise.

Preparing to write a novel is a combination of planning and going with the flow. Focus and precision come later with the writing, and then much later again, the editing.

Perhaps this method derives from indecision in a job which requires decisiveness, but I prefer to think of it as the uncomfortable process of invention. Margaret Atwood has a great quote on this. She compares writing to 'wrestling a greased pig in the dark'. This startling image rings true for me, not least because it is close to how I have long described my work as a person-centred counsellor. I'd switch the pig for an oiled exercise ball. My job, in maintaining appropriate and sustained focus and so on without the interference of my own life and influences, was not to grab the ball but to balance on top of it. Writing is somehow much more challenging and painful. Margaret Atwood's idea of grappling with something hysterical, violent, slippery and dangerously evasive that you can't even see, sums up the agony of the writer trying to nail a project. It is the source of the nauseous disorientation. The trip to Cluanie and Glenelg was causing me a similar queasiness.

My way of counterbalancing all this confusion is to make attempts at being disciplined. Getting up at the crack of dawn, or before, is usually good, then doing everything possible to keep going for as long as possible. Sometimes I just have to admit I'm beat, but usually there are tricks I can employ to make this happen. For instance, if I'm on a first draft, I have to write a thousand words before I stop. Sometimes I'll write three thousand, other times I'll be struggling at eight hundred. In that case, I'll make myself find another two hundred words and shove any old thing onto the page just so I can stop. The next day these forced words may be the best or the worst and may need to be kept or removed accordingly, but the same is true of the easy three thousand. Hemingway said you should only stop when you know what the next bit is going to be, so that it's easy to start again in the morning. I find this a good idea but difficult in practice. On this particular trip, I had no plan of action for either the trip or the writing. There was no obvious way to proceed. Therefore road noise and other things which seem more interesting or fun than writing had become distractions. Grappling with greased pigs or oiled exercise balls requires a serious amount of focus. Lack of focus makes the journey, literary or actual, more difficult to relax into and just enjoy. I was getting nowhere in particular.

Counselling and writing, as I do them, have many similarities. I approach them both with the notion that everyone has their own profound logic to what they do. Therefore we all have redeeming features but also the capacity for wrongdoing. I like this quote from Christopher Isherwood: 'I am a camera with its shutter open, quite passive, recording, not thinking. Recording the man shaving at the window opposite and the woman in the kimono washing her hair. Some day, all this will have to be developed, carefully printed, fixed.'

This seems about right, recording not thinking. However, the sense of camera doesn't always come easily to me. It usually arrives with a later draft when I've climbed down off my soapbox and removed all the emotional stuff of my own which is not relevant to the story.

This is the parallel process idea and the necessity for counsellors not to act out their own concerns in the counselling room. Like Isherwood's inner camera, a good person-centred counsellor reflects back to her client that person's inner world. She does this without embellishment because her job is to help the client understand their own particular and peculiar inner world, not her own. Therefore the counsellor has to listen carefully. I try to listen carefully to the people who appear in my books so that they can grow wings and become their own fully formed characters. They should be quite distinct from myself, with their own moral codes and feelings.

In all this discussion I have left my actual self on the tiny road to Glenelg, an exciting but treacherous road if ever there was one, and to which we must now return. The road does indeed wind its single-tracked way up the mountain, turning at such a degree you half-expect to meet yourself coming back, and climbing at so high a gradient I thought the van would fall over backwards. Even there the traffic is much heavier than anticipated but halfway up I found out why. A large sign said 'Mam Ratagan' and a gap opened between the trees to a stony car park and some picnic benches. Mam Ratagan is not someone's grumpy gran. According to *Scotland for the Motorist*, mam means 'a large, round or gently rising hill' and a rathad is a road, so Mam Ratagan is 'the large hill road'. Which has a beautiful simplicity and amply describes where I was.

I pulled in and was immediately breathless and slightly dizzy at the view. It was nothing short of magnificent with vistas across Loch Duich to a whole range of hills at the other side, up the valley to Morvich and over to the Five Sisters Mountains. The ground fell away almost immediately and disappeared into woods and down to the loch. There was even a beam of light coming down through puffy clouds from God Almighty on high. Again I had a mild sense of vertigo, that if I leant too far forward to see down the hill I'd probably tumble head over heels into the loch below. The day was still bright and warm, so once I'd had my fill of gazing and gasping, I got out my notebook and perched at one of the picnic tables to continue my joyful scribbling, occasionally gazing through binoculars to the other side and sipping tea from a proper china cup as is only appropriate in a little old campervan. Smug with my mug. I was only slightly alarmed when some overseas tourists pointed their camera at my van while I was in there making my second cup.

I know the mountains I saw are the Five Sisters because one of the visitors to the Cluanie-side car park earlier was a tourist guide with four charges. I took a sneaky photo of him in my wing mirror to remind myself because I found his enthusiasm for passing on the joys of his country endearing and mildly exaggerated, which made me laugh. It must have been nice to show people round with the sun shining. This same group appeared halfway up Mam Ratagan and I took the opportunity to avail myself of his local knowledge and quiz him about which petrol stations nearby might sell LPG gas. Vanessa is a dual-fuel machine and runs on both gas and petrol. The petrol gauge was faulty and anyway I preferred gas for environmental reasons, plus it's cheaper. I had spotted a petrol station through the binoculars, but unfortunately it didn't sell LPG. Broadford on Skye was the nearest.

The rest of the Glenelg road was green and undulating, the long fertile valley it eventually passed through like the Shire of Tolkien's hobbits. A river meandered along the flat bottom beside fields while the road clung to the northern slopes of the valley. There was a surprising number of houses and I wondered why I'd never known about this beautiful valley before.

Finally, arriving in Glenelg, I observed one of my principal rules of campervanning which is to get as close to the sea as you possibly can. In this instance I parked *on* the beach and close to a small number of unoccupied caravans. The beach was stony so this was possible. It seemed a daring thing to do, offensive even to others, but a sign nearby confirmed parking was ok by offering clear advice on what I mustn't do there – don't leave rubbish or pee – which I already knew, thanks.

It was a spectacular but weirdly oppressive spot and the place where, the following day, I would wake to discover my leaking toilet. In the meantime, I decided to make contact with my family and explore my surroundings while I was at it, so I set off along the shore towards the village.

There was no signal whatsoever, and as I walked back feeling small and lonely, I thought about my husband who had also come to this spot alone. The beach did not feel like a happy place, which was confusing in itself. I wanted to leave, but this strangeness had also made me sleepy. Even scribbling didn't come easily. I went to bed early and woke too soon.

The following morning there was the *terrible stink* and I quickly realised my toilet was leaking. I packed up in double-quick time and arrived at the Glenelg Ferry for Skye at seven o'clock, excited by the prospect of getting the hell out. There was the added bonus of the ferry being run by the community. Unfortunately a large notice informed me the first ferry was at ten o'clock. Had I been in a better frame of mind, and without a hideous mess within my bunker, I might have stayed and watched the early morning mist evaporate, listened to the birds and written a chapter or two of this book. I wasn't and there was, so I hot-wheeled all the way back up Mam Ratagan, down the other side, through Shiel Bridge, past the garage with no gas, over the sea to Skye (via the Bridge) and all the way to Broadford.

It seemed significant that at every stop on this trip there was a cuckoo calling. Perhaps cuckoos were thriving that year or maybe it was their time of year to mate. Either way, I felt accused. What did I think I was doing? I had no idea, but it was definitely cuckoo.

In Broadford the LPG pump was horizontal. For non-gas users who might not know, LPG pumps look similar to petrol ones but with different nozzles. Being recumbent was not good. The cheerful attendant told me there was gas in Portree as well but that their pump was also broken. If they're both broken, I thought, maybe someone could fix them?

My frustration was building. Not only had I not so much as lifted the laptop out of its cupboard, I had barely thought about it. Multiple practical problems were developing. As well as the broken toilet and hardly any gas, the faulty petrol gauge meant I couldn't tell if the tank was full or empty. I had never used petrol for any length of time so I had no sense of how big the tank was and therefore how far I could travel between the far-flung petrol stations of the north. This meant my only option was south where I knew where the LPG pumps were. Meanwhile I'd have to rely on frequent top-ups of petrol, and a petrol can for emergencies.

It was all getting too much. Home would have been nice but I didn't let myself even think the thought.

Suddenly I needed a friend. I'd intended going to Glenuig to visit her later in the week, but sooner would have to do. This involved another ferry back to the mainland. I was fast approaching the completion of a circle. On arrival I found my friend comatose on her bed with a migraine. She was projectile vomiting high-vis yellow bile into a filthy towel and unable to hold down even a sip of water. Her dog sat in the next room with a worried look. I had never witnessed my friend's migraines before, in fact I'd never seen anything like this, and was alarmed. It is a terrible thing to be so helpless in the face of such suffering and not know how it will end.

But through the fug of her illness, she insisted there was nothing I could do, that it would pass in its own time, and could I bring her another towel? She fell asleep again. She has always told me there is nothing to be done but wait, but it was extremely hard to follow orders in these circumstances and leave her in peace. So I sat at the picnic table outside and checked on her condition every twenty minutes. She told me afterwards she didn't remember my arrival and our conversation at all and was unaware of my sneaking in to check on her.

Out on the bench the sun was beaming down. I got out my notebook and wrote. I wrote all afternoon. Perhaps it was more parallel process with my friend, but I vomited hundreds of words onto the page as I moved round the circular picnic table chasing the sun. Bees were buzzing in her colourful garden and at the bottom of the hill her pigs were snorting and churning up the ground. Blue tits, finches, thrushes and blackbirds were calling between the eaves of her various outhouses and the trees. Busy, busy. I berated my lack of proper 'work', my lack of focus on this trip, my inability to help my friend, my helplessness around her croft where there is always something to be done, and in summary, my general lack of progress in any direction whatsoever.

Fortunately, and with no medical intervention, her health recovered through the evening. She was tired the following morning but otherwise fine. Then, quite expectedly, I was lounging in jammies in a warm kitchen. I was swapping stories and having a laugh instead of suffering at the hard coalface of creativity. But this was not part of the plan. With a sigh, I abandoned all hope of more writing for the time being and concentrated on the toilet problem. Practicalities, as we've seen, are always a good antidote to the heady pleasures (and tortures) of writing. I wished my friend well and applied myself to finding a new Porta Potti.

The problem took me driving round further loops and tangents. I still couldn't contemplate giving up the trip, so I turned south for the open shores of Kintyre and the certainty of the familiar.

But Kintyre was a long way off and at the end of lots of winding roads which, while lovely in themselves, are tiring in an old van. This was especially when, at last, I just wanted to get down to the job in hand. I needed this trip to get easier. My adventure spirit and courage were exhausted. I took myself to a quiet layby surrounded by trees and had a little think.

I wanted to go home. It was a guilty thought but the possibility of giving up also appeared like a treat. I stared out at lovely Loch Awe for all of three seconds and started for Glasgow.

At the top of Rest And Be Thankful (or Fly And Be Happy if you're going downhill), I pulled into the picnic area for a final cup of tea from the burger van and watched the endless traffic ploughing up the hill through the rain. I chastised my lack of application to that great and apparently noble task of writing ... when suddenly I realised my face was in fact metaphorically blackened, my hands too which were calloused and bruised. My clothes were filthy and I was cold and wet, metaphorically and actually. I had the odd but very real sensation of having worked very hard and that this is a familiar feeling and one usually followed by a reward, if only being able to stop. It was like I had been writing for days but I couldn't go home triumphant because I felt I had little to show for all this hard work, only a few scribbled ideas of what I hoped to write about later, if I ever got my act together.

With a start, I realised this *is* the hard coalface of writing. I had come away to write, and to reconnect with that inner muse and all I seemed to have done is fret, or write about fretting, or fret about writing. But every bit of this is part of the process. It's like the wood and the trees you can't appreciate when you're amongst them but which turn out to be a thick forest of creative possibilities. I wondered whether all this time I'd been grappling a greased pig in a dark wood without even knowing it.

I reopened my notebook and realised I'd written the basis for the 'Campervan Love' chapter and half of 'Can You Fix It?' It was like the muse had got up in the night, stolen out to the forest, and written two whole chapters while I slept on in the van.

I came over all post-modern and felt rather proud of myself. I really had worked hard. It wasn't a pleasant trip but it was certainly interesting, complicated, varied, weird, disconcerting and, above all, remarkably productive. The whole thing had lasted five very intense days.

There, specifically, is your parallel process, various parts of me working hard in different ways towards the same end result, seeming to feed off each other but without letting 'me' know. The end result can be called many things but they are all bound up together in one bundle: satisfaction, peace of mind, processing difficult feelings, overcoming a challenge, and writing those chapters. Without my realising it, these various parts were more integrated within me than I had imagined.

In one final extra parallel, this chapter has proved the most difficult to write. I have meandered greatly and wandered in fields of doubt. Somehow the strange and difficult process that I lived through on the Loch Cluanie trip has seeped into the business of explaining it to you, including a sense of wonder and fulfilment that I have arrived at the end. On some trips, the wilderness is so potent I don't know what I've accomplished until the trip is over.

Time for tea and a walk.

Get Lost

It's not unusual for me to take a day to pack up and leave. Sometimes I become very anxious, often without realising it. Even before the difficult Loch Cluanie excursion, which was enough to put anyone off, I worried about everything working, whether I'd chosen the right destination or even if I should go at all. I fret about leaving something vital behind, or whether the solitude will be cathartic or miserable. The only thing to do, finally, is leave.

Similarly, there is a moment of indescribable agony which preludes many creative sessions. It may be fleeting or imposing. This is when I'm scaling the greased ball or looking for the oily pig in the dark with which to grapple. Perhaps the greater the agony, the more worthwhile the endeavour; it's hard to tell. Maybe I'm writing something ambitious which requires more thought. Therefore, I must give it the attention it deserves.

This means allowing a little wandering about in my head. There may be monsters and burning bushes in there, exotic dancers, lost souls or birds of fantastic plumage. These may be figurative or real and are likely to come with ridiculous, exaggerated or straightforward plots. They may jostle for my consideration. The thing which cries loudest could only be a distraction from the quietly fascinating story waiting its turn.

Sometimes this is not a pleasant place to be. It's alarming and full of self-doubt. All those negative derisory voices chime in, the ones we've all heard, voices of people who ridicule my efforts or offer faint praise, voices I've internalised and think I don't believe but actually in some small way do: these are the birds of prey hidden in the bushes.

At times like this I need distant support, people I can phone who (often unwittingly) remind me who I am and what I'm about. But I also need solitude. It is only by sticking with this inner wilderness and paying attention to it that some sense is made and a route through it is found, the richness of the landscape tapped. It is no coincidence that I find this most possible when I'm in an actual wilderness.

I try to remember that fears and doubts are only a matter of perception, and that they pass. I therefore actively see them off in good fashion. They are not helpful. Nothing interesting or innovative was ever done by paying heed to thoughts of this kind and I have many good examples to follow. Christ, for instance, went into the desert and lived in apparent torment before facing his greatest work. So did Siddharta Gautami, otherwise known as the Buddha, and Henry David Thoreau and Mahatma Gandhi.

By allowing some roving, the hope is my muse will find her way through it. This is one of the reasons writing often requires massive stamina, because there is an element of hard, sometimes spiritual work. Albert Einstein once said: 'It's not that I'm so smart, it's just that I stay with problems longer.' He was a nuclear scientist, not a writer, but the point is still well made.

The need for stamina is obvious with regard to novels, which take ages to write. I'm guessing it's true of all forms of writing, or indeed all art forms. It takes stamina to continually return, like the mindful Buddhist, to the still point, the Zone, or to listen closely to your inner muse for long periods of time. Nurturing that part of your existence can be a lifetime's work, as can combatting the negative birds of prey in the bushes.

Being present in the moment, fully alert and mindful, is vital but mindfulness and this kind of concentration take more than determination and stamina. They require courage too, the courage to confront the unknown in ourselves and to be open to our own inner craziness without trying to avoid it, change it or explain it away. At times it requires the kind of blind faith found in religions that leaves me cold. Religious blind faith would seem to be anathema to free thought and to exploring inner wildernesses. Trust in something that has worked for others, and more importantly trust in yourself and your daft ideas, works creatively, even if at times it seems like a direct pass to the asylum. Buddhism is the only 'religion' I'm aware of which supports this personal trust. I follow it as a philosophy rather than a religion because it requires no leaps of faith and is based on practical good sense and a deep understanding of the human condition.

However, this is not an argument for Buddhism. It's an argument for wilderness. It's not about nonsense such as 'trusting in the universe' either. People didn't get to the top of Everest by trusting the universe to provide either good weather or rescue teams. The faith I'm talking about is not external but about trusting that whatever bubbles to the surface of your inner quagmire you will deal with it, and also that whatever its nature, it is of value.

American writer, Rebecca Solnit, has written: '… to be lost is to be fully present, and to be fully present is to be capable of being in uncertainty and mystery.' She suggests this type of lostness is a conscious choice rather than something that has happened accidentally, a deliberate losing of oneself. She goes on to say: 'That thing the nature of which is totally unknown to you is usually what you need to find, and finding it is a matter of getting lost.'

Tricky one. Ye olde slippery pig.

It is much more difficult to get lost when you are surrounded by the practical demands of 'normal' daily, earning-your-living life, the feeding-the-family or fixing-the-toilet business. This is perhaps what I was trying to do on the round trip to Cluanie and Skye. I wanted to get lost but instead became bogged down with practicalities, and I was scared. But, of course, I was metaphorically lost. I just didn't know it. There were good reasons for being fearful and paying attention to practicalities, as is often the case. It was the tussle between practicalities and facilitating my inner wilderness that ultimately bore fruit. By the time I'd realised my folly and headed south towards Kintyre, I'd depleted my inner stamina and the best thing was to go home, regroup and feed my spirit. I had been lost in the wilderness and it was exhausting.

The difficulty is knowing when I am simply giving in to distraction, but this is the nature of wilderness. I have to be willing to risk being an idiot or lazy or stupid. I'm often all three and occasionally the explorer and writer in me get to be the hunter-gatherers of fascinating ideas. Again, the Buddhists are there with help. Luckily Buddhism is big on lists and they always make things easier. One of my favourite lists is the list of distractions. You can use it to check what's going on when you're not getting lost enough. Then, of course you have to scrub the list because the list itself so easily becomes the distraction. Am I making you dizzy?

Actually in Buddhism these distractions are generally known as 'hindrances' and you'll be pleased to know there are only five, though those five do cover a multitude of what Christians might call sins. They are known as the 'Five Mental Hindrances'. There is also a system of antidotes in the form of five specific meditations, each one designed to counter one of the five hindrances. In the hope it might prove useful, I offer you snippets of these because they sometimes help me stay on track. If they seem helpful, I suggest you read one of the specialist books in the bibliography for more information or contact a Buddhist group in your area.

The first mental hindrance is sensual desire. This includes

craving for sex, food, friends, lovers, material things or situations. It is a series of 'what ifs'. The human condition is characterised by a monkey in a fruit tree who climbs on and on seeing a better fruit on every next branch and never being satisfied with the one in its hand. A good antidote to this is the understanding that everything passes, everything fades and nothing stays for long. A desire that obsesses us today will be meaningless tomorrow. Therefore another good antidote is recognising the desire for what it is: a desire. This often diffuses its power and the sensation leaves us naturally.

Anger is the next mental hindrance and it has its antidote, obviously but not easily, in working on a sense of loving kindness towards other people and also towards ourselves because that's where most anger starts.

The third mental hindrance consists of 'sloth, torpor and boredom'. I love these words, which so onomatopoeically sum up that drowsiness that overwhelms us when we have a difficult task. This is an important hindrance to writing because … Oh dear, a pause in the writing. I'm laughing out loud here all by myself because immediately I'd written 'because' I wandered off to have a look at Facebook, then made more tea, sat down to check emails and finally painted my toenails bright blue. And all this in the face of the very limited time I have available to write just now. I am not writing this in the campervan because a storm was predicted for Kintyre today and because I know my house will be empty, apart from a rather demanding cat. Therefore the conditions for serious concentration, perhaps even some real submersion, are better than usual, *but extremely time-limited*. Painting toenails is never *ever* either necessary or urgent. If I'm not careful, I'll soon be going for that twenty-minute power nap which so easily slides into a full hour-and-a-half sleep cycle. And then it won't seem worth starting up again with only a few hours left of the day. All of this is complete nonsense, including the storm in Kintyre which could be avoided by the use of wheels to carry me to more sheltered parts of the peninsula until it passes. You see how this works?

It is true that good things sometimes come of such boredom and avoidance. I have knitted several jumpers. But such successes are designed (by absolutely no-one) to make the distraction activity seem more worthwhile than getting yourself lost in writing that novel. Sometimes, it's true, it's hard to tell when sleepiness is genuine or merely your body trying to stop you doing something difficult like facing the endless possibilities of the inner wilderness. My own personal motto for this is stolen from Nike (with whom I have no truck otherwise) and that is 'Just do it'. This is the antidote. Another antidote is 'Just stop doing it'. Perhaps it is the wrong thing to do. The point is all these displacement activities are easier (yes, even cable-knitting) than actually being with that inner space, the contents of which we suspect are not going to be good news. Actually we are just avoiding the truth which surely is more important than anything else. And if the truth is not worth writing about, I don't know what is. When boiled down, the antidote might be to face the truth.

The fourth hindrance is restlessness and worry. When confronted with the gates to the middle of everywhere, it is easy to allow other situations to become more pressing and more distressing. My trip to Kintyre while reading *Way of the Wanderers* is a case in point. A series of other scenarios, real and imagined, mine and those of others, toppled my equanimity to the point that I had to rescue myself from hindrance four (restlessness and worry) by being present in the 'now'. The next day I fell into hindrance three (sloth, torpor and boredom) and knitted most of a (admittedly very beautiful) jumper. I am only too capable of wandering from one hindrance to the next.

It is easy to lean on familiar ways and allow worries to infiltrate. It is also more than possible to actually create things to worry about in order to avoid the big wide silent space that is the inner wilderness. I am extremely skilled at this. What I need is perspective and the only way to get this is mindfulness. I stop and focus on my breath. This instantly brings the barrage of pointless thoughts to a standstill. Having done that, zooming out of my life and wondering how this small problem will look in ten years' time also helps. Don't forget the Pali word for mindfulness includes 'remembering'. That means remembering what's important and that mindfulness meditation is your direct route back to it.

The last mental hindrance is doubt. All projects worth their salt are likely to cause some level of doubt. The unknown is a place which you have not explored yet and has no proven worth. In some weird kind of way the antidote to this is similar to that for sensual desire: recognising doubt for what it is, observing its approach and how it operates but not getting involved in it. I try to employ some simple hands-off observation. I also try to have a rule whereby, if I've set myself a task or made a plan, I have to stick with it until a certain predetermined point. When I reach that point I can reassess the original idea and whether it works or not, then decide if it's still worth pursuing. Barriers of doubt are part of the process. They are only hurdles to be overcome and can prove to be rich seams of ideas.

But beware. When I first learned meditation I used to have all sorts of wonderful thoughts and ideas during every session. I could never retain them until after I'd finished, so they were mostly lost. This was how it seemed, anyway. To rescue some of these amazing insights, I put a notebook and pen beside the meditation cushion so that I could come out of the meditation for a second and capture these little gems as soon as they arrived, then dart back in. I can hear all the serious Buddhists I've ever known howling with laughter. (But come on guys, it was an innocent mistake.) Various things happened: first, these thoughts never seemed as good when I read them over after the meditation; second, they soon stopped arriving with any frequency; and third, I was so busy staying alert to their arrival that I lost all focus on the meditation. This is what you call a lose/lose/lose situation.

I didn't really believe this meditation thing was worth doing. I was holding other things as more important than the task in hand. I wasn't taking my meditation seriously enough. Hence the Zen laughter ringing round the walls, and the metaphorical whack across the back of my head.

This holds true for writing. I have to suspend all disbelief in the project until enough of it has been explored, then keep going well beyond that line, preferably to the point of the ridiculous. Then, if necessary, I can abandon it, or decide to carry on. Ridiculous is often good.

As well as observation, the antidote to doubt is a willingness to let go of the end result. It is a willingness to not know, to be lost in the wilderness. Do I repeat myself here? Apologies, but if you want to create anything real, meaningful and interesting, you need to get lost. This means learning to go with the flow without interrupting it. It means allowing the crazy thoughts in my mind to erupt onto its surface, observing them, and letting them pass so they can grow or wilt. Now, I'm amazed how much material I retain through my meditation, and how the good, the bad and the ugly sort themselves out quite naturally anyway, as they do in the film.

I once took an evening class in drawing and painting at Glasgow University. It was run by a woman called Irene Macneil whose philosophy was to always find something good in everyone's work, no matter what. Obviously this was good for confidence because it allowed me to fool myself that I had the teensiest wee bit of artistic talent. I learnt lots of new skills in visual art and practised them as best I could. The biggest and most important lesson Irene taught me was the value of letting go of the thing you have in your head and seeing where your work takes you of its own accord. She advocated treating every project as an experiment, not as a journey towards an end which is already predetermined, but an adventure in the possible. This was massively freeing. It no longer mattered if the finished painting was 'good' or not, and I had a lot more fun. In her own way, Irene was inviting me to wander. This often meant the end product was also better because it was valued for itself, not because it lived up to expectations.

Incidentally there's another parallel here with person-centred counselling. Research shows that when people begin to show more compassion towards themselves, they are also kinder and more accepting of other people.

Andy Warhol once said: 'Don't think about making art, just get it done. Let everyone else decide whether it's good or bad, whether they love it or hate it. While they are deciding, make even more art.'

So those are the five mental hindrances, roughly Buddhist-style.

Here are some of my hindrances: Facebook, my troubled friends whom only I can rescue, housework and cooking for adult children, computer spider/mahjong or knitting, fixing cars/vans/houses/stuff, and sheer indolence. Recognise any of them? All of these things have their place in life. The problem here is the proportion of your day that you spend on any one of these, or indeed on the whole lot.

Finally I have to mention mental activity, which is arguably the umbrella under which all hindrances reside. As a woman of words I spend a lot of time thinking. Many times my friends and family have interrupted a good think, or a submersion in the Zone, with their brief and minor demands, or to quickly tell me some good news, like the post's arrived. Studies show it takes a full twenty minutes to get back to where you were after such an interruption. I know I look as if I'm just staring out the window but actually there's some very important daydreaming going on, perhaps even some wandering in the wilderness. It is possible that I place far too high a value on mental activity over all others. Perhaps I snarl a little when someone breaks my train of thought to ask when dinner will be ready. Perhaps I still worry too much about losing that extra-clever storyline, that miraculous image, that stupendous turn of phrase. Perhaps I am still very very human. Perhaps I make no apology for this. It's my work, after all. I try to be kind.

The chief antidote to unwanted mental activity of any kind, and indeed to all distractions, is mindfulness meditation. This is your greatest tool and is available to you at any time or place. The same principles can be used to keep coming back to the writing or the wilderness. However, it is true that even with an awareness of these hindrances and their antidotes, it can still be immeasurably difficult to get down to writing, so is there another way?

Yes. Morning pages. I learnt these in the book *The Artist's Way* by Julia Cameron which has lots of basic tools for fostering your creativity and helping you to keep going when you're stuck. The best tool by far is 'morning pages'. For a full account of how to do this and why, please read the 'Basic Tools' chapter in this wonderful book. My method of doing morning pages is to get a sheet of A4 narrow feint paper and a good pen that runs smoothly. Then I write down everything that comes into my head. I do this without stopping for a second until I reach the end of the second side. If I can't think what to write I write, 'My mind has gone blank' or 'I don't know what to write' and other stupid obvious things. It is important not to stop. As soon as I've done it, I rip it into little pieces and put it in the bin. This is a form of psychic vomiting. Everything gets spilt onto the pages without correction. It's not good writing, and it doesn't have to be. That's not the point. This activity is for depositing all the distracting worries and angers and concerns out of the forefront of your mind and onto paper, giant and petty, both. All of it can be dealt with later, or simply observed and dumped. It's like the worry tree and should have a similar effect, but it includes every form of rubbish your mind could contain. Hughie.

Often I notice the same annoying worry, joy, sadness or person featuring every time I do morning pages. Sometimes I am ashamed of what I say or surprised by it or by how I say it. Sometimes I'm just bored. Sometimes I have fabulous ideas and find I've stopped writing to think about them, but as soon as I'm aware of stopping I put a cross in the margin and carry on. If I have crosses in the margin at the end, I go back and read that one line, transfer the gist of it into my notebook, then rip up the original page. The ripping-up is especially important if you are angry with any of the people you live with …

In many ways this is a direct route to being, here, now. It clears out all the psychic junk so the jewels can shine through. For years I did morning pages religiously every time I sat down to write. If my writing time was limited, I still did my morning pages. If all I had was an hour I'd morning page for half of it. That's how important it was. On holiday in parched France I wrote about the roasting weather and the stresses of that family holiday, then wrote a chapter of a novel set in a muddy field in torrential rain.

It is also a great way to sneak past your inner censor. Like it or not we all have one, or several. At times I've felt like there's a whole battalion in there. I'm trying to think through a storyline and nothing's happening, or I'm suffering from sloth and torpor and can't find any interest. If I can summon the energy to do a morning pages exercise with a slant on the problem, sometimes that funny little daft idea will present itself and I'm up and running again, or at least sitting down and thumping the keyboard.

Incidentally, Julia Cameron based *The Artist's Way* on the AA (alcoholics this time not automobiles) twelve-step recovery programme, equating choosing an artistic path to releasing oneself from addiction.

Resilience

Being suddenly alone after my second marriage was perhaps the biggest shock I'd ever experienced. I refused to accept it and therefore fought the break-up on all fronts. After we broke up a second time, I decided that, whatever else happened, I needed to learn how to be alone, and that even within a relationship I needed to be more self-sufficient and more resilient. So I set out to learn. The third and final time we parted company, I stood up and walked away before I even realised I was doing it. Much of this book is about what I learned.

I have a lot to say about being alone, so it's hard to know where to begin. An online search about 'alone' revealed most people's perceptions of 'being alone' are about not being with someone else, especially that special someone, as opposed to simply being alone for its own sake. Alone is thought of in relation to its opposite, rather than as a concept in its own right. Coupledom and company are seen as the norm, and singleness and aloneness are odd. Even today, in this world of individualism, being single is not as acceptable to us as being part of a couple. Even the word 'odd' implies an extra entity outside the convenience of things being in twos. There is almost a higher value placed on being in company in general rather than being on your own. Someone declining a night of eating out with friends in favour of staying at home alone is likely to be considered weird or at least suspected of being unhappy in some way. Audrey Hepburn disagreed: 'That's how I refuel.'

People who choose aloneness as a habit rather than occasionally are often thought inadequate, as if they can't cope with 'society'. We assume there's something wrong with the alone person, not the crowd, if the alone person chooses aloneness. For women especially, but by no means exclusively, there is the added jibe of being selfish. The mores of our job as women are to look after other people and hold the family together. We are expected to be the central cog in the family's social wheel. Time alone is considered a luxury, an indulgence. It should be an hour in the bath or at the gym. A stepping out and not an adventure which is worthy in itself.

In a recent radio interview Guy Grieve described chucking his highly successful marketing career, which he found meaningless and soul-destroying, to spend a year in Alaska three hundred miles from the nearest road. He was surrounded by bears, circling packs of wolves and worst of all (apparently) by moose, and he didn't mean the Scottish variety. His interviewer, Clare English, used my mother's line a few times: 'Oh come on, you don't really mean …?' She repeatedly suggested that this life-changing adventure was selfish and that selling 'space', as he put it, couldn't possibly be meaningless. She seemed unable to understand how a year spent in the wilderness could be such a vital and significant experience. How I squirmed at her refusal to get it.

Guy Grieve's year was surely a monastic type of experience, the ultimate reset button. I can't imagine how his wife must have worried as she struggled at home with their children. But as he pointed out, and claimed his wife knew all too well, when your partner is dying inside, a complete reset is the only option (my words). The high level of stress amongst men, especially between forty and fifty-nine, has been well documented. Men of this age now account for roughly a third of all suicides (men and women) in the UK. Clearly desperate measures are sometimes needed.

Most of us spend less and less time alone resetting ourselves, and when we do we're often on social media, and therefore not fully alone, or we are watching other people on TV or in films which in itself is a form of social contact. We're not really being alone because we're not alone with our thoughts when we do these things.

A young friend of mine can't be alone in the house without a TV on somewhere. Many people have TVs, computers or tablets in every room. Another friend uses the radio as background noise without really listening. When we're out, we check our phones or have music blasting into our ears, often both. Tannoys tell us things we already know or warn us of non-existent dangers. Piped music follows us into the toilet. I mean, toilets are surely special spaces for emergency alone time with custom-built seats for peeing while you're at it, aren't they?

It's the lonely in a crowd thing. We are surrounded by people on a train, yet we feel alone so, instead of talking to the person next to us, we check Facebook, text a friend, look up the news and tweet. We seem to need some form of contact with other people all the time, but often not the real individuals close by. Perhaps we don't all need to go to the same extremes as Guy Grieve. Maybe most of us don't feel we need time alone. Maybe we've forgotten or never knew what being properly alone can bring us. Maybe that's why there are all those misconceptions about what the lone person is up to and why.

I think we are in danger of losing the ability to be truly alone in a way which is reparative, progressive, healing, constructive, diffusive, invigorating and feels downright good. We need to be alone some of the time, if we are to be fully functioning human beings. Perhaps it is our lack of confidence in being able to think our own thoughts that makes it so difficult. In such a welter of communication there is little time to stop and think clearly and consistently. For instance, without incomprehensible station announcements on the train to and from work there might be the potential for unwinding, repairing, remembering, rethinking, exploring, feeling good and so on while you travel. I suspect it is that mental freedom and the potentially life-changing quality of solitude that scares others. It also has the potential to sustain.

It doesn't always work that way. There are also many people who have too much time alone thrust upon them by circumstance, for instance single parents, the elderly or people without work. Some of these people, the elderly in particular, are often grand masters of being alone and have learnt through necessity how to deal with loneliness. This is a different thing entirely. The difference is choice. Inviting such people to be expansive in circumstances not of their choosing is unkind and daft. Even Virginia Woolf, queen of bold in so many ways, said: 'Alone, I often fall down into nothingness. I must push my foot stealthily lest I should fall off the edge of the world into nothingness. I have to bang my head against some hard door to call myself back to the body.' Ouch. Her solitude doesn't sound remotely rejuvenating. This is our biggest fear about being on our own, that we might scare ourselves out of existence or never find our way back.

Such things frighten me too, and sometimes I'll postpone a trip if I'm not in the right frame of mind. But perhaps it is that disembodied feeling I had at Ronachan, or the mortification of the flesh which I'm sure Guy Grieve experienced while starving in the minus fifty temperatures of Alaska, which can trigger the reset. Being alone is fun, once you've got the hang of it.

For a start there's arrival. As we've seen, sometimes it takes me a whole three days to 'arrive' where I am and be with myself. I used to always stop at Ronachan on the Kintyre trips, sometimes even spending a night there, to do this. In the car park I'd stop beside the screen of six-foot marram grasses then hurry through the bracken and wildflowers. At certain times of the year this was a battle because the greenery was often tangled and very large, forming a natural assault course. As I stepped at last onto the beach I'd let a long sigh out into the wind and stand there gazing over at Jura and Islay. This was Arrival with a capital A. It was a primitive sense of coming home which was also extremely physical in an unconscious sense. I've noticed this sensation of deep and immediate physical relaxation when I first put my foot on the sand or rocks, the non-living earth. I am earthed. In Kintyre the air and sea are both astoundingly clear. On an outcrop of rock there, I often perch to gaze into the swaying seaweed in the water below and the sand beneath the water, watching shoals of little fish dart about. I sip my tea and gradually all those jangling thoughts begin to dissipate. I have done this in company and the experience is never as immediate or profound.

Here is something I wrote while sitting on Ronachan's rocks. It's basically a transcription of the sounds happening around me. This one's for reading out loud, so I hope you're not on a train. Watch out for the seagulls.

Rocks of Ronachan
(after Edwin Morgan)

schurp, schlop, schlock, schgloop, schsssss … aaahhh
boodly woodly, a booble-oodle woodly oodly
tss tss t-t-tsstss
peese!
schup, schloop, schlop schgloop woop woosss
whhooossss!
aa-aa-aah haa!
brr-rrr-rrr

ee-hee, ahee, aye, ah! Haha. Haha. Haha. Ha. Ha.
(haha, haha, hahaha, haha, haha, ha, ha, haha, haha)
wow!
ha ha ha.
wow!
Sschloosh, sschlosh, ah, sschloosh, ah, schss, schss
...
schrraaaaarrrrr! schlop, schlup, schrarr!
tss-tss
a-peese!
tss, tss schup, schlip
pss – tss – kss – tss – pss – schssss ...
...
attaloodle – oodle – oomps – scraash,
scroosh n scrosh, tish tosh pish posh wash
ah ha, ah hum, ah ha, ah hum.
... ...
ah sschlah, a schluff, a schlurpa, a schler
up
a schloss, schlosss, schloss, tish, gosh n flush.
whaaawaaoowaaaaaooaaa ... keschlup.

Water is often involved in this moment of arrival. On
another trip, this time northwards, I set off in the morning
hoping to make it to a campsite near Ullapool on the northwest
coast. The bulk of the journey was on motorway then up the
fast, busy and notoriously dangerous A9 to Inverness. From
there, the road cuts across through the mountains. A few
miles beyond Garve I pulled over into a layby just north of
Inchbae Lodge and next to the Black Water. Sometimes I need
to establish what I'm there to do: write. It's easy to forget in
all the hassle of getting there. So I got into the back, made
tea and opened up the laptop. I was effectively arriving at my
work, but not in the corporate sense. I was engaging with my

beloved task and dispelling nagging doubts that I'd lost the thread of my story. I wrote until the battery began to run down then set my mind to practical tasks, namely filling the water tank. I had neglected to refill it before leaving home but luckily there was the river close by.

A flattening of the grass suggested I was not the first person to gather water there. After a few yards the path was joined by another and a short distance further it became clear two wheels had passed at some time not distant. Then the grass gave way to smooth worn old stones which inclined sharply towards the water. It was a wide shallow river, unhurried, constant and whispering quietly to itself, a great contrast to the urgency of the busy road just the other side of the bushes. Little birches and hazels lined the water's edge and insects flitted through the sunshine. The day had been mostly bright but with occasional sudden showers, which means there were constant dramatic changes of light, clouds filled with foreboding followed swiftly by blinding sun rebounding off every wet surface, and sometimes sun and downpour both at once. Such was the bedazzlement of that moment that I could barely see and had to close my eyes for a minute to stop them weeping. Fortuitously, during this self-inflicted blindness the noise of traffic abated and I could hear the water and the birds and the wind in the trees. I opened my eyes and the world had become almost black and white, each dark shape picked out by a rim of sunlight. It was impossible to discern detail of any kind or have any sense of scale. The hill opposite could have been a mountain or a hillock, near or far, the trees might have been huge but I could have been huger. All very weird and magical. Then, just as I feared I might be losing my marbles, I noticed a straight line leading out across the water from where I stood, rocks set just beneath the waterline, with sunlight caught on the rimming water. I was by an old ford. In my mind

I heard horse's hooves on the stone and saw a gaggle of people waiting to cross, bundles on their backs, skirts being wheeched up over bare feet, children's hands being grasped for protection against the current. For a second I was standing there beside all those other people who I imagined might have journeyed through this spot. I waited, holding my breath to hear the real birdsong in the trees, and soaked up the warm low constancy of the breeze then felt my breath soften, my shoulders melt and my joy rise.

I was there, right there in my awareness and ready for that trip, and the natural world was there to greet me. It's still there, quietly getting on with its work while I ignore it for weeks on end in the city, cocooned in my centrally-heated life.

Cocoon

we sleep against the night
cushioned in the silence
between these walls
padded with shelves and gadgets

sea change is gradual
movement perpetual
likewise wind and river
the play of trees
fall of rain
rise of pollen

new life pushing through
while we sleep against the night

That arrival was massively comforting, as arrivals always are when I do truly and properly arrive. It needed no partner with whom to share the experience. It was enough of itself to give me confidence to get on with the adventuring, whether by laptop, foot or wheels.

I clambered into the cab with renewed confidence. The previous two trips, including the Cluanie one, had been fraught with anxiety. I'd been unsure whether I'd have the stomach for more. Another unhappy trip, no matter how productive, would have had me wondering why I do this at all.

I had driven a little way along that road through the wilderness (though there was so much traffic, this being the high season, I'm not sure it deserves the title) when I spotted my mother coming toward me in her bright red Volkswagen. What was she doing there? My stomach churned. As soon as I had reception I phoned her and found she was not in the wilds of Easter Ross but safe at home in Glasgow. Much as I love her, it was a relief to find she has a doppelganger. A cup of tea or dinner would be fine but it wouldn't stop there. With whose mother does it ever? And who ever wrote the greatest novel of all time with their mother in the BnB next door waiting to explore the area?

Then I checked in with my husband. We were progressing well with another reunion and I wanted to reassure him the trip was on the up and not the down. He told me he'd hired a car and was coming to join me for a night.

What?

'Yes,' I stammer. 'Good. Here are my coordinates.'

I did offer, you see, so it was my own fault. And he and I were in that delicate stage of needing mutual encouragement about 'us' and fabulous locations in which to reinvent ourselves. The beautiful wild place I was in was one I would have liked us to internalise, if I wasn't meant to be writing. I pointed out how much he dislikes Vanessa Hotplate and told him if he wanted we could stay in a BnB. Really I wanted him to love Vanessa as much as I do, but looking round her meagre insides I knew this was foolhardy. I had packed for a lengthy trip which was to take in an attendance at a book club to read sections of my novel. I therefore had books for selling, extra clothes so I could be smart, knitting because I couldn't write all week, a gas heater, towels plural and six kinds of footwear. It was late August, the time of year when clothes for all seasons are required. I was packed to the gunnels. There was simply no room for him plus a bag, and I was keen not to put him off the whole business of campervanning on a budget.

But mostly, I'd only just started this trip. I needed to write or I was likely to behave badly. I know that's terrible but I also know this is how it works. I went into overdrive. I rushed to the supermarket in Ullapool and stocked up with grub, then parked in a beautiful campsite and got back to work. I got down to it first thing in the morning too and gave myself a word deadline which, if I truly applied myself, I'd manage before they threw me off at noon. In other words, the imminent arrival of another was like rocket-fuel.

It was also a complete change of tack. He knew about this conundrum. My job, having 'arrived' in my writing, was to stay present. My job with my beloved was also to stay present, but with him. In very different ways, he is another solo traveller. This much we have in common. He enjoys long-distance walking and cycling and, as it turns out, living alone. Our mission, had we chosen to fully accept it, was to be fully present with each other.

The notion of staying 'present' is another one I learnt in person-centred counselling. It means being fully available to your client, fully concentrating on being with him or her. This takes skill and practice and is akin to mindfulness. Indeed, a Buddhist teacher I encountered years ago on retreat told me my work as a counsellor was in many ways a form of meditation. This effectively meant I was meditating for five hours a day, which seems unlikely, but I was pleased to have so many extra Brownie/Buddhist points.

In counselling, to be fully present with another, you need to be fully present with yourself first. It means being able to be aware of yourself and your own feelings, whatever they are, and being able to use them appropriately and without pressure for the good of the client. In many ways the job of the counsellor is to help people achieve this presence with themselves. It is of course a different scenario in close personal relationships like marriages, friendships and other committed partnerships, but the importance of being emotionally and psychologically available holds true. 'Arriving' has a lot to do with being 'present'. Sustaining it is the tricky bit. It's easier to get hold of a greasy pig than it is to keep hold of it.

There's another counselling concept I like, that of 'fragile process'. This is where the client's sense of themselves, or their awareness of themselves, is extremely delicate, usually through a difficult upbringing of some kind during which the child they were has been taught that what they say, think or feel is not important or valid. Their inner reality has been denied and in response they often learn not to trust their own most basic perceptions. This void is often the result of some unconscious teaching on the part of the parents, but the effects may be potent nevertheless. Counselling can help repair that damage and clients learn, perhaps for the first time, how to listen deeply to themselves. Taken to extremes, a person can have almost no self-awareness, in which case the task of the counsellor is even more delicate. The slightest interruption when the client is examining some aspect of themselves or their life from their emerging own perspective, can throw them off course entirely. The counsellor has to stay emotionally alongside, letting them know they have heard, but without directing or interfering in any way. This is extremely difficult to do, not least because the client is working so hard to explore that inner reality and is most likely very scared. They need reassurance but may get upset or angry if you interrupt them or get it wrong. This is because you have made them lose their way. What they are afflicted with, poor souls, for this is painful stuff, is fragile process.

Sometimes when working on a writing project which is ambitious or challenging, I find myself going through something similar. I need, very much, to be alone and uninterrupted in order to look inward or to fully experience what my invented character is going through. I often need an open-ended period of time to be alone, if it's at a particularly difficult stage. If I have that limitless time, I may only use a completely focussed half-hour. Sometimes I can write in busy cafés but not usually for long. Writing can feel like a bad bout of self-inflicted fragile process in which I have to tease out the truth. The danger is losing my voice to Margaret Atwood.

My point is about the impending presence of my husband, the loss of concentration, and the impossibility of entering that magical uninterrupted Zone once he's here. A time limit had been set, and not by me. As Thomas Mann said: 'Solitude gives birth to the original in us, to beauty unfamiliar and perilous – to poetry. But also, it gives birth to the opposite: to the perverse, the illicit, the absurd.'

Peril, absurdity, illicitness, unfamiliar beauty and of course poetry. Wow! How I needed solitude! But faced with company, I was more than able to maximise my remaining time alone.

My husband knew, more or less, why I was there, so I had to assume he too wanted a bit of illicit beauty or absurd peril and would act accordingly. I knew he knew because he had reassured me he was only coming for a day. This was a round trip of five-hundred-and-seven (and a half) miles. There was hope for us.

As fast and furious as I imagined he was haring up the A9, I clung onto my fragile process, ignoring all distractions which in a greater time pocket might have infiltrated my focus, like the man who parked his pick-up right behind me in a layby and just sat there, or the fabulous rock formations over the road. Greta Garbo didn't want to be alone. She wanted to be 'let alone'. There is all the difference.

Redraft

The first draft of this book was finished. It had been simmering in the 'Campervan' file, a tiny icon in the top corner of the desktop, for two months, cooking up some objectivity by being forgotten about. I needed to come back to it fresh. But two months had become three and then four and it was obvious that our old friend Fear was holding me back. In this case, it was fear of failure, and no further progress could be made until I faced the truth: Was it any good? Would it pass muster?

These are unspeakable questions. So unspeakable I can only wonder if other writers and artists go through the same extraordinarily crippling doubt. What if, after all this effort and time, it's complete and utter rubbish. I was facing the possibility that, on a profound level and over a protracted period of time, my judgment was worthless.

This is a terrible stage in the writing process, and induces a pain similar to the agonies I went through trying to paint when my kids were tiny. The weeks since the end of month two after completion had been full of distractions, prevarications, evasions, avoidance, self-deception, false promises, delusion, self-hatred and fibs. And almost physical pain. Desperate measures were needed.

There were times during these intervening weeks that I'd dithered at the laptop writing 'important' emails instead, or sorting out other less pressing pieces of work. During these dedicated writing sessions, I'd begun new projects, had brainwaves that I'd stored for future use in the notebook, cleaned the house, applied for day jobs, weeded the garden, sympathised with people who needed my assistance/support (not) and so on. I suppose, on reflection and seen in this light, these sessions of agonising weren't all wasted. But too much tea was drunk, even by my standards, and this book wasn't going anywhere. During these sessions of self-torment I sometimes quite literally forgot what I was meant to be doing, rarely located the file behind the icon, opened it less often and almost never did any actual work on it. On a couple of rare occasions when I did open the file, I panicked, closed it again and went out and thought about getting drunk but couldn't, given my inability to handle alcohol. Instead I whinged to friends, bought clothes I didn't need, knitted a lot, knitted some more and got very bad headaches. This continued for some time until I realised the awful truth: I had arrived at an impasse.

Perhaps this level of skill in procrastination is a form of madness. Maybe it's an art form in itself. Maybe this is writers' block. Like any other brick wall, banging my head off it was beginning to hurt. And it was making me grumpy.

As in so many other situations, the solution was, of course, the campervan. A day trip was called for, or perhaps longer, but certainly a campervan outing. I had to make further avoidance impossible or I'd lose all my friends.

To do this I needed a day of luxury and kindness. I therefore dug out clothes that made me feel like something special was about to happen, which in terms of the book it was. I've reached this desperate point many times before, in fact with all my other projects, and the solution is always the same. I must feel good but also be comfortable and focussed. This is most easily done on a good day weatherwise, but not so good as to make it impossible to stay indoors. Realistically, I live in Scotland so I adjust my glamorous clothing accordingly. I'll probably wear mascara and perfume, 'In Love Again' by

Yves Saint-Laurent, ironically. It'll most likely be a dress, not an evening dress but still special, perhaps the one with the giant flowers in all colours of the rainbow, clean tights, favourite underwear and newly polished shoes. There will be blue, purple or vermillion nail varnish, though this is mainly so I can't prevaricate again by painting my nails as I work. There may be music on as I drive to my destination, or not, depending on what best feeds the muse, the inner child, the grumpy little artist inside me who has been turning her back on me and refusing to play. It is her I have to persuade, reassure, cajole and bribe into making an appearance. Getting down to it has to be irresistible to her.

I have occasionally managed to get back to redrafting my books by going to nice coffee shops, but the eyes of neighbouring customers make me self-conscious about glamming up, and the squabble I'm about to have with myself is best done away from the public eye or there is a danger of distraction or even abandoning ship. If I'm heading in the van, I've probably already tried cafés by that time. Time has to be bought in cafés with teas and cakes, and this is counter-productive and a distraction from the work in hand.

Cakes and other delicious things are blatant bribery. It's hard to argue with someone who's been thoughtful enough to seek out your favourite nibble. I'm trying to remove the option of quarrelling with myself because me, myself and I are all driving each other nuts. We're all exhausted with this argy-bargying that's been going on. It's just that one of us is shouting 'Forward!', another has bolted herself to the floor, has her fingers in her ears and is singing 'lalalalala', and the third is running between the two offering up solutions. Enough. Someone has to take charge.

Therefore, the next task is gathering all my favourite kinds of food, preferably of the instant type requiring the simple opening of packets. Oatcakes and banana are good, roasted seeds, apples, sugar-snap peas and so on if you're naturally healthy, but more likely (this is meant to be a treat) chocolate, biscuits, sweets and top quality crisps. Part of the function of the food is to keep my hands and mouth busy. There is something very physical about this moment of truth. I need even the smallest outlet for tension. If I was still a smoker I'd probably faint from the amount of nicotine action required. But Jaffa cakes, pistachio nuts and cherries are a much better option, or whatever is in season at the corner shop (usually chocolate chip cookies). I then allow myself to eat whatever I want in whatever order or combination I want, party style, no rules, which means peanuts, dolly mixtures, clementines and sausage rolls all on the same plate.

The van may or may not need to be pristine, depending on whether cleaning it feels like a putting off or a gathering of speed. The view out the window has to be good and, depending on how many weeks or months I've been avoiding, a spot nearby may be enough but more likely a truly spectacular outlook such as Kintyre or Assynt with their great grandeur may be required. Obviously the van needs to be travel-worthy to get me there, but given the amount of activity involved in avoiding the current task, I've probably already sorted any practical problems. If not, fixing it may be an urgent concern, and therefore a source of some stress, which is exactly the thing I'm trying to avoid. This is one thing which may need direct action. If little me, the writer, is anxious to get going it may take a lot to keep her calm as she sips coffee in the mechanic's waiting room.

I bring a printout of the entire document, even if there won't be time to read it all. This is a source of environmental guilt, but the printed word is as much a tool of my trade as the telephone is for a receptionist. I have a fine-nibbed turquoise pen with turquoise ink and the word 'PILOT' written on the clip. This is what I am, the pilot, and turquoise is preferable to red. A document with red ink scrawled all over it tells me I've done something wrong. We all learnt this in school. Turquoise is serious and special. I don't use that pen for anything else.

I often worry that even once I've done all this preparation I still won't be able to get down to it. But it seems rude. To the muse, I mean. How could I not show up at the coalface after all that? Even at my age I'm still capable of a degree of belligerence (ask my mum) so sometimes I just need to be gentle but firm. I will stay there until I've read some pages, enough to convince me I'll be able to go on when I return to civilisation. I'm a chaperone to my inner child who is travelling alone to a foreign country. She needs to know she's safe but also to keep moving and have an end destination in sight. With luck she'll find herself in a playground full of wonder at the way my project works. I'm hoping she'll get lost in the words just as I want any other readers to get lost. Alternately, I may stumble over paragraphs but see solutions and feel compelled to fix them. If either of these things happen, I know the idea fundamentally works, that the writing is ok, that the overall logic of the book is consistent and worthwhile, there is still fun to be had going back and perfecting it, that there is a way to do so. If this is not the case, the pages go back in the envelope until I can think of a more radical plan. This is the appalling prospect I'm trying to avoid. It is this possibility that is the fuel which drives me to find solutions to bad paragraphs, chapters that don't work and structure which needs to be ripped apart and rebuilt.

For this book, I set off one evening in summer after a hearty dinner. The laptop and printout were snuggled together under the bench. My giant double-layer Tupperware box was stuffed full of fruit, oatcakes, nutty biscuits and cheese, and a large bar of hazelnut chocolate, all bought specially for the occasion. The cupboard was packed, as always, with a great variety of teas. My hot-water bottle, special jumper and a dress were in the clothes box. I felt a resigned determination, a slight gritting of teeth, a sense of heading off down a tunnel with only a dodgy torch for company, but I was also excited. It was like opening a present. It could be another pair of socks, but it could just as easily be the one thing that was so precious I didn't even dare ask for it. My insides churned with the possibilities. I tried to think of other things, failed, and nearly missed my turning.

It had taken me the best part of a day to make myself leave the house.

'What? Are you still here?' my daughter had said, then my mother on the end of the phone, and then myself as I stood at the door trying to think of other things I'd need to stay behind for. Finally, there had been no more excuses and I climbed into the cab and drove.

As the light began to fade over the hills I chose a small, rough and ready layby a little back from the road amongst some trees and close to a burn. There was little wind, but the thrum of running water was my constant companion through the night. I woke with the daylight, shortly before my alarm was due to go off. A couple of blackbirds were calling each other between two trees, and further off I could hear the metallic hammer of a thrush. I peered through the gap in the curtains. Other birds I couldn't see or identify were busy in the bushes that lined the burn and one even tiptoed across the roof and threw its little shadow over the opaque skylight. I sat breathless beneath it until it flew off, then opened the curtains on the off-road side, the one which backed into the trees. There was something indescribably intimate in this, as if I'd walked into someone else's early morning bedroom. The light fell through the dew-laden trees in patches of gold. I made tea, opened the Tupperware box and set both within easy reach of the bench on which I'd slept. Then, forsaking the lovely dress and the shiny shoes this time, I dug out the manuscript and the pen and got back into the sleeping bag still in jammies and my favourite sloppy-joe jumper. The little bird ticktacked across the roof again, stopping every so often to whistle.

I took the manuscript from its envelope and drew a line through the title, *Deep Campervan Joy*. That would have to go. All the birds seemed to fall silent. There was no traffic on the road and the trees stood listening. I glanced through the window at the light sitting on a clump of nettles. A tiny winged beastie was upside down within the window space. There was a comma missing in the first sentence. I put one in, but on reaching the end of that little paragraph, the opening line seemed superfluous, awkward. I took it out. The new opening line was far better. I swapped one word for another and made it better still.

I took a large mouthful of oolong tea, clutched the mug to my chest, opened the road-side curtain and took in the expanse of hill that rose in layers of grass, hedge, forest and moor on the other side of the valley. Then returned to the manuscript.

On. This simple word pulsed through my head, through my fingertips. The familiar editing symbols and markings which are a secret second language for me, washed through my mind. I remembered the excitement of editorial cutting that I first experienced when rewriting my first novel (on the instructions of an errant agent) from a giant tome to tiny sliver of a book and, later, the reshaping of it into the book it now is.

I opened a bag of satsumas and consumed the lot without noticing, adding a faint but lasting orange whiff to the now heavily turquoise sheets.

On. I made more tea, grabbed the biscuits and ate them alternately with the grapes.

All seemed to be well, just the occasional sin of inelegance, inaccuracy, bad spelling or punctuation. A tentative flutter of relief trembled in my chest, then grew to form a certainty that whatever mistakes lay ahead, the work was worth pursuing and all my previous efforts had not been wasted.

But after some indeterminate period of time (I'd forgotten to look at my watch when I started), probably somewhere between two and four hours, I came across a moment of extreme doubt: the structure and reasoning of the entire thing seemed wrong. I had repeated myself on two separate issues in several different ways. Panic set in. The possibility of deleting the lot and returning to my earlier professions of counselling or social work seemed attractive. I got up and paced the only two short steps you can pace in a van of such minisculosity. Just at that moment, a large saloon car flew into sight, roared towards me, growled past and vanished round the bend. I flung the curtain over again and fumed in horror in the shadow. The book was a disaster. I ate a bar of chocolate and glared at the blue tits in the nearby branches. I thought of all the people who'd encouraged me in this insane project, and wondered why, and considered in what tones I was going to tell them of its failure.

It was time to clear up and move on, as if having created this embarrassing blunder I had to escape from the gazes of the birds, insects, trees and hills which had been witness to my foolishness. I washed, dressed in ordinary clothes and tidied everything away, stuffing the manuscript behind a cushion for easy access. Then I drove fast and then slow, then fast again, my brain searching while not searching. I tried and failed to ignore those relentless inner censors who threw scorn on the whole thing. Then I swerved into a layby on the edge of a village.

It was the order of the thing. I got in the back, made fresh tea and lifted the pen. The tea went cold. So did my heart. *I love this section*, I thought, *but I love that one too*. They said the same thing. They both had to go. I wrestled the storyline to the ground. I pushed myself to stick with this apparent cruelty and went home exhausted and downhearted. When I got there, I was still considering dumping the whole thing.

But the following morning I woke to find I had accomplished a great deal. I thought of phrases I liked, of the fortuitousness of having two sections on one subject and a choice. I thought of the whole book as a voyage of discovery not just for the reader, as any book is, but for me as its writer too. I realised finished products aren't everything and remembered the terrible finality of the moment I sent the final unchangeable version of *Mavis's Shoe* to the publisher.

The journey of this campervan book was everything and I had just crossed a great chasm. I saw the incredible amount of work still needed and wanted to continue.

Two months after that trip I had to repeat the excursion, including treats and attractive clothing. I had again failed to continue work on the book. But in the meantime, I had at least identified a problem. I'm a fiction writer and I was writing nonfiction. I was applying fiction rules to nonfiction writing. Silly me. You couldn't make this up.

So I wrote two lines on each chapter and sent the summary to my brother, Colin Salter, a nonfiction writer. He went through it and immediately divided the chapters into four types of subject matter and suggested a different chapter to open with. We spent an hour discussing it and miraculously, without even needing to read it, he managed to identify the problem and also the solution. It was a lightbulb hour.

Safely ensconced once more in the back of the van with views of the hills of North Ayrshire, I wore this time a stripy red-and-yellow mohair jumper and munched on blueberries. Green farmland stretched as far as my wandering eye could see. Emmental cubes, oatcakes and peppermint aero chocolate bars were scattered across my table. I rearranged the chapters, not in the order Colin had suggested, but along roughly the same principles. I chose another opening chapter, deleted a few more, wrote some new ones to suit, saved the whole lot and stuck the file behind its icon. Obviously this didn't all happen in the same day but over time and in several equally pleasing locations, reducing the food bribery and sugar content each time until at last the book made sense.

Where We Are Now

Ode to Killiegruer, West Kintyre

By a sea of grey and pink,
the birds as calm as you like,
your Irish accent in my ear,
and a breaker a great mile long
turns with a roar and a boom
to startle me looking on
and the surface an icy glint,
sun reflecting a peachy pink,
heat still in it at eight in the eve,
the seals shout and roll and bob,
a swift, another and another
my hat and shades a shelter,
a towel across my burning feet,
the air passing hot and cool and hot;
there is no Ireland, no Islay or Jura,
or even a Machrihanish.

The sea is busy always;
it roars and shouts and roars some more,
though the sun is ready to drop,
and seems to have lost its way
the horizon hides in the haze,
and sea blends with sky, seamless,
dreamless, calm and lazy.

The majesty and the grace,
the unthinkable unthinkingness
of every rock and life.

This is the place I love the most, Killiegruer in Kintyre. And it's spectacular. I have that deep sense of calm when I go there, as if my whole metabolism has slowed down. On this trip I was only disturbed by the anxiety that I had to go home soon and that I had to write a chapter before I left. I therefore wanted to write, but not to finish. I just wanted to be, here, now. And for a while to come.

Rain was forecast later and my body yearned to spread out on a proper bed. I'd run out of milk and my food was low too. The nearest shop was only a mile's walk away. I wouldn't starve, even with what I had. But perhaps a natural end was on its way.

The back door of the van was open. Outside there was a stretch of grass about six feet in length then the tops of a couple of boulders. Out of view beneath them was a sandy beach. In view, beyond that, were some outcrops of pink sandstone with lime green slips of seaweed draped across them and a couple of gulls picking their way amongst the rock pools. Then the big wide open sea. On the horizon there was a dot which on inspection through the binoculars turned out to be a small yacht making its way round the southern end of Islay. Luckily the weather was cooling but not stormy. There is some pretty treacherous coast over on Islay and then nothing until you get to America. Through my southern-facing window I could see further round the Kintyre coast to Machrihanish, just a streak at the water's edge, and right in beside me at disturbingly close range a caravan with an awning and a whirligig full of wet swimming costumes. On the other side, two hooded crows were picking bugs and worms out of the camping area. There was only one tent, a little blue dome, which was as far from me as it could get and beside a picnic bench. Beyond it the coast curves back inland to the River Barr and further on again there was a house just visible against the hillside. Behind me was a lush flat field with a small herd of Friesian cows quietly munching their way across it. The road runs along the back of this but is far enough away not to encroach. The sound of waves always drowns out the traffic anyway.

It's difficult not to sit and stare out to sea for hours on end, to watch the clouds come and go, the sun bursting through then hiding again. It is the loveliest thing to sit at the back of the van and see the wagtails bob across the daisies in the grass, the gannets plunge into the waves, the gulls gyrating overhead and other people wandering across the rocks with their little nets searching for crabs or drifting down the golden sand barefoot with their dogs.

There are raised beaches beyond the green field and road behind me with a sudden steep rise then flattish fields at the top. I once watched hundreds of seagulls playing in the updraughts there. They'd approach the edge of the field on the top from inland, then were whipped southwards by the eddies coming up the hill. It looked like fun. I guess if you live to be fifteen and you're a gull you'll know how to enjoy yourself.

This time I had the campervan stand with the best views, the last one in the row. This is the most sought-after position and usually you have to book to get it. That time I just got lucky. It meant I had all the conveniences of a caravan park and could still pretend I was in the wilds, as long as I only faced west or north. I could sit there all day, and frequently do. When I'm back in Glasgow in the rain, I travel to that spot in my mind and imagine the sea in all its different moods.

But today my thoughts are fleeing north again to Assynt. Perhaps you're wondering what happened in Lochinver and whether my husband and I managed to work things out or if the whole thing was blown out of the water again. Or perhaps you're not interested. Perhaps it's not relevant at all.

We met up near Ardvreck Castle, a tiny and astonishingly beautiful monument to savagery and violence if ever there was one. It's easy to guess the reason for the location. There are clear views in all directions so you wouldn't miss the approach of enemies. Built about 1490 by the MacLeods of Assynt, the castle sits on a rocky promontory of land that sticks out into Loch Assynt. On the day we were there it had become an island because of heavy rain.

In 1650, the castle became famous when the MacLeods captured the Marquis of Montrose, who was a royalist, and handed him over to the Jacobites. He was taken to Edinburgh to be hung, drawn and quartered as a traitor. However, twenty-two years later, in 1672 the MacLeods, who were a bloodthirsty lot and spent much of their time fighting their neighbours, were put to siege by their main rivals, the MacKenzies. The siege lasted two weeks with the MacKenzies victorious and the MacLeods no longer in charge of Assynt. In 1726, the MacKenzie laird built a mansion nearby called Calda House. He and his wife had a taste for greater luxury than the castle. Unfortunately the clan couldn't afford this luxury and having fought everyone in sight to gain control of all Assynt, weren't managing the surrounding land all that well either. While still in possession of the house, the MacKenzies' fortunes had failed so badly, they knew the inevitable was about to happen. Their own principal rivals, the Sutherlands, were poised to take over. Then in 1737 the house mysteriously burnt down. Some say because the MacKenzies were drinking on the Sabbath, others that it was deliberately torched by MacKenzie supporters to end the Sutherlands' occupation. Some local accounts state the entire household perished in the inferno. The details are lost in the mists of time. Finally, in 1757 the estate was bought by the Sutherlands. Meanwhile, Ardvreck Castle remained intact until 1795 when it was struck by lightning, arguably a comment by God, and has been ruined ever since.

I didn't make it across the water to the castle, though other tourists had paddled over in bare feet, but I had a wander in the ruins of Calda. There was a Buckfast bottle halfway up one wall suggesting I wasn't the first voyager from Scotland's central belt. Buckfast calls itself a tonic wine, comes in a green glass bottle with a mustard yellow label and is popular with underage drinkers in and around Glasgow. I gather it is now available in pub optics in certain Lanarkshire hostelries. It was highly visible in a spot only accessible by someone drunk enough to take the idiotic risk of getting to it.

If you look closely at the land surrounding the castle and mansion, you can see how prosperous and alive the area once was. Oddly straight lines suggest disused roads and pathways, rucks in the grass tell of dry-stane dykes around fields, and green patches among the heather suggest houses and kitchen gardens. Set amidst the stark grandeur of the mountains, this is Clearance country. The Clearances were a blight which happened across Scotland in the early nineteenth century, but with extreme cruelty and little concern for human welfare particularly in Assynt. Between 1812 and 1821 over one-hundred-and-sixty families were evicted from land their families had farmed for centuries. Their well-farmed and fertile land was seized and the area divided into five sheep farms. Having been replaced by sheep, the people themselves were forced down into the over-crowded coastal areas.

Back in the present day, I had arranged to meet my husband in the car park. I had time to search the nearby hills for the grinding stone which ground the other stones for making roads.

'Well, this is romantic,' he laughed as we approached each other in the grandeur of the Moine Thrust, another of those geological fault lines like the Great Glen. The mountains on one side of Loch Assynt are five hundred million years old, while those on the other are three thousand million years old (wow!) and they meet at the fault and rub together or, to be more specific, the one climbs over the other. No wonder the castle has a history of antagonism. One side rocky, the other brown with heather, but sharing the wild cold wind, the bright sunshine and a brilliant blue sky. A meeting place of contrasts indeed.

Laughing at ourselves was perhaps the only way forwards in our strange disengaged circumstance. I don't like romance. Its chemical imbalance brought up by that old devil dopamine. I try to resist the soaring of my heart in such conditions. It's nothing but trouble. It keeps me striving for things that experience has shown me are impossible and also extremely painful in the pursuit thereof.

The truth is I was excited and touched that he would travel so far. He even agreed to spend a night in my little tiny ancient, well-used and slightly broken campervan. It wasn't entirely true that there were no beds to be had in any of the local BnBs, so it was his choice. Suffice to say we had a truly wonderful interlude in Clachtoll Bay and environs, and it turned out Vanessa's previously untested king-size bed worked. Much caution had already been thrown to the considerable wind over the previous weeks, and we both therefore allowed a slightly celebratory mood, this for the first time since our gradual reunion.

However.

This is not a guy and gal meet each other, fall in love and live happily ever after sort of story. Oh no. I have come too far for that and the stakes are so much higher.

According to the American motivational self-help author, Wayne W Dyer: 'You cannot be lonely if you like the person you're alone with.' I had spent much of the previous year learning to like that person enough to stop putting her through anything that was going to make her deeply unhappy again. I also learnt to write and keep writing, that writing is quite simply what I do and that I need to keep doing it in order to live, and that nothing, but absolutely nothing, must get in the way of that.

So, from placing husband and family first at very nearly every turn, I had moved the centre of my gravity, in both senses of the word, to my work. This may not look all that radical in any outward sense, but in a personal sense it was huge.

Another diary entry from last year: 'If he took decisive action, ie bought a campervan and made me a concrete offer regarding us, then I'd listen.' Isn't that sad? Am I that easy? Buy a campervan and I'm yours? Or is it not just that we both desperately needed to change and put each other, and our wider family, into a healthier perspective; that we needed a paradigm shift within ourselves as individuals but also as a couple? Somehow the purchase of a campervan might have signified all that.

Unfortunately the sad truth is we didn't buy a campervan together. We just discussed it many times. We managed a small paradigm shift but we needed a seismic one, and it didn't happen. So we went our separate ways.

A year before the Clachtoll trip and four months after he'd moved out for the second time, I wrote this:

'I do actually feel extraordinarily happy. It would seem madness to move from this spot (Kintyre). I am learning how hard it is to fully pay attention to me and recovery. Part of me objects to my need for recovery. I'm so lucky. My life is full of all the things I want and need. Except him. I think now I'd like to be held again, to be within a circle of trust built by two people.'

I had been reading Kapka Kassabova's *Twelve Minutes of Love*, a book in praise of the passions of tango dancing. It was impossible not to think about sex and intimacy and to remember early nights he and I had enjoyed on a Cuban dance floor. But Kassabova also talked about Guillermo, a tango artist and teacher. Guillermo's love affair was with his art, an art form which imitates a passionate affair with another person. Guillermo's true love was tango itself. He was not confused about any of his dance partners. His art was enacted love but he loved his art over all else. There was much for me to learn.

But it seems I'm a slow learner. We were briefly reunited not long after, one of several attempts. The pain of that particular failed reunion was such I brought down a curtain on the whole thing and returned briefly to Kintyre for solace:

> Waves roll into the rocks.
> A ship has passed many miles away.
> The roar of Westport Beach echoes
> the hum of Glasgow city.

Unfortunately this was also Vanessa Hotplate's maiden voyage and one which she too spectacularly failed, returning home on a lorry due to a tiny fault with her key. The plummet from ecstasy to despair, which often accompanies mechanical breakdown, was extraordinary. But I picked myself up, found the spare key, and went to Wigtown Book Festival alone. And enjoyed it. In fully accepting the end of my relationship, I began a period of sore but simple mourning with all the various stages identified by the best clinicians.

Christmas was especially difficult. It skewed my view of the precious single life that I had built and made me desperate not to be single any more. It should have been a time of relaxation, a quiet period with no work commitments and a chance to sort myself out or to write. It didn't work that way. For single people, the Christmas period is to be borne, or tholed as they say in Scots.

But I have wheels and will travel. In fact Hogmanay brought peace and hope. I spent it in Glenuig with my friend who had suffered that terrible migraine. Despite being teetotal because she had learnt alcohol was one of many causes for her affliction, she had an open house on the booziest night of the year. The Hogmanay bells rang out to a small group of interesting, admirable and warm-hearted women seated round her kitchen. At two in the morning the serious carousers arrived and the party began in earnest.

This was also the point I left them and returned to the van. I began the year in a sleeping bag wearing the previous day's clothes, clutching two hot-water bottles and with two heavy blankets wrapped about myself. I slept like the proverbial log. At nine in the morning I started for home. Apart from the soles of my friend's feet sticking out the bottom of her real, presumably comfortable and actual proper bed when I went to say goodbye, the first sign of human life was eighteen miles away at Glenfinnan, a shepherd and his sheep. A couple of centuries earlier Bonnie Prince Charlie had gathered his clans in Glenfinnan, raised his royal standard and laid claim to the two thrones of Scotland and England. Despite auspicious beginnings and considerable support, this didn't go well for him. I was hoping for better luck so I raised a cup of tea there in the back of the van and celebrated my survival of another Christmas season. The year turned and so did I.

Finally, back home, I stopped moving. Even my work rate was less frenetic. Preparations were afoot for *Rue End Street* to be published and I began writing the book you have in your hands. I had arrived in my own life. I knew that when I had done everything I could with my day, I might occasionally feel lonely or even empty, but that if I waited I might learn to love that gap and all would be well. Eventually I did.

I was moved and comforted by a poem written by Jane Holland, herself a solo campervan writer. She had taken an old English poem, 'The Wanderer', which was written by an unknown hand before the tenth century, and had adapted, 'transgendered' and renamed it to be 'The Lament of the Wanderer'. Here is an extract:

> The best we can do, not knowing the future,
>   is to stay resolute, resisting our grief,
>   the terrible grip of its torments, and keep faith
>   with ourselves, refuse to forget.

This is Buddhist tonglen – not flinching from the reality of suffering, but resisting its grip nevertheless.

This book is a first person narrative. The musical equivalent of a first person narrative is probably the solo. The most intense, the most moving, the most personal and often the most meaningful pieces of music are frequently by solo instruments or voice. Think of the Bach cello suites, or traditional Scottish songs sung by Margaret Bennett or Sheila Stewart, or Griselda Sanderson's solo nyckelharpa pieces, or spoken poetry. Somehow we are allowed right up close for those few minutes and what we find there is something more penetrating and passionate than any multi-instrument music. Often seeming to come straight from the heart, solo music is the most direct communication between musician and listener, and carries a greater intensity. We love it, but can't listen for long. It is the truth, but it overwhelms us, like the truth of the Cowal sky at night or the brilliance of the sea at Kintyre.

But what if your whole life is a first person narrative or a solo cello suite? What if we are all solo artists singing to each other, and then listening? We better make it good. We better sing the truth.

That spring, after a long drive, I arrived in Kintyre. Unlike my usual solo excursions to this part of the world, on this occasion I came to meet two friends who had hired a motorhome for a week. They'd asked me where I'd recommend and naturally Kintyre is where I directed them. The sun had shone throughout their week and they'd had a great time. I met them in Killiegruer Caravan Site just as the weather changed. We greeted each other in howling wind and torrential rain while breakers crashed on the shore only a few feet away, then hurried into their luxurious motorhome.

Some would argue it was a shame about the weather. Anne, the site owner, was upset that my friends only saw the place in this deluge. I had never been there in such extreme weather. The worst had been a night in Fugue Ducato when the wind had been so loud through the railings on the roof I'd had to use earplugs to sleep. Winter storms here are too wild to be safe, a phenomenon I'd heard about but never experienced. Three caravans were lost one year on the same night in the same three minutes which also took down hundreds of trees across Scotland. My friends were unseasoned campervanners, so I could understand them being a little nervous, even though it was only late summer.

In the event, their double-glazed, fully sealed motorhome kept the storm out more than adequately without so much as a jiggle to the suspension. While we ate handsomely from their multi-ring hob and oven, my friends demonstrated the many virtues of this fine spotless vehicle. They were however compiling a list of faults to raise with the hire company. None of which were serious. It was the fanciest thing on wheels, with three double beds, a million different light fittings, an all-mod-cons kitchen and a shower room to match. While the storm continued to rage outside, embarrassment crept up on me that my own van was such a wreck. Fear snuck in there too. Perhaps it really was dangerous? Maybe the wind would topple it on its side in the night, death in a campervan.

I wanted to abandon it. I wanted them to invite me to stay in one of their super-comfy beds. I didn't want to be alone in the cold and dark of a small space with the wind racing through the holes round the door, past my cold ears then on out the gaps between living space and cab, which I hadn't yet got round to fixing. I pictured myself emerging from my little van the following morning bleary-eyed and unslept, but glad to be alive.

Noticing my reluctance to leave, at last they offered me a bed. I nearly took up their offer. But suddenly pride got the better of me. Warm damp air came swirling in. 'Quick,' they said, 'close the door.' So I stepped outside and did.

The breeze blew me swiftly back to Vanessa where I quickly made up my bed, heated a hot-water bottle and brushed my teeth. Vanessa shoogled about with every squall of Westerly, the rain sounded on the roof like bacon frying, and yes, the wind did race through the gaps, tickled my nostrils and exited through the front, but I was warm as toast and the wind rocked me to sleep in no time. I woke briefly through the night and listened to the gentle patter of rain above my head, a caress which grew and receded like the breath of a kindly giant.

In the morning my friends cleaned and packed, and I waved them a cheerful goodbye. The weather was beautiful. Over the course of the day the wind dropped, the sky turned a rich blue with puffs of cumulous nimbus periodically making the light change with great rapidity. Over the next two days I wrote more words than I've ever written in that time-space before, finishing comfortably near my finishing line.

The last of these days of paradise gave way to a clear warm starlit night. I roused myself from the laptop and stood against the front of the van, the landward side and searched above me for Ursas Major and Minor, Orion and his belt and the Northern Star. I leant back across the slight incline of the bonnet and gazed up at the shimmering Milky Way in all its astounding enormity and beauty.

Unfortunately the lights from the toilet block were a little off-putting. My rods and cones were confused between the darkness and the electric light, and were starting to ache. So were my arms from trying to shield them. I determined to come back out again later to have another look at the night sky after lights out. I was just about to leave when I glimpsed a shooting star and then shortly after it another. It was only when a third star raced across the same small patch of the sky that I began to suspect it was seagulls or bats scooting briefly across the beam of light from the toilets. It was time for bed.

Back in the van I discovered the toilet was full and unusable. There was nothing celestially uplifting about that. Cursing my own negligence, I decided trying to empty, clean and refill it in the dark probably wasn't the best idea so I went to bed with fingers crossed, completely forgetting my plan to wait for the toilet lights to go out so I could view the great cosmos. It was three in the morning when I woke again with an unstoppable need, found the trusty green bowl and soon after tiptoed barefoot in the dark across the grass to empty it on the rocks by the beach. Turning back to the van, I saw the whole big wonderful sky spread out above it full of diamonds, the iridescent, effervescent Milky Way shimmering across the centre of a glittering glowing glorious sky.

'Thanks for wakening me,' I said to no-one in particular and paused a second on the doorstep. 'Wow!' I breathed and 'Ooft!'

Then I crawled back into bed for a deep and dreamless sleep.

Bibliography

The Wisdom of No Escape, Pema Chödrön, Shambhala Publications Inc (2001) and Element, HarperCollins Publishers Ltd (2003)

No Mud, No Lotus: The Art of Transforming Suffering, Thich Nhat Hanh, Parallax Press (2014)

Twelve Minutes of Love: A Tango Story, Kapka Kassabova, Portobello Books Ltd (2012)

The Artist's Way, Julia Cameron, Pan Books (1995)

Camper Van Blues, Jane Holland, Salt Publishing (2010)

The Highlands of Scotland, Ward Lock & Co Ltd (1937)

Scotland for the Motorist, A A (Fifth Edition 1933)

Recollections of a Tour Made in Scotland, Dorothy Wordsworth, edited by William Knight, Macmillan, (1924)

RSPB Birds of Britain and Europe, Rob Hume, Dorling Kindersley (2006)

The Hydro Boys: Pioneers of Renewable Energy, Emma Wood, Luath Press Ltd (2005)

Emergency Kit: Poems for Strange Times, Jo Shapcott (Editor), Faber & Faber (2004)

Everything that follows is based on recent, real-life experience that has been proven to work: Professional Survival Solutions, James Shepherd-Barron, Penguin *(2010)*

The Cloud Collector's Handbook , Gavin Pretor-Pinney, Sceptre (2009)

'Things', Fleur Adcock, in *Sixty Women Poets*, Linda France (Editor), Bloodaxe (1994)

'Cow', Selima Hill, in *Sixty Women Poets*, Linda France (Editor), Bloodaxe (1994)

Feel the Fear and Do It Anyway, Susan Jeffers, Century (1987) and Vermillion (2007)

Into the Wild, Jon Krakauer, Pan (1996)

No Country For Old Men, Cormac McCarthy, Picador (2006)

For There is Hope, Martin Stepek, Fleming (2012)

*Asterix and the Pict*s, Jean-Yves Ferri & Didier Conrad, Orion (2013)

Zen Mind, Beginner's Mind, Shunryu Suzuki, Weatherhill (1997)

Funnybones – various titles, Janet and Alan Ahlberg, Puffin

Can't You Sleep Little Bear? Martin Waddell and Barbara Firth, Walker (1987)

Way of the Wanderers, Jess Smith, Birlinn (2012)

Among You Taking Notes, Naomi Mitchison, Phoenix (written 1939–1945) (2000 edition)

The Poor Had No Lawyers, Andy Wightman, Birlinn (2013)

Austerity Britain, David Kynaston, Bloomsbury (2008)

A Field Guide to Getting Lost, Rebecca Solnit, Canongate (2006)

'The Loch Ness Monster's Song', Edwin Morgan, in *From Glasgow to Saturn*, Carcanet (1973)

USEFUL WEBSITES:

http://plumvillage.org for the Plum Village Mindfulness Practice Centre, France

http://motorhomeparking.co.uk/scot.htm for local authority rules and provision on motorhome parking

http://oulipo.net/ official Oulipo website, in French

http://pitchup.com for viewing and booking websites